DEATH

AND

ETHNICITY:

A

PSYCHOCULTURAL

STUDY

Richard A. Kalish
and
David K. Reynolds

This Monograph is published by the
Ethel Percy Andrus Gerontology Center
University of Southern California
Los Angeles, California 90007

RICHARD H. DAVIS, Ph.D.
Director of Publications and Media Projects

THE UNIVERSITY OF SOUTHERN CALIFORNIA PRESS

ISBN 0-88474-032-3

Library of Congress Catalog Card Number 76-18380

Preface

The past decade has seen an incredible increase in writing, research, and educational programs concerned with death, dying and bereavement. When Ed Shneidman, then chief of NIMH's Center for Studies of Suicide Prevention and RAK first talked about the possibilities of funding this project, there was the sense of adventure, of probing into new territory, undertaking large scale research on non-medical aspects of death and bereavement. The territory is no longer untouched; others have also ventured in, but the expanse will accommodate many teachers, writers, and investigators.

We feel strongly that rigorous quantitative and qualitative research is badly needed on the matters that have concerned us here. We feel even more strongly that clear thinking and planning are needed. This era is in danger of replacing old myths and stereotypes with new myths and stereotypes, slightly more accurate and less destructive perhaps, but nonetheless not always appropriate. We hear the words "death with dignity" spoken by everyone, a few of whom seem more concerned with a dignified death than a dignified life for the dying. We hear debates over the extent to which psychedelic drugs or psychotherapeutic processes may prolong meaningful life, and wonder whether we are not entering a new cycle of denying death and developing new rationales for such denial.

The intent of this project is to emphasize that death occurs to unique individuals living within particular sociocultural settings. Those who provide and plan services need to recognize both the differences among groups and the differences among individuals within these groups. They need to provide options for those who are representative of their group and options for those whose wants and needs are atypical.

In the pages that follow are a large number of statistics, accompanied by our attempts to integrate these statistics, to relate them to the words and

i

numbers of others, and to develop some meaning from the entire fabric. We hope that those who plan projects, programs, courses, and services concerned with death and bereavement, and those who fund, plan, direct, and work on these projects, programs, courses and services, will invest some of their time in these pages. We hope that the statistics and the interpretations will be used in debates about service needs, that our work will soon be superseded by the work of others built on ours, that a variety of people will expose us and praise us, damn us and laud us. We hope that this book does not lie unnoticed because the value of our project, the meaning of the effort that went into it, depends on the impact it has on students, on service providers, on policymakers, on researchers, and on those who are or someday will be dying or caring for the dying.

The lists of names of those who participated actively in one way or another with this project is lengthy, and we will acknowledge them only in terms of the general role that they performed in our work. Needless to say, it is these individuals and those who were kind enough to answer our questions who were primarily responsible for whatever has succeeded in this report; for its inadequacies, we must look back at the two of us.

Those who helped carry out the research: Eddie Alexander, Lafayette Hanible, Veassa Johnson, Brian Ogawa, Richard Reubin, Patricia Salazar, Annamarie Simko, and the UCLA Survey Research Center, its staff, and its interviewers. Those who read and commented on part or all of the manuscript: Oscar Caneda, Margaret Clark, Jacquelyne J. Jackson, Robert Kastenbaum, Christie Kiefer, Joan Moore, Koji Omaye, Patricia Salazar. Those who typed, edited, or helped in other ways: Joel Cantor, Soichi Fukui, Eleanor Kwong, Claudette Martin, Janet Masuko, Thomas Noguchi, Barbara Saito, Alice Sederholm, Edwin Schneidman.

And finally, thanks to Richard Davis and others working with the publishers whose enthusiasm helped sustain our own.

Contents

1

Introduction

Human beings are the only members of the animal kingdom that can anticipate their own death and potential extinction of their species. No other animals can plan their lives or their individual actions with future death as one determinant. This very ability to anticipate death is a source of feelings of meaningfulness and uselessness, anxiety and love, resignation and denial, achievement and failure. It generates poetry and art and music and building and conquest and deceit and delusion and pain. Death can have heroic size or pitiful smallness, perhaps in direct relationship to our perception of the heroism or pettiness of life.

Up until recently, most books and articles on death made reference to the taboo nature of the topic, many referring to Gorer's description of death as the contemporary pornography (1959). This is obviously no longer the case, as the writings about death and dying have rapidly increased from a trickle to a stream to—at present—a veritable flood. The authors include academics and professionals from all conceivable disciplines, plus numerous lay persons who have described, often with great sensitivity, their own feelings and experiences with death and loss.

Not only is death described in words, but it is also depicted by pictures and music. Look through an art gallery and note the frequency with which death appears—from the ubiquitous paintings of Christ on the Cross to the death-ridden work of Edward Munch to the pop art depiction of the Kennedys, King, and Marilyn Monroe. Death on the battlefield and at home is displayed from the Louvre to the sculptured murals adorning the walls of Angor Wat and nearby temples. The theme of death in music, both symphonic and popular,

1

while probably less common and less impinging than in literature and the graphic and plastic arts, is still prevalent.

Although socio-philosophic currents of today are sufficient to produce a growing body of research and writing about death, they do so in the face of strong cross-currents that work against such efforts. While most persons will verbalize the importance of caring for the dying and of helping people deal with their own death and the death of others, actual practice falls far short of the ideal.

Death has always been studied, discussed, written about, by medical scientists, theologians, philosophers, and anthropologists. In a very different context, other professions required an understanding of the significance of death: mortician, life insurance agent, cemetery owner, grave-digger, florist, policeman, physician, nurse, lawyer, social worker, and clergy. Yet even those lives and livelihood revolved, in varying degrees, around death, have found ways to avoid the existential reality of it. Perhpas they, more than others, needed to do so.

WHY THIS RESEARCH

When we began this research, the studies of attitudes, values, and expectations relating to death and bereavement were already being conducted and published in increasing numbers. With one or two exceptions, however, all had been conducted with highly specialized populations. Respondents included groups of elderly, of college students, of mental patients, of health and mental health professionals, and of the dying and the bereaved themselves. They included written questionnaires, personal interviews, observations, field studies, and even investigations measuring perceptual defense, reaction times, and physiological changes to death-related words.

For the most part, the nature of the populations being studied precluded meaningful comparisons from being made. True, we could compare men and women, students and non-students, Protestants and Catholics, but even these comparisons had to be made within restricted populations. (An immense sample of *Psychology Today* readers has made its opinions known, but again the lack of representativeness of this population prevented generalization to the broader spectrum of national opinion.)

Nor had any comparisons been made between groups of varying ethnocultural backgrounds. Whatever the ethnicity of the respondents of the published research, it could only be assumed that the few non-Anglos responding were not a sufficient proportion of the sample to merit comment by the authors.

We launched this study with two major convictions. First, we believed we needed to learn much more about how a cross-section of a general population felt concerning death and bereavement. This would provide us with information about the psychological, the "pan-human" responses to death and grieving. Second, we wanted to understand better how and why groups differed in their views of death and bereavement. This would help us understand how values, roles, and other social-structural features affect the ways in which ethnic communities view death. Further, we wanted to draw information from a variety of sources and through a variety of methods, rather than depending totally on one kind of source or one research tool.

We firmly believed that we could gain information and understanding of use to both the theoretician and the practitioner. Further, we hoped that our findings and our interpretations would find an audience among non-professionals, as well. The salience of the death of self and the death of others is hardly restricted to professionals.

For the theoretician—the academic and research people concerned with death and bereavement, with adult development, with personality and social theories, with ethnology—our study aims at presenting some hypothesized relationships among aspects of personality and culture and orientations toward death. We shall present enough information about our procedures, our sampling, and our data so that these scholars can decide for themselves the significance (statistical and social) of our findings. They can use our data for their theories and build on these data for their own subsequent studies. At the very least, they can profit by avoiding our pitfalls.

For the practitioners, we have presented some alternatives for living. We have tried to set these alternatives into a meaningful historico-cultural context. We have discussed what we feel are some of the consequences of various alternatives of meaning and behavior related to death.

For the non-professionals, we hope to offer the opportunity to gain insight into their own feelings and to understand better the feelings of others. In both our personal and our professional lives, we continue to encounter people who must help someone else to live more effectively for a brief period, who must enable others to die as comfortably and satisfactorily as conditions permit, who are forced to think about their own finite nature and what it means. In the few years since we began this project, we have noticed a greatly increased willingness to discuss death and to be overtly aware of the overwhelming importance of the social, emotional, and economic concerns that arise from death. Although our writing is addressed primarily to professional theorists and practitioners. we hope that everyone interested in the subject will add something to his/her understanding.

AN OVERVIEW

Our project has two central foci. We are concerned with the ways people verbalize their thinking about death, dying, and grieving, as well as the related ways they actually behave. Thus, we have gathered two kinds of data. On the verbal level, we have interviewed community residents from each of four major ethnic groups in the Los Angeles area, taking care to include diversity of age and sex while controlling for socio-economic class differences. We have also interviewed specialists from each community. These specialists, e.g., physicians, deputy coroners, ministers, morticians, insurance agents, are often able to consolidate their personal observations into meaningful generalizations and suitable hypotheses for directing our research probes. In addition, we explored the printed word. We have examined both fiction and non-fiction to learn more about how death is handled by various ethnic authors.

On another level, we have selected several settings in which death-related behavior can be observed. For example, we have made observations in funeral homes, terminal wards in hospitals, cemeteries, and nursing homes. We have worked with the Los Angeles County Coroner's office, the Los Angeles Suicide Prevention Center, and other agencies. We have been host to three one-day conferences, each focused on one of the three ethnic communities involved in our project, to which we invited as participants knowledgeable professionals from the relevant community. These conferences were to let members of these communities know about our research and about our availability to keep in touch with them as our findings emerged.

Sources of Information

1. Community Survey. The major investment of our resources has been in the community survey. Drawing on our preliminary observations and extensive pilot interviewing in the various communities, we constructed an interview schedule, which, translated into Japanese and Spanish, was carried into the four communities. It is described in detail in Chapter Two.

The interview schedule itself covers four general topical areas:
1. One's own death—thoughts, dreams, plans, expectations, wishes, fears, worries, and one's own funeral;
2. The death of others—telling another of impending death, frequency of experience, mystical experiences;
3. Survivors—acceptable and unacceptable grief reactions, expectations in mourning behavior;
4. Death in the abstract—tragedy of different types of death, mass death, life after death, suicide.

In-depth interviews of two hours or more were also conducted by our staff using the same interview schedule. An attempt was made to get at basic feelings underlying the simple responses to our questions. The precise meanings of the questions, concrete illustrations, and verbatim responses gathered by our staff have added some depth and richness to our data and have allowed us to interpret our findings more meaningfully.

2. Newspaper Analysis. We selected the four newspapers most widely read in these four ethnic communities, and performed a content analysis as to how each of them reported death. All reported deaths within the ethnic group were coded for cause, place, age, sex, survivors, religion, occupation, the general tone of the article, and the philosophical implications of the article. The non-English newspapers were analyzed by fluently bilingual research assistants. This phase of our project is reported elsewhere (Reynolds and Kalish, 1976), but will be referred to in this book.

3. Interviews with Professionals. To supplement our informal discussion and our structured interviews, we conducted unstructured interviews with professionals from each of the ethnic groups. Nine of these were with Black Americans, over 20 with Japanese Americans, 17 with Mexican Americans, and 11 with Anglo Americans. Those interviewed included nurses, physicians, funeral directors, insurance agents, policemen, psychiatrists, priests and ministers, nursing home administrators, social workers, students, coroners, cemetery workers, newspaper editors, and some patients and family members of patients.

In addition, the project staff members participated in the three conferences mentioned above, in professional meetings, and in student-organized seminars. Of considerable value were the weekly staff meetings that were conducted much more like seminars than like traditional staff meetings. Not only staff members, but graduate students, visiting scholars, and others were in attendance.

4. Observations. Observations were conducted in several settings and under varied conditions. Staff members attended funerals for each of the ethnic groups. They also visited hospital wards, cemeteries (including Memorial Day observances), nursing homes, and the County Coroner's office.

5. Our Staff. The staff members reflected a breadth of background: Black American, Japanese American, Mexican American, Anglo American; Catholic, Jewish, Protestant; women, men; students, non-students. But mostly young—not by our choice, but by circumstances. And all life-oriented. Perhaps death-related research attracts such people, for the researchers in our study, and in others with which we are familiar, are among the liveliest we have encountered. In fact, we found that neighboring office workers were surprised to learn and sometimes "forgot" the nature of our research because, somehow, we just did not fit their stereotypes of persons who would be studying death.

We have attempted to integrate what we have learned from all these sources of information with what we have learned through our own reading, observing, intuiting, and talking. That attempt at integration formed our early manuscript drafts. But we remained concerned that we were trying to be expert in too many areas, and we submitted each chapter in the book to at least three individuals whose credentials we felt qualified them to criticize our interpretations as well as our statements of fact. In some instances, these credentials were doctorates and years of study; in other instances, we believed that having lived as a member of a particular ethnic group and having been aware of oneself as a member of that ethnic group were more important credentials than diplomas and academic experience; in many instances, we received help from persons who were qualified by both criteria. These reviewers helped us immeasurably.

Throughout the coming pages, we will have occasion to refer to other studies that have produced comparable data. Two of these are of particular consequence and deserve elucidation. The earlier was conducted by Dr. John W. Riley, Jr., in 1963 whose data are available in two sources (Riley, Foner and Assoc., 1968; Riley, 1970). The study was carried out by the National Opinion Research Corporation on a nationwide probability sample of 1500 respondents over the age of 15. There is no readily available comprehensive source of the findings, but the two works cited above include partial compilations.

The second study was conducted by Dr. Edwin S. Shneidman through a form published in *Psychology Today* (1970, 1971). The magazine readers—and presumably whoever else cared to—filled out the questionnaire and returned it to the journal. Over 30,000 forms came back, accompanied by better than 2,000 letters. Shneidman's sample, although much larger than either Riley's or ours, was inevitably much more biased. His respondents were primarily female (63%), young (79% under 35), single (53%), high income (66% with earnings over $10,000), college-educated (19% with graduate degrees and 48% with college degrees), and self-declared liberals (72% stating they were either "somewhat liberal" or "very liberal" versus only 8% equally "conservative"). When referring to either Shneidman's or Riley's surveys, we will not always bother to provide formal citations.

THEORETICAL FRAMEWORK

Our theoretical framework evolved from our data rather than vice versa. The more we worked with the numbers and the more we thought about the people behind the numbers, the more we realized that one particular organizational structure emerged triumphant. This structure consisted of a broad gestalt formed by several dimensions, inter-correlated but far from identical.

One set of responses and reactions could be labelled as individualistic, secular, ahistorical, pragmatic, intellectualistic, cognitive, and scientific. Opposing these were the concepts of familistic, historical, affective, emotional, romantic, sacred, traditional, and ceremonial. We are reluctant to add gemeinshaft and gesellshaft to these terms, although they obviously come to mind. Nor do we feel we are representing the "old" and the "new," since the counter-culture is never still and defies such categorizing.

This framework was amazingly pervasive. Many, perhaps most, of our variables had responses that could be ordered along these dimensions. Further, the age cohorts, ethnic groups, educational categories, and religiousness self-ratings could also be ordered along the same dimensions. Inevitably there were reversals and inconsistencies; occasionally one dimension was unrelated to the general pattern for one or a few related variables. For the most part, however, the framework held together. Whether we were asking about whom to call in case of a suicide attempt or if a dying person was better off knowing that he was dying or what was the most likely event to produce the end of the world, our questions seemed to elicit answers that made sense in terms of these dimensions.

We have avoided the temptation to refer continually to these themes, since we feel the data speak fairly well for themselves. Further, our major purpose is to show how death-related phenomena and behavior can be understood in terms of the general socio-cultural and social psychological patterns of a group or community. We are similarly aware that we have not developed any kind of theory of behavior or of structure or of groups. What we have tried to do is provide a theoretical framework through which our data and our insights can achieve some order and which, we feel, permits our findings to make better sense.

THE REST OF THE BOOK

In deciding how to organize the materials, we found that every chapter should come first and every chapter should come last. We reconciled this irreconcilable conflict by beginning with a description of the community survey and the persons we interviewed. The next chapters compare the ethnic groups (also providing an overview of the data), followed by comparative findings based upon age, sex, education and religiousness. The subsequent section presents ethnographic descriptions of three ethnic groups, the "Anglo" sample presenting such a diverse composite of nationalities and cultural characteristics that we could produce no useful thematic summarization for this sample. And we finish the manuscript with a relatively brief discussion chapter and a summary. For the most part, we left our tables (with significance levels) for the appendix, where they appear in very small print, not because we did not want readers to use them but because we did not want readers to have to pay for them.

Throughout the book, we have attempted to integrate data, theory, speculation, results from other studies. Occasionally, our own values intrude. As one preliminary reviewer stated, "You are expecting the reader to shift levels whenever you do, or to develop that special perspective that allows you to keep your own balance whether clambering among specific findings or coining eternal verities." We plead guilty. We have tried to present our data in the broadest possible context, even if it means that readers will need to shift levels abruptly with us. We believe that the reward will be worth the effort.

Two other compromises of a more practical nature were necessary. First, it became increasingly apparent as the study proceeded that the Anglo group was not an ethnic group in and of itself, but a combination of ethnic groups. This criticism could be directed to some extent at the other three communities also, but we believe that the shared ethnic experience of Blacks, Japanese Americans, and Mexican Americans produced somewhat more coherence to their data. Therefore, we considered the Anglo group as a comparison group, rather than a specific ethnic community. This decision resulted in a subsequent decision, i.e., not to attempt an ethnography of Anglos as we provided an ethnography of the other groups.

Second, it is impossible to provide all the raw data, percentages, chi square tests, correlations, and so forth. We selected those we believed most important. The basis for the compromise was a simple one: we knew that adding more pages would add more cost. We also know from experience that only a small proportion of readers would make actual use of the information we deleted. We recognize that some readers will be frustrated because the specific piece of information they want is not available.

2

The Survey
and the Sample

While the more critical and the more academic are eager to read a fairly detailed description of research procedures and methods, many readers are satisfied with a brief explanation of what happened so that they can get to the results and discussion as quickly as possible. To try to satisfy both groups without compromising either, we begin this section with a moderately comprehensive description of the way in which we developed our community survey, then we turn to discussing the nature of the sample we obtained and some of the characteristics of the interview setting.

COMMUNITY SURVEY: ORIGIN AND DEVELOPMENT

From the very beginning of the research program, we were aware that the community survey would be our major task, requiring the greatest investment of time and money and generating the greatest amount of data. We were thus obligated to make certain the results were worth the effort.

The task in the initial stages was that of generating ideas, trying to determine how vital and meaningful these ideas were to various subgroups in the community, and beginning to evolve some hypotheses that would be worth testing through our eventual survey. We also attempted to be alert to the customs, rituals, habits and terms that we needed to know. We were particularly concerned that we not inadvertently include questions or use phrasing that might be distressing or insulting to any of the ethnic groups. For example, we decided not to ask anything about family income, political affiliation, or personality characteristics. We felt that our topic was inevitably going to touch upon some sensitive issues, and we wished to avoid raising the anxiety/antagonism levels any higher.

We completed three substantial revisions before our initial pilot testing. Each of these revisions consisted in part of screening every item with the entire staff in a group session—those who have done this will know how much more critical people usually become in a group setting. The fourth revision was pilot tested on eight to ten persons by each of four staff members. Respondents were selected without sampling procedure, but all four ethnic groups, all adult age groups, all social class groups, and both sexes were included.

Following the next revision, the fifth, we had the questionnaires translated into Japanese and Spanish by highly competent bilingual persons. They were then translated back from Japanese and Spanish into English by others fluent in both necessary languages. Any discrepancies between the two English versions were evaluated, and resulting changes were made in the Japanese and Spanish versions. We emphasized in our instructions to the translators that we wanted the survey to have not only the same literal meaning, but the same flavor, i.e., we were not concerned with a highly literate or technically accurate version, but wished to have the wording comparable in style and connotation to the English version. (Later analysis of results from English- and non-English-speaking respondents indicated no meaningful differences in responses attributable to translation, with one possible exception for the Japanese Americans.)

Once again our staff field-tested the questionnaire, in three languages this time. Their respondents for this run were more diverse than before, and they interviewed people they did not know, rather than restricting themselves to their friends. The sixth revision was then given to the Survey Research Center at UCLA, with whom we had been in close contact throughout this process. They suggested some additional changes and field-tested it in the community with their interviewers, also in all three languages. The changes that came about due to this final pilot run were incorporated into what amounted to the eighth version. With only minor changes in wording, this was the form that finally went into the field. The questionnaire can be found in the Appendix.

Throughout the interview we permitted the interviewee various degrees of personal distance from the questions. This personal involvement varied from "Did you _____?" and "Would you _____?" to "If you were Mr./Mrs./Miss Brown/Sanchez/ Yamada would you _____?" and "A friend of yours (with the same characteristics as the respondent)—Should he/she _____?"

Groups of questions were introduced with carefully-worded lead-ins not only to provide the respondent with some sense of what was to follow but also to encourage people to answer freely without fear that their notions or feelings were strange. "Of course, there are no right or wrong answers. I only want to know your feelings about them." "Here are some ideas we have heard in our preliminary interviews. Do you agree or disagree with them?" "Here are some reasons why people don't want to die. Tell me whether they are very important to you, important to you, or not important to you personally." "People differ in the *ways* they show grief and the *length of time* they mourn." All these served to established the "set" that we recognized that people might respond in various ways to these questions and that all sensible variations were equally acceptable to us.

The level of abstraction varied among questions. Preliminary interviews indicated that most questions needed some grounding in concrete context before respondents could answer meaningfully. "Should a dying person be told?" was sufficiently vague to elicit only a number of clarifying questions from our interviewees and not the codable responses we desired. Clearly, people respond differently to the death of a parent than to that of a child or to that of a spouse; they may want quite different funeral arrangements for a relative than for themselves; they react differently to sudden death and slow death, to homicides and suicides and accidents. So on the final interview schedule, the questions became: "Now I am going to ask you some questions about a few situations we have invented. First, imagine that a friend of yours is dying of cancer. He/she (make the friend the same sex as the informant) is about your age. His/her family has been told by the physician that he/she will die soon. Should your friend, the patient, be told?" Later, we prefaced a series of questions with "Here is another imaginary situation." Thus, although the contexts were concrete, we allowed the respondent some personal disengagement from the questions.

On the few questions that required the respondent to keep in mind and select among several alternatives, the interviewers handed out a laminated card with the alternatives printed on it (and their appropriate translation on the reverse side).

Topically, the interview covered such items as frequency of contact with death and dying persons, funeral attendance and gravesite visiting, wishes and plans for the respondent's own funeral, thoughts, expectations, and attitudes toward his own death, beliefs and experiences with life after death, communications related to dying, norms and expectations in grief and mourning, suicide, and death-in-the-abstract.

SURVEY RESEARCH CENTER AND ITS INTERVIEWERS

The UCLA Survey Research Center had established a cadre of skilled interviewers from its several years of successful work in Los Angeles. They also had experts with sophisticated awareness of the demography of Los Angeles County and ready access to recent census material, and they had already conducted some studies among minority groups in the community. We required that every interview be conducted by a person who was visibly of the same ethnicity as the interviewee. Thus, the SRC not only needed Spanish-language interviewers, but they had to be of Latin origin. We made this decision with full awareness that we were exchanging one type of experimental error for another. We were familiar with the literature that shows the ethnicity of the examiner as a significant variable in the response of the person being questioned. We learned, by experience, that the subject matter of our interview did not negate the effects of this variable. During our pilot interviews one very patient Black American woman was interviewed *twice*, once by an Anglo woman and then by a Black man. On one item she gave a different response, realized it, and remarked that she had not wanted to hurt the Anglo interviewer's feelings by stating her desire to have a Black American funeral director officiate at her own funeral.

When their backgrounds differ, responses may be more guarded, more sparse, more socially acceptable. On the other hand, interviewers might consciously or unconsciously distort responses from members of an ethnic group with which they identify; again we run the danger of socially acceptable responses appearing, this time because of interviewer bias.

We decided that the latter danger was less than the former, and we opted for interviewers, bilingual when necessary, of the ethnicity of the interviewee. An interviewer who found a person of a different ethnic group answering the door was instructed to go on to the next dwelling.

The SRC serves only non-profit organizations and is non-profit itself; it maintains high standards for its interviewers and its staff. They were responsible for recruitment and training of interviewers and coders (most coding, however, was done during the interview), as well as the actual selection of the sample, in response to our instructions. Since most of the interviews were conducted by women and since many were conducted in high crime-rate areas, the SRC provided a male companion to accompany the interviewers into neighborhoods where most other survey organizations often do not go.

Four of our own staff participated in the interviewing, following their attendance with the SRC recruits in all interviewer training sessions. Our purpose in this was two-fold: first, we felt we could add to the number of cases for the final tabulation; second, and more important, we believed that our own people would be more insightful and more helpful, if they had undergone the same experiences as the interviewers. The people who analyze and discuss the results are seldom active participants in getting the data.

All interviews were conducted during four consecutive weeks in October and November, 1970. Coding of routine items was done during the interviews; additional coding was done by the interviewers immediately after the interview. Coding of four more complex items was done by our staff, based upon verbatim written reports of the interviewers.

SAMPLING

A sequential outline of steps in obtaining the interviews seems to be the most effective way to present our procedure.

1. We had decided to conduct a minimum of 100 interviews with members of each of four ethnic groups in Los Angeles County. Each ethnic sub-sample was to be divided equally between men and women over the age of 20; and we wished to over-sample among those in the later years, so that we would be assured of sufficient numbers of older persons to permit age group comparisons.

The Survey Research Center achieved these goals amazingly well. We ended up with 434 respondents, nearly 9% more than anticipated. Of these 109 were Black Americans, 110 were Japanese Americans, 114 were Mexican Americans, and 101 were White Americans. The sample divided almost exactly half men and half women (215 and 219). The mean age of all respondents was in the middle-late forties; nearly 37% were between 20 and 39 years of age, with just over 35% being in the middle two decades, and 28% being 60 and over. There were no significant differences between ethnic groups in age or sex distribution (see Table 2-1).

2. A common error in many studies that encompass more than one ethnic group is to ignore social class differences between the groups, then to attribute behavior or attitude differences to the "ethnic experience," rather than to social class differences. Nonetheless, the opposite error is also possible, i.e., the social class distributions for each of our four ethnic groups were sufficiently different that insistence upon controlling fully for social class in the sample selection would be to restrict our selection within at least one or two

TABLE 2-1

AGE AND SEX OF RESPONDENTS BY ETHNICITY

		Black American (%)	Japanese American (%)	Mexican American (%)	Anglo American (%)
A.	Age				
	20-29 years	24	18	23	26
	30-39	12	14	16	14
	40-49	23	24	20	15
	50-59	14	14	14	18
	60-69	19	11	13	13
	70 and older	8	20	15	15
	Mean age	45.7	49.0	47.0	47.6
B.	Sex				
	Males	49	54	46	50
	Females	51	46	54	50

ethnic groups to a totally unrepresentative sample of that group. We were caught on the horns of a dilemma—we could sacrifice either across-group comparability or within-group representativeness.

We opted for a compromise, compensating for some of the problems plaguing other cross-ethnic studies. We obtained the median family income ($7,046) for Los Angeles County, as indicated in the 1960 census. We then eliminated from possible sampling every census tract in which the median income was above the median income for the County.

In evaluating the success of this sampling device, we decided against the normal measures of social class, obtained by some formula involving job status and educational level or income. First, we did not wish to inquire about income; second, job status differs considerably from community to community, and we felt it could not be adequately quantified for our purposes; third, women and retired persons are especially difficult to evaluate. We ended up with years of formal education as a crude measure of social class (see Table 2-2).

Educational level was highly related to age, but not at all to sex. Our having over-sampled the elderly and the low-income groups produced an anticipated below-average educational level. Most

TABLE 2-2

EDUCATION, OCCUPATION AND MARITAL STATUS
BY ETHNICITY

		Black American (%)	Japanese American (%)	Mexican American (%)	Anglo American (%)
A.	**Education Level**				
	Mean years	10.6	12.4	6.5	11.1
	Median years	11.6	12.0	6.0	11.8
B.	**Occupation**				
	Unskilled	38	14	25	15
	Skilled	34	46	34	41
	Professional	6	4	1	12
	Housewife	16	28	40	29
	Other	7	8	0	4
C.	**Marital Status**				
	Married	50	71	73	66
	Never married	13	16	10	10
	Widowed	21	13	8	12
	Divorced/Separated	17	0	9	12
	(No answer)	(2)	(0)	(4)	(0)

respondents were either unskilled (nearly 25%), skilled or white collar but not managerial or professional (about 40%), or housewives (under 30%). Highly significant differences for educational levels were obtained between all pairs of ethnic groups, except between Black and White.

Again, we felt that our compromise had worked. We reduced, but could not possibly eliminate, educational/social class differences, while in so doing we under-sampled, but did not exclude altogether, medium- and high-income respondents.

3. We now faced the task of selecting a quota sample of approximately 100 persons from universes that ranged from 100,000 up to over one million (recall we had already eliminated roughly half the County population). Our next step was a practical one, a function of the immense geography of Los Angeles County. We took a compass and drew a circle marking a 20-mile radius from the downtown Civic Center. All our sampling would be within that area.

4. We then needed to find areas of high ethnic density. In so doing, we had to make another decision. Members of all ethnic groups live in most sections of Los Angeles. To decide not to sample, for example, Japanese Americans from an area that is primarily Black, or not to sample Blacks in an area primarily Anglo, is to bias our sample. The alternatives, however, were impossible: to locate every one of Los Angeles's 762,844 (1970 Census) Blacks, then select a sample randomly until sufficient N's of each demographic category appeared in our sample would have been even more impractical. We decided that persons living in areas of high density of their own ethnicity are more likely to have more homogeneous death-related value systems than those living in areas dominated by members of other ethnic groups.

We then mapped all areas of high ethnic concentrations for each of the four groups and divided each of these concentrations into ten approximately equal-sized geographic areas to insure geographic spread within the Los Angeles area. For the Mexican American and Black American populations, the basis for selection of census tract was 1960 census figures; any tract containing 45% or higher concentration of that ethnic group was brought into our pool. In almost every instance, the ethnic density had considerably increased by 1970, when we conducted our survey. For the Anglo area, we used Los Angeles County Health districts.

The Japanese Americans provided a more difficult problem, since they do not constitute 45% of any census tract. We determined areas of concentration by means of (1) an inverse telephone directory, (2) the Southern California Japanese American Telephone Directory, (3) data compiled by the Los Angeles City Unified School District (Report #303), (4) the City Planning Commission Map "Distribution of Japanese, June 1953," (5) field mapping of boundaries, (6) non-White categories of the 1960 census, and (7) discussions with Japanese American community leaders and realtors. The task was substantial, with questionable districts being verified by driving around in the late afternoon to observe who was on the streets. The aim was to be inclusive, to tap all those areas with significant Japanese populations. We were satisfied that we did not omit any large pocket of Japanese Americans existing within the 20-mile radius.

5. To select the Black, Mexican, and Anglo Americans, we turned to our density maps and randomly selected two census tracts from each of the ten high-density areas previously mapped. Within each of these tracts, blocks were randomly selected. For the Japanese respondents, their ten areas being smaller, we selected blocks directly.

The resultant sample blocks were spread geographically throughout the 20-mile radius; all were in predominantly lower-middle and lower income neighborhoods. Interviewers were instructed to continue going to randomly-selected blocks in each area until they had completed ten interviews at ten different households on ten different blocks in each of the ten geographic areas. Once a block had been assigned to one ethnic group, it was excluded from consideration for other ethnic groups.

The interviewer was instructed to begin at the southwest corner of each block and proceed clockwise until he had completed one interview. He was permitted to inquire at a household where on the street a family of the appropriate ethnic background might be found; he could then proceed directly to that house without calling at intervening houses.

Each interviewer was given ten preferred blocks plus ten numbered alternates, also drawn randomly. If he could not complete his ten interviews in an area after trying on the ten preferred blocks, he was instructed to proceed to the other ten blocks in indicated order.

All Black American and Mexican American interviews were completed within the ten preferred and ten alternate blocks for each area. In the low-income Anglo areas, however, we encountered numerous blocks and, in fact, whole census tracts that were now populated by Blacks. It then became necessary to select at random five additional census tracts in those areas—each with randomly drawn preferred and alternate blocks, so that our interviewers could complete their quotas. Additional alternate blocks were also necessary to complete our interviews with Japanese Americans in two of the selected areas.

Thus, it is clear that in drawing our sample we elected to make some reasoned compromises.

1. We sacrificed complete geographic randomness by selecting areas with lower- and middle-income families and relatively large proportions of the respective subcultural groups, and by remaining within 20 miles of downtown Los Angeles.

2. We sacrificed complete randomness in selecting household units by requiring interviewers to interview only at households of their own subculture group and allowing them to inquire about the presence of the appropriate sort of household at a household of some other ethnicity.
3. We sacrificed complete randomness in selecting individual respondents within a particular household by requiring quotas to insure age spread and sex differentiation.

In retrospect, we feel that our sampling methods were totally appropriate given the practical limitations placed upon the project by time and money. The possible effects of the sampling biases are discussed in those chapters where their influence might be felt.

INTERVIEWEE REACTIONS

In recent years, there has been increasing reluctance on the part of potential participants selected for commercial or academic interviews. Some of this reluctance has arisen out of social pressure by members of militant organizations (ethnic, age, sex), for understandable reasons. First, only rarely is the interviewer non-Anglo or elderly, and even more rarely is the director of the research project elderly or non-Anglo. Therefore, the old and the Black, Japanese, and Mexican American interviewees are giving their time and effort for a young or middle-aged Anglo American to get paid, sell his product, or earn academic credits. Second, in spite of promises over the years to act upon the results of surveys, such action virtually never takes place. Suspicions are high in some communities that the surveys are conducted to enable members of low-income groups (age or ethnic) to be more effectively exploited. One well-educated and articulate Black American accused us of trying to learn how to get Blacks to die with greater docility.

In spite of the good intentions of academic researchers or government survey directors, the people in the communities being asked what they want and think and expect are tired of answering surveys instead of getting services. We were careful to inform both our staff members and our interviewers that we were aware of past failures, and that we could give no assurances that any action programs would emanate from our study. We hoped, however, that we would obtain information that providers of services could use to understand better the very meaningful problems of those they served.

In spite of these difficulties, and in spite of the sensitivity of our topic—each prospective interviewee was informed of the nature of the study before beginning—we had only a moderate turndown rate. On the average, three of every five qualified respondents agreed to be interviewed. This ranged from 52% of the Mexican Americans to 69% of the Black Americans (J 66%, A 54%). We compared this response rate to other studies. For examples, the Survey Research

Center conducted a Los Angeles Metropolitan Area Survey about the same time. Their refusal rate was about half of ours; however, their interview topic was much more neutral and they did not have nearly the same proportion of respondents who were elderly, low-income, or non-Anglo. Mintz (1970) conducted a study on suicide in the city of Los Angeles and had a 65% acceptance rate (compared to our 58%). However, his sample included relatively few non-Anglos and elderly, both of whom have a high turndown rate. (In a sense, the claim that non-Anglos have a high turndown rate runs counter to our data. However, the experience of other investigators has been that non-Anglos have had a high turndown rate.)

To indicate the nature of the task we presented to the interviewers, they needed to make some 5300 calls to obtain the sample of 434. Of these, the two major reasons for not finding a person to interview were that no one was at home (42%) and that no qualified interviewee was at home (38%).

The Anglo interviews lasted an average of 71 minutes, compared to the significantly briefer mean of 61 minutes for the Blacks. We have no way of determining the relative degree to which interviewer and interviewee contributed to these figures. Nine percent of the Black interviews, but only two percent of the Anglo interviews were thought by the interviewer to be less than acceptably frank, but again we cannot determine the degree to which ethnic defensiveness or individual-interviewer defensiveness may have affected these results.

An hour of intensive questioning about death and dying cannot help but leave an impact upon the respondent. Although we could make no claim to providing interview-therapy, we were deeply concerned that we not leave distressed people in our wake. Thus, at the end of the interview, we asked directly, "What effect has this interview had upon you?" Nearly three-fourths of the Mexican Americans and approximately one-third of the other groups gave positive responses; relatively few (B 9%, J 18%, M 4%, W 11%) were unhappy. Personal anxieties were most frequently mentioned as the bases for negative responses, although 5% of the respondents criticized the interview or research design in some fashion. The value of the interview as a learning experience, as "making me think about some important matters," and simply as an interesting and thought-provoking experience was mentioned in support of the event. Obviously those who were too fearful or anxious would, for the most part, have refused to participate in the interview initially. We also recognize the possibility of response bias in an attempt to please the interviewer. And we might assume that some of the implications of participating in the interview—both positive and negative—would not occur until later. Six months later, in our follow-up subsample of 120 persons, three reported feeling depressed or frightened following the interview and nine had made some concrete preparations for death such as taking out life insurance, making a will, selecting a gravesite, and arranging to donate their bodies to medical science.

This very small number of negative reactions, plus the willingness of over 90% of those with telephones to give the interviewer their number for future calls should we need to clarify a question, led us to believe that respondents felt they did benefit from their participation. Feifel (1963) reports that he was warmly thanked by the terminally ill patients whom he interviewed, and Ross (1969) mentions the warmth with which her discussions with terminal patients were received. Riley (1970), in discussing the comments of those interviewing 1,482 adults in a national sample, states, "Almost without exception, the interviewers reported that people, typically toward the end of the discussion, expressed feelings of relief, almost as though some load of unexpressed anxiety had been lifted from them" (p. 35). The opportunity to express oneself to a concerned outsider on a topic usually considered taboo commonly results in expressions of relief and gratitude even in psychological autopsy investigations of suicides and equivocal suicides in Los Angeles. Some quotes from our respondents were:

"It's brought some things out consciously—they were always there—just brought them out."

"Well, it brings back a lot of memories. I cried and it helped."

"It made me realize I should be prepared for death."

(Or, conversely) "It's silly and stupid."

Were the responses we received accurate representations of the feelings of the respondents? How much conscious and unconscious distortion took place? To what extent were people responding on the basis of attitudes that were created by the interview itself? Obviously we cannot give reassuring answers to these questions. They underlie all research—indeed, all endeavor—in which one person asks another a question.

We did seek to deal with these matters in several ways. First, we administered a brief telephone follow-up to a 30% sample six months after the interviews were conducted. This gave us some sense of the consistency of the responses over time. We were surprised that the changes were so few. (See pp. 22 for data and discussion.) We also included within the initial interview several items that served as partial checks on each other, e.g., we asked about attitudes toward visiting graves and about frequency of visiting graves. Again, we found considerably consistency. And we employed a variety of other research techniques, primarily non-quantifiable, both to broaden and deepen our understanding and to test our survey results. These included content analysis of ethnic newspapers, unstructured and semi-structured depth interviews, and observations. Our final evaluation was to decide whether the data made sense, whether they could be integrated into theory or could help to generate new and meaningful theory. We felt that—with few exceptions—our data were appropriate for these tasks.

Of course, for a respondent to state that he would prefer to be told of his impending death, for example, while healthy, seated in his living room, and conversing with a polite stranger is quite a different matter from stating the same preference while lying in the immediacy of a hospital room, feeding tubes, and oxygen apparatus. Situational variables are undoubtedly important in determining our attitudes and even in creating who we are. Thus, the strategy of tapping many settings and many observers' recollections served to give us some sense of the situational "embeddedness" of our interview responses.

For example, although 15% of our respondents reported knowing a family member telling a dying patient of his impending death and nearly 25% felt that, if anyone, a family member *ought* to do the telling, Glaser and Strauss during their extended research into terminal illness *never* witnessed a family member disclosing the probability of impending death to his dying relative (1965, p. 31), and they report hearing of only one such case.

Each reader will need to decide for himself the adequacy of our methodologies and our application of theory to results. We have attempted to offer a sufficiently explicit presentation of both methodology and results to enable him to do so.

DATA ANALYSIS

Our primary statistical tool for data analysis was the chi square test of differences between sample distributions. We made the following chi square tests for responses to each item on the questionnaire:

—responses by four ethnic groups
—responses by each ethnic group paired with each other ethnic group on those items showing significance in the previous analysis
—responses by three age groups
—responses by sex
—responses by four educational levels
—responses by three religiousness levels
—responses by sex within each ethnic group
—responses by three age groups for males
—responses by three age groups for females
—responses by three age groups for each of the four ethnic groups

In addition, we computed 't' tests of the significance of differences between means for pairs of ethnic groups on selected variables with continuous data.

We also selected variables for factor analysis, using the Kaiser Varimax program, based upon a correlation matrix previously corrected for attenuation. We felt that the results of our factor analysis provided us with only a minimal increment of insight into our data. As a result, we have made very little use of it. Our factors verified the obvious, rather than opening up new avenues for consideration.

When we began to look carefully at selected items in the correlation matrix, we again felt we were provided with only a minimal increment of understanding. The effects of the demographic variables, i.e., ethnicity, age, sex, education, and religiousness, appeared to underlie almost all of the inter-item correlations, except for such obvious relationships as finding a high correlation between wanting to be told when one is dying and feeling that others should be told when they are dying. Not all relationships were this predictable, but we again felt that the most meaningful contribution that we could make through the community survey was in terms of differences and similarities among sub-population groupings.

Other statistical tools were used in individual situations. These will be explicated at the appropriate points in the manuscript.

CAVEAT EMPTOR

At this point, we should clarify our use of statistical significance, especially in regard to chi square. We are fully aware that chi square does not state direction. It merely indicates that the obtained frequencies differ from the theoretically expected frequencies. However, in order to discuss our results in narrative form, we have used a shortcut. In the coming chapter, and elsewhere in this monograph, we have spoken of Group A having more or less (or significantly more or less) than Group B, or we have spoken of a trend or a significant trend. What these statements mean is that a significant chi square was obtained, and our observation of the data indicated that differences or trends could be defined. We have provided tables in the Appendix to help in checking our accuracy. The alternative to this approach would have necessitated an impossibly awkward style of writing.

Readers may note that statistical significance is not always cited in the subsequent pages. Unless otherwise noted, every time we speak of a difference or a trend, it has emerged from a chi square (or other measure) significant at the 5% level of confidence or beyond. We have often omitted the differentiation of the .05, the .01, and the .001 levels of confidence, although, again this information can be found in the tables in the Appendix.

TWO ATTEMPTS AT VERIFICATION

Two possible sources of questionnaire/interviewer error were amenable to checking. First, we were in a position to telephone a sample of respondents at a later point in time, to look into the reliability of responses over time. Second, we could compare persons interviewed in Japanese or Spanish with comparable persons interviewed in English.

Follow-up Study

How stable are survey responses? What happens to the respondent after participating in an interview? These two questions haunt all survey research. We decided upon a tactic that, although it would not lay them to rest, at least could provide us with some estimate of what occurred after the interviewers left the door.

We engaged upon a telephone survey of a 30% sample of respondents, using a limited number of items. Since we had obtained the telephone numbers from 80% of the original sample, we selected from this group 15 males and 15 females of each ethnic group for callback (we had forewarned them of this possibility before obtaining their telephone numbers). Nine old questions and four new questions were used for the interview, which was conducted by the Survey Research Center interviewers six months after the initial study. Because of moving, illness, and other reasons, we had to make many more telephone calls to reach our sample size than originally anticipated.

The questions we selected for the follow-up study were chosen to provide us with responses to representative issues. We also attempted to use some issues that seemed to us highly stable and others that we felt might be susceptible to change. Comparisons were made for the entire sample, for males and females, for each ethnic group, and for each ethnicity by sex. Statistical analysis was done by chi square with correction for attenuation where appropriate and correlated proportions where the former would not suffice.

Our results were surprisingly stable, considering the time period, the nature of the questions, and the arousal potential of the survey in the first place. On only two of the nine questions was any significant difference obtained. For Black men and for Black women, a significant difference was found at the time of the telephone interview regarding their fear of death; the change was from being unafraid to being neutral or neither afraid nor unafraid. A second significant difference was found for males, Mexican males, Mexicans, and the total sample. These groups all changed in the direction of feeling that people should be allowed to die if they so wish.

No significant changes—and often no changes at all—were found for (1) whether the dying wish to be told, (2) when to begin dating after the death of a spouse, (3) how the last six months of life would be spent, (4) extend of belief in after-life, (5) whether the preferred funeral director would be of the respondent's own ethnicity, (6) how often the individual thinks of death, and (7) whether the body should be buried or cremated.

We also asked the 120 telephone respondents four additional questions, related to what had happened since the first interview. Four women and three men had made additional preparations for death; the men had all taken out life insurance; the women had made such changes as making out a will, making plans to donate their bodies to science, selecting a gravesite, and discussing plans with others. Since we have no baseline data of how many such decisions are normally made within a six-month period, we cannot evaluate the impact of our interview with certainty.

Fourteen persons, six men and eight women, stated that the interview did affect their lives. Four men and four women said that it made them think more about death, while two women and one man commented that the interview contributed to feelings of depression or mild anxiety; the others gave positive responses but were not specific.

Only one person responded affirmatively to our asking whether any answers should have been changed. Obviously, only fairly vivid circumstances would have enabled the interviewees to recall the original questions sufficiently to respond positively. After the interview, one Anglo woman had had a very strong premonition, along with what she described as a "funny feeling," that her granddaughter would die; the girl did die, in an automobile accident shortly before Christmas.

The handful of significant changes came to only six out of 135 tests for significance and—furthermore—were interdependent, i.e., a significant change in Black women could produce a significant change in Blacks.

Following our principle of taking people's statements at face value, unless persuaded otherwise, we can only assume that the attitudes toward death and bereavement are quite stable across time.

Matched Pairs

Although we had translated and back-translated our English interview schedule into Spanish and Japanese and were basically confident of its accuracy, we decided to run matched-pair comparisons of responses to English and non-English forms of the interview. We felt that if no significant differences appeared, our results probably were not affected much by the language in which the interview was conducted.

Our samples (J-N=28; M-N=20) were matched for age. The Japanese Americans in three age categories: 20-39, 40-59, and 60 and older, and the Mexican Americans in two age categories: 20-45 and

46 and older. The samples were also matched by sex and education (Japanese Americans, 2 categories: less than high school graduate and high school graduate and above; and Mexican Americans, 2 categories: grade school and none, and some high school and above). We also matched our Japanese American sample by religion: Buddhist, other, and none. Nineteen of our Mexican Americans were Roman Catholic, one was Protestant.

We compared their responses to all 173 non-continuous variables and analyzed them by X^2 with correction for attenuation.

Among the Mexican American matched pairs, we found two items that were significant beyond the .05 level of confidence; nine such items were found differentiating the two groups of Japanese Americans. These could well be chance findings, and analysis of the individual items indicated only that those preferring the language of origin were more inclined to respond in a traditional fashion.

The most important meaning of these findings is not the differences that were obtained, but that so few differences were obtained and that these differences did not suggest any errors in translation or other sources of confusion in the two non-English presentations (with one possible exception discussed in the chapter on Japanese Americans).

3

An Overview of
Death and Ethnicity

Two eternal truths about human beings are, first, that people differ from each other and, second, that people are similar to each other. Any attempt to communicate psychological insights must straddle these two truths, with a bow to one truth often incurring a buffet to the other. In this chapter, probably more than any other in this book, we defer to the latter. We will emphasize the over-all data with only modest attention to the role of such groupings as sex, age, education, and religiousness, which are discussed in other chapters.

Here we will attend to summary data, while simultaneously providing sufficient information to enable readers to grasp the extent of and meaning of differences among the ethnic groups. For the present chapter, we ignore the fact that the universe represented by our sample of Japanese Americans is just over 100,000, while that represented by our sample of Anglo Americans is over 5,500,000. We do this outrageous thing, this turning of sample into universe, because the alternative was to become impossibly ponderous, overloaded with our data.

Each of the chapters is organized differently, reflecting our attempt to integrate the data in whatever fashion makes the best sense, rather than trying to fit each set of results into a single structure or framework. This chapter, then, begins with an overview of the encounter with the death of others, moves on to the communication with those who are dying, discusses grief and mourning, and proceeds to a description of encounters with one's own death. Finally, we summarize those items that do not differentiate ethnic groups.

ENCOUNTERING THE DEATH OF OTHERS

Relatively few people have not had some encounter with the death or dying of other persons (see Table 3-1). Only 18% of the entire sample did not know anyone who had died in the two years prior to the interview, while almost that many knew personally at least eight persons who had died. Most of the deaths encountered were from natural causes, but nearly one-third of the respondents had known at least one accident victim during the previous two years, although only a handful knew people who had died from suicide or homicide.

Over one-third of the respondents had visited or talked with at least one dying person during the previous two years, and two-thirds had attended at least one funeral during the same time interval, while one person in twelve had gone to eight or more funerals. About 60% had been to a funeral during the previous year, compared to 55% of a primarily Anglo American sample over a decade ago (Fulton, 1965) and only 22% of a large British sample covering adults of all regions and socio-economic classes (Gorer, 1965). Visiting the grave (other than during funeral services) was less common, over half not having made such a trip during the past two years (Table 3-1). A 59-year-old Anglo man expressed one extreme reaction: "Don't keep running there. There's nothing there. I guess it's okay on Decoration Day." A Japanese American woman provided the counterpoint with an explosive "Twice a week! *Important* to visit the grave!"

TABLE 3-1

		B (%)	J (%)	M (%)	A (%)
(014)	"How many persons that you knew personally died in the past two years?" None	10	17	19	26
	8 or more	25	15	9	8
(023)	"How many persons who were dying did you visit or talk with during the past two years?" None	62	58	61	68
	2 or more	16	17	15	18
(020)	"How many funerals have you attended in the past two years?" None	33	16	40	45
	8 or more	9	17	2	4
(022)	"How often have you visited someone's grave, other than during a burial service, during the past two years?" Never	71	36	56	59
	4 or more	4	39	17	15

Two points strike us as especially significant in this context. First, except for visits to the grave, the Anglos are obviously less in contact with the dying and with death than are the other ethnic groups. Second, and more meaningful, death and dying are very much a part of the experience of adults. During a two-year period, over two out of three adults have attended at least one funeral, and more than 25% have attended three or more; most adults have been friendly with at least two persons who died, and 25% have known five or more; and nearly 40% have visited or talked with at least one dying person. Perhaps—and only perhaps—we have denial mechanisms that exclude the affective impact of death and dying, but we most certainly do not escape continuing contact with this ultimate reality of life. Even the intimacy of touching the body at the funeral was considered acceptable by a majority of all groups except for the Japanese (B 51%, J 31%, M 76%, A 51%), and, although Blacks and Japanese would hold back, over half the Mexicans and one-third of the Anglos would be likely to kiss the dead person. One woman explained, "I don't know why—I just couldn't do it—touch the body." (Kiss the body?) "Oh, no." She paused a moment. "I don't even like to kiss him *now*."

In 1915, G. Stanley Hall could write, ". . . it appears that the first impression of death often comes from a sensation of coldness in touching the face or hands of the corpse of a relative, and the reaction is a nervous start at the contrast with the warmth which cuddling and hugging were wont to bring" (p. 551). Hall's data had been gathered some two decades earlier. Although much reduced in frequency, such experiences are undoubtedly still not uncommon. These findings, and others to be discussed later, cause us to believe—with Donaldson (1972)—that we have proclaimed this to be a death-denying society too often, and that the concept should either be effectively operationalized or else discarded.

The term *denial* is used both sociologically and psychodynamically, with relatively little overlap between the two usages. We will use the term in this volume only when there is evidence that the individual is utilizing defense mechanisms to protect himself against awareness of death or something death-related. We will use the term *death-avoiding* to cover—we feel with more precision—such acts as not liking to go to funerals. Parsons & Lidz (1967) also question the common assumption that ours is a death-denying society, stating, "American society has institutionalized a broadly stable, though flexible and changing, orientation to death that is fundamentally not a 'denial' but a mode of acceptance appropriate to our primary cultural patterns of activism" (p. 134). And Kastenbaum & Aisenberg (1972) ask why we so fear the fear of death.

In integrating these findings, we see that Anglos are likely to have the least contact with the dying and the dead, are probably more death-avoidant, although they do not admit to greater fear of death. Perhaps more salient, our data suggest that the avoidance of death is not a global concept, but must be restricted to more specific occurrences, i.e., what kind of avoidance behavior to what kinds of death for what reasons.

Attendance at funerals correlates significantly with having visited a dying person, and the correlation is substantial (r=0.41), but neither of these variables correlates substantially with willingness to inform a person of his own death (r=0.17 and 0.19 respectively). Both individual uniqueness and cultural roles contribute to the variance. Thus, although age, sex and ethnicity are predictive of reliable differences in how one responds to each of the numerous kinds of death-related encounters, considerable variability is evident even within these categories. In short, being Black, being old, and being female all help predict how an individual will respond to each of several kinds of death-encounters, while being an elderly Black woman will be even more predictive. However, considerable individual variation does exist among elderly Black women. Furthermore, knowing how a person will react to one kind of death setting (e.g., attending funerals) provides only limited predictive accuracy in determining how they will react to another setting (e.g., informing a dying person).

Before leaving this issue, we should point out that for *some* individuals, death-avoidance is sufficiently pervasive that they do exhibit avoidant behavior in a wide variety of situations. Even when their overt behavior does not appear consistent with such avoidance, they pay a penalty in anxiety or extensive use of defense mechanisms. Sometimes they display counter-phobic behavior through a virtually ritualistic attendance to planning their own funeral or establishing their own claim to immortality. Probing this issue would require depth interviews or similar methodologies.

Kastenbaum (personal communication) offers an alternative way of viewing these variables. Rather than utilizing only the concept of death-avoidance, he suggests applying the approach-avoidance mode of traditional psychology. Thus any given behavior could be viewed as the result of the interaction between the motivation to approach and the motivation to avoid. Not visiting graves could then be interpreted as having a low approach value rather than a high avoidance value. This strikes us as an important refinement and may help avoid some non-parsimonious assumptions about motivation when the root of the behavior (or lack of behavior) can be viewed as an absence of felt need.

COMMUNICATING WITH THE DYING

Ever since Glaser & Strauss (1965) published their monograph, *Awareness of Dying*, the issue of whether the patient should be made aware of his coming death has been discussed—sometimes heatedly—

among physicians, nurses, clergymen, behavioral scientists, and others. More than half our respondents felt that a dying person (described as approximately the same age and of the same sex as the interviewee) should be told that he is dying, but many more Anglo Americans favored this approach than members of other ethnic groups (B 60%, J 49%, M 37%, A 71%). One Black American stated, "I think the person would want to know. Those things should not be kept a secret unless they are too old and can't stand the shock." An older Anglo man explained, "Yes, but in a roundabout way. No two people are alike, so you can't treat them all the same. I know one person who was told, but the doctor was too blunt and it about killed the whole family. He should have done it in a more roundabout way—gradually—work up to it." A woman presented the opposite position: "I wouldn't want to know. If she knows, she would worry."

The task of communicating was left primarily to the physician, with some member of the family listed as the second most appropriate choice. All ethnic groups responded in this fashion. For example, "The doctor, assuming the guy can take it. Also have to take into account how well the doctor knows the patient, how much confidence the patient has in the doctor, the ability of the doctor to relate to the patient, what the family members think . . . Cannot say definitely any one person." Although survey data often do not reflect it, respondents constantly express the need to approach matters individually, to take individual differences into account.

Although over half the respondents felt that dying friends should be informed, three-fourths wish, themselves, to be informed. Only among Mexican Americans does this drop to as low as 60% (B 71%, J 77%, M 60%, A 77%). Each ethnic group has a higher proportion of persons wishing themselves to be informed than feeling that others should be told. The two groups that are most familistic, the Japanese Americans and the Mexican Americans, show the greatest discrepancy between their own desire to know and willingness to let others know, reflecting a strong desire to protect and a note of paternalism perhaps.

Physicians are also much less likely to feel patients should be informed than the patients are, while both physicians and laymen, according to several studies, are more likely to want to be told themselves than to feel others should be told (reviewed in Hinton, 1972; also Feifel, Hanson, Jones, & Edwards, 1967).

The results of other studies do not differ appreciably from ours. Hinton reviews four studies in which patients and their relatives were asked whether a cancer patient should be enabled to learn about his condition: the results were overwhelmingly affirmative, ranging from 66% to 89%. Feifel & Jones (1968) found 77% wished to be informed, drawing from both physical and mentally ill and normals; Vernon (1970) in a primarily youthful sample found a 71% favorable response.

Numerous authors make a very strong case for informing a terminally ill person (e.g., Ross, 1969). Koenig (1969) has gone so far as to tabulate the articles that provide the pros and cons, and ends up with a distinct majority favoring some method of permitting the dying to become aware of their impending death.

That the task of informing the dying is not an easy one is attested to by the admission of the respondents that only a handful (between 4% and 7% of each group) had ever told anyone he was dying and that fewer than half of the remainder felt capable of serving as informant in such a situation (B 51%, J 47%, M 19%, A 52%). An elderly Black American woman answered, "I don't think I could tell anyone. I'd just tell him when the Lord's ready, He will call him." An ex-medical technician was forced by circumstances to answer a man who "was literally almost cut in half . . . I told him that it didn't look too good but that we were taking him to the hospital where he would get the best of care. He never made it to the hospital." Of 295 Catholic and Unitarian women who were asked whether they were afraid of encountering a dying friend, Chenard (1972) found that equal thirds were "a great deal," "some," or "a little or not at all" afraid. There was no difference between the two religious groups.

GRIEF AND MOURNING

The loss of others through death is immensely painful. Such loss gives rise to sadness and melancholy, anger, resentment, guilt, fear and anxiety, and sometimes to a search for meaning, a turning toward or against God, the desire to lay blame on someone or something, the attempt to find a reason for the death.

The death of another disturbs us in several ways. First, it may remind us of our own finite nature, of the obvious but avoided truth that we too shall come to a termination of our existence on earth—which, for some, means termination of all existence. Second, the death of someone close removes something from our own lives—we no longer can relate to that individual, no longer receive his warmth, friendship, support, no longer depend upon him or gain pleasure from his depending upon us. This is object loss—it is also objective loss. Sometimes the loss removes from the family, the business, the institutions, the community, an important part of that structure. The tragedy of the loss is often related to how much dislocation and upset occur in the lives of the survivors.

Third, the intricate set of social obligations and interactions that death brings to a close are often not ready for total finality. The survivors may be angry at being deserted and attribute the death, in an unconscious and mystical fashion, to willfulness on the part of the deceased (this response may be intense following a suicide). They may feel overwhelming guilt in their real or fantasized role in his death, for their perceived failures in offering attention or concern or—in some instances—for their relief that the death has finally occurred. Things undone and unsaid can no longer be compensated for, although the funeral service may offer some opportunity for self-absolution. Expressions of guilt have come up spontaneously in all subgroups, i.e., ethnic, age, sex, education.

In describing the feelings of a wife subsequent to her husband's heart attack, Schoenberg & Stichman (1974) point out that the woman often berates herself for not having made certain that her husband had eaten more moderately, worked less intensely, exercised more, and worried less. Or, in the case of the wife that had done these things, the self-condemnation would be for having nagged her husband unduly and thus raised the tension level of the home. The double bind is evident in many instances following loss.

Although the ability to express one's grief openly is frequently encouraged by professionals in the mental health field, our respondents displayed considerable reluctance to do so. Fewer than half would worry if they could not cry (except for Mexican Americans, 50% of whom responded in the affirmative). Three-fourths of the Blacks, Japanese, and Anglos would "try very hard to control the way (they) showed (their) emotions in public," although less than two-thirds of the Mexicans agreed to this. Nonetheless, a great majority of all groups and almost all of the Mexican Americans would "let (themselves) go and cry (them)selves out" in either private or public (B 64%, J 71%, M 88%, A 70%). Apparently emotional expression is appropriate, even encouraged, in private, but is expected to be constrained in public. One woman explained her feelings about the entire matter: "I would do whatever felt natural." Here, however, our observations indicate a real discrepancy between expressed norms and observed behavior in the Black American community. Perhaps attempts are made to control public expression of feeling, but they do not appear successful, since crying, moaning, wailing and fainting are commonly observed.

Two-thirds of the Black Americans and over 80% of the others would carry out their spouse's last wishes even if they were felt to be senseless and inconvenient. Such responses might arise from guilt, but we feel that the motivation is more from a sense of obligation, a recognition of the importance of the dead person and perhaps a kind of denial (we would not assume this to be emotionally unhealthy) that the relationship has been severed. Simmons (1945) describes how effectively final wishes can bind the survivors in some cultures.

A family member would usually be sought for comfort and support in time of bereavement, although clergymen were also cited with moderate frequency. Less often selected was a friend, and about 8% of the respondents said they would not turn to anyone for comfort. Support for the bereaved is not only emotional, however. The death of a spouse requires practical help, such as keeping the household going. Most people would seek this help from relatives (B 50%, J 74%, M 65%, A 45%), but friends, neighbors, and fellow church members were picked by nearly one-fourth (B 42%, J 9%, M 14%, A 45%). Previously we found the Anglos least likely to participate in rituals for the dead; now we find that they have fewer expectations of their family in times of crisis. It would appear that the mutual obligation structure is weakest in Anglo families in the Los Angeles area.

The extent to which a particular death is perceived as tragic seems to vary as a function of the age, the sex, and the kind of death involved (Table 3-2). And the different ethnic groups differ considerably in their evaluations. Particularly striking were the strong Anglo feelings about slow deaths and about the deaths of infants and children, and the relative unanimity about the meaning of the deaths of the elderly.

TABLE 3-2
WHICH SEEMS MORE TRAGIC

	B (%)	J (%)	M (%)	A (%)
(068)				
Sudden Death	39	43	41	20
Slow Death	58	50	50	68
Equally Tragic	3	7	9	12
(Don't Know)	(−)	(−)	(−)	(6)
(074)				
Man's Death	10	34	9	16
Woman's Death	38	29	36	25
Equally Tragic	50	36	55	52
Other	2	2	0	7
(Don't Know)	(6)	(−)	(5)	(13)

	Most Tragic	Least Tragic	Most Tragic	Least Tragic	Most Tragic	Least Tragic	Most Tragic	Least Tragic
(069 & 073)								
Infant's Death (0-1 year old)	14	24	8	18	13	25	17	14
Child's Death (around 7)	26	5	24	2	25	1	44	0
Youth's Death (around 25)	45	2	43	1	48	0	32	2
Middle-aged Person's Death (around 40)	8	2	22	2	6	5	5	1
Elderly Person's Death (around 75)	6	67	1	74	6	69	0	82
Other	1	1	3	3	3	1	1	1
(Don't Know)	(2)	(−)	(−)	(−)	(4)	(−)	(2)	(−)

TABLE 3-3

In general, after what period of time would you personally consider it all right for a (person of respondent's age group, ethnic group, sex)

		B (%)	J (%)	M (%)	A (%)
(110)	To remarry;				
	Unimportant to wait	34	14	22	26
	1 week - 6 monts	15	3	1	23
	1 year	25	30	38	34
	2 years or more	11	26	20	11
	Other/DK/Never	16	28	19	7
(111)	To stop wearing black?				
	Unimportant to wait	62	42	52	53
	1 week - 1 month	24	26	11	31
	6 months	6	7	7	5
	1 year or more	5	14	28	1
	Other /DK	4	11	3	11
(112)	To return to place of employment	39	22	27	47
	1 day - 1 week	39	28	37	35
	1 month or more	17	35	27	9
	Other/DK	6	16	9	10
(113)	To start going out with other men/women?				
	Unimportant to wait	30	17	17	25
	1 week - 1 month	14	8	4	9
	6 months - 1 year	24	22	22	29
	2 years or more	11	34	40	21
	Other/DK	21	19	18	17

Death and loss are not only personal matters. They are also social. Society prescribes standards for grief and mourning, and each individual grieves not only from his personal sorrow, but in a style which is the product of early socialization and later social dictates. This is especially obvious in the length of time the mourner is expected to refrain from returning to usual behavior patterns. Although nearly one-fourth of the respondents felt that the widow(er) could appropriately remarry at any time after the death of his spouse, over half the Japanese Americans and Mexican Americans felt at least one year's wait was necessary, many feeling that two years or more would be preferable and some stating that remarriage was never appropriate. Since the question (and those following) was asked in terms of the age, sex, and ethnicity of the respondent, answers to this item were related to age, i.e., many of those who said remarriage was inappropriate were speaking of an older person remarrying (see Table 3-3).

Respondents were understandably more lenient in stipulating how long the bereaved should wear black. Over 40% of the Japanese Americans and over half of all other groups felt that black clothing was unimportant and need not be worn. In a major study of bereavement in England, Gorer (1965) interviewed over 350 men and women who had lost a close relative during the previous five years. Of these, 37% wore no symbolic clothing or armband, and only 20% wore anything for longer than three months. Relatively few of our respondents felt that black should be worn beyond six months, but we have no data directly corresponding with those of Gorer. Similarly, a majority of all ethnicities felt that a week or less was ample time to remain away from work, roughly half of these indicating that the bereaved person should be able to return to work as soon as he wished.

Going out with others of the opposite sex was treated more conservatively, although a young Mexican American woman made the point that this would be all right "As soon as you felt no guilt about it." Less than one-fourth felt that waiting was unimportant, with the median response being between six months and a year. The Blacks and the Anglos were consistently more casual than the Mexicans and the Japanese, seeming to form a pattern in keeping with funeral attendance and other family interactions. About 30% of those who responded stated that they would begin to worry that mourning was extended too long if crying and grieving lasted as much as a couple of weeks; a slightly larger proportion would not be concerned for at least six months; while the remainder opted for an intermediate period, usually between one and three months.

How do you know when grief is not normal? Around 30% did not know, but the remainder displayed considerable variability. Half the Blacks indicated that they would look for abnormal behavior, compared to 27-29% of the others; one-third of the Blacks and one-fourth of the Anglos (compared to 15-16% of the others) would look for withdrawal and extreme apathy. The Mexicans were alert to the bereaved under-reacting, i.e., not showing any overt signs of grief or, as one said, "When they can't cry" (34% compared to under 10% of the others). Two out of five Japanese gave answers that could not be coded in our available categories. The issue needs to be pursued, because it gives promise of major differences in expectations of the various ethnic groups.

ENCOUNTER WITH THE DEATH OF SELF

Do people fear death? We don't know. All we can say with certainty is that study after study has shown that people *say* they do not fear death. How valid are these comments? Again, we don't know. University students displayed the same reaction time lags to death words that they did to sex words, while their galvanic skin responses and reaction times to death words were significantly and substantially greater than to neutral words (Alexander, Colley & Adlerstein, 1957). But does this suggest greater fear? It could imply excitement, fascination, or even response to the unexpected.

Most studies of fear of death have been conducted with specific age groups, especially with either university students or the elderly. These are discussed in the chapter on age, so that comparisons can be made with proper age groups. However, a few investigations have cut across age lines. Neither Scott (1896) nor Hall (1897) asked directly about fear of death in their questionnaires, although Hall did say 20 years later, "We long to be just as well, strong, happy, and vital as possible, and strive against everything that impedes this wish or will . . . We love life supremely and cannot have too much of it . . . while we dread all that interferes with it" (p. 569). Feifel and Jones (1968) combined the seriously ill, the chronically ill and disabled, the mentally ill, and normals into one sample, with roughly equal numbers in each category. Of this conglomerate, 71% verbalized no fear of death.

In Hinton's observations of the terminally ill, he felt that "as many as two-thirds of those who died under fifty years of age were clearly apprehensive, whereas less than a third of those over sixty years were as anxious" (1967, p. 84). Of Chenard's Catholic and Unitarian women, 11% were very much afraid, 21% were not at all afraid, and the rest were split between some fear and little fear (1972).

In a recent national survey, conducted by the Harris Poll organization under the auspices of the National Council on the Aging, individuals in a large sample were asked to respond to the open-ended question: What are the worst things about being over 65 years of age? Fear of death was given as an answer by 9% of the total sample, but by only 6% of those 50 years of age and older. This compares with 62% of the sample who indicated that poor health was one of the worst things about being old and 33% who stipulated loneliness. Blacks mentioned fear of death only 2% of the time, compared to 10% for the non-Blacks (other ethnic groups were not represented in sufficient numbers for breakdowns) (National Council on the Aging, 1975). When the same respondents were asked to list what they considered to be very serious problems of old age, fear of death was not among the 12 most common concerns listed either by those between 18 and 64 or by those 65 and over.

Riley (in Riley et al, 1968) reports that only 4% of his national survey sample "gave evidence of fear or emotional anxiety in connection with death" (p. 332). Other studies, although based upon samples limited by geography, age, or education, found comparable results ranging up to around 10% or so indicating fear of death. Our respondents were either more frightened of death—or more truthful in their responses. We asked, "Some people say they are afraid to die and others say they are not. How do you feel?" The interviewer coded the response in the categories *terrified/afraid*, *neither afraid not unafraid*, or *unafraid/eager*. Only two people could be clearly categorized as *eager*, and about 2% gave responses classified by the interviewer as *terrified*. Because of these small numbers, we combined those categories with adjacent ones, as indicated just above.

Using this approach, over a quarter of all respondents were classed as afraid of dying (B 19%, J 31%, M 33%, A 22%), while just over half were unafraid (B 50%, J 50%, M 54%, A 53%). About 2½% were uncodable, and the rest were classified as neither afraid nor unafraid. Why we received such a low proportion of persons claiming to be unafraid is difficult to say. Perhaps their having already participated in some 30 minutes of death-related discussion heightened their anxieties—or perhaps it enabled them to reply with greater honesty. To be consistent with our policy of assuming face validity of any statements, unless substantial evidence suggests otherwise, we propose that our data represent accurately the feelings of the respondents at the time the question was asked.

One respondent commented, "So many say they are ready (to die), but I don't feel near ready. Judging from the way I got frightened at the earthquake, I'm not near ready." A Mexican American man said, "I *say* I'm unafraid, but if I had time to think about it, and I knew I would die shortly, I don't know—I guess I would certainly be concerned." And an Anglo American man put his view succinctly: "You are *nuts* if you aren't afraid of death."

This leads to the question, how stable are attitudes toward death? Ivey and Bardwick (1968) have shown that death anxiety of women varies as a function of their menstrual cycle—as do other kinds of anxiety. We know of no other evidence on this issue. However, we suggest no mystique for death attitudes—they undoubtedly vary as a function of situation, mood, experience, and shifting cultural milieu, just as all other attitudes vary.

Whatever a person's attitude might be regarding death, what has influenced these feelings? For this question we provided the respondent a card with 10 alternatives, plus an eleventh, "OTHER (SPECIFY)." Over one-third of the respondents selected the statement, "The death of someone close," as having influenced them the most (B 26%, J 41%, M 39%, A 35%). "My father died when I was 5½ years old. I was very close to him, and when I heard of his death, I ran away from home and went into the woods. I was gone for 2½ days. I felt as if my whole world had collapsed, as if I had no one to turn to any longer. I was desperate. I cried a lot." Second most frequently selected was, "Your religious background" (B 40%,

J 13%, M 21%, A 25%). Nearly 19% stated that having been close to their own death, or believing themselves to be, was their greatest influence. Reading, conversations, the death of an animal, mystical experiences, funerals or other rituals, the media, were all listed by only 5% or less of the sample.

Shneidman's survey, while not drawing from a comparable sample, obtained some parallel results. Of his respondents, 35% stated that introspection and meditation most influenced their attitudes toward death; we did not include that alternative, but we doubt whether many of our respondents would have selected it. Second and third most frequently mentioned by Shneidman's sample were the death of someone else and religious upbringing (19% and 15% respectively); these fit quite well with our data. Over one-third of Shneidman's group stated that existential philosophy influenced their present attitudes toward their own death more than such concerns as pollution, violence, television, war, poverty, and so forth. We believe that very few of our respondents would have selected that alternative.

Although 19% of the respondents felt that either actually being close to death or thinking they were close to death had the greatest impact upon their attitudes, over twice that many had—at least once—believed that they were close to dying (B 48%, J 31%, M 49%, A 37%). Of these, exactly half of the Blacks and Japanese asserted that the experience had affected their lives, slightly under half of the Mexicans and Anglos agreeing also. Unfortunately, responses to the question of how the experience affected them were so scattered, that the categories became too small for serious consideration. Here, too, the response to near death was highly individualistic, varying with circumstances, cultural background, and other experiences before and after the event.

Do people often think about their own death? Kennard (1937) informs us that the Hopi "man who thinks of the dead or of the future life instead of being concerned with worldly activities, is thereby bringing about his own death" (p. 492). Simmons (1945) does not mention any other example of this, but a number of respondents in our study—proportionately more Black Americans than others—referred to being worried that talking about death would bring it about. Scott's sample of 226 adults indicated that only 7% never "dwelt on death or suicide," while 60% responded in such fashion that they obviously gave at least some thought to the matter (1896). Vernon's student sample showed only 45% who said they thought only "rarely" or "very rarely" about their death (1970).

Additional studies add numbers, but little insight. Feifel and Jones (1968) in their investigation of a primarily mentally or physically ill sample, found that 44% thought of death "rarely" and 42% occasionally. Fulton (1965), using a mail survey with a limited percent of response, also found that 40% rarely or never thought about death, while 12% dwelled on it frequently or all the time. And in 1963, Riley's national sample (1971) splits into almost equal thirds, stipulating "often," "occasionally," and "hardly ever/never." Shneidman found 5% of his respondents thought of their death once a day, while 21% contemplated it no more than once a year. In a study of persons 45 years of age and older, drawn from Black, Mexican, and Anglo American samples also in Los Angeles, 35% stated they thought about their own death "not at all," 65% "occasionally," and 9% "frequently" (Bengtson et al, 1976). Interviews in retirement communities found that fewer than 10% stated that they thought of death very frequently, while nearly 15% claimed not to think of their own death at all (Mathieu, 1975).

How do our respondents compare? Sadly, almost none of the studies produced directly comparable data. Nonetheless, there is reasonable consistency. Over one in six thinks daily about his death, while over one in four contemplates his termination at least once a week (B 34%, J 10%, M 37%, A 25%). On the other hand, 25% say they never think of their own death, and over twice that proportion claim that once a year is the most often that thoughts of personal death arise (i.e., combining "Never," "Hardly Ever," and "At least yearly") (B 41%, J 69%, M 38%, A 47%). One person makes the valuable point that, "One does think about death, but doesn't remember how often."

If conscious thoughts of one's own death are highly variable in terms of frequency, dreaming about one's own death is much less common, with less than 30% admitting that they ever have such dreams. Middleton's (1936) university students reported equivalent figures, only 37% indicating such dreams.

Another much-discussed aspect of the process of dying is that of the efficacy of the will-to-live or, conversely, the will-to-die. Weisman and Hacket (1961) discussed the post-operative deaths of six persons, all of whom anticipated their subsequent deaths and none of whom died from obvious medical causes. The professional and popular literature is filled with other examples (e.g., Kalish, 1965). Except for the Mexican Americans, the overwhelming majority of each group agreed that "People can hasten or slow their own death through a will-to-live or a will-to-die" (B 88%, J 85%, M 62%, A 83%).

One Japanese American funeral director suggested a statistical study to verify his own observations that a highly disproportionate number of deaths occur within one month of the deceased person's birthday. Such research has, in a sense, been conducted. Phillips and Feldman (1973) found a significant reduction in deaths during the month prior to the birth month and a substantial increase in deaths during the month of birth and the month following; this was verified on several independent samples, apparently confirming the perceptions of the funeral director. This information suggests that the dying person has some control over the actual time of his demise. A most graphic case described to the senior author was by a young woman studying for her doctorate whose mother was terminally ill. Although the older woman had been seriously ill for several months, she appeared in good spirits and alert until the day following her daughter's doctoral preliminary orals (the most demanding single day of her graduate program), when the mother died peacefully in her sleep. She had frequently expressed the double concern of wanting to know that her daughter had been successful (she was) and of not wanting to place the burden of a death upon the immensely important event.

Many supernatural and mystical feelings surround death. Thus nearly half of all respondents were affirmative in answering, "Have you ever experienced or felt the presence of anyone after he had died?" (B 55%, J 29%, M 54%, A 38%), and one-fourth of these were manifested while awake and were perceived through the senses. This issue and the data are discussed at greater length elsewhere (Kalish and Reynolds, 1973). Pursuing feelings of mysticism surrounding death, over one-third of the Mexicans and between 12% and 15% of the other groups had experienced the "unexplainable feeling that (they) were about to die." We explicitly eliminated from our count instances in which these feelings occurred during dreams.

Even more persons had had such a feeling about someone else (B 37%, J 17%, M 38%, A 30%), and over 70% of these respondents stated that the presentiment was validated by actual death on at least one occasion. We feel strongly that these data have an important message to professionals who work with the dying and the bereaved: mystical feelings, "being in touch with his ether," "sensing the vibes," or actually having vivid and realistic contact with the dead, all these experiences are commonplace to large segments of the American public, and it is time they cease being approached as inevitably pathological.

In some settings, people routinely express their desire to die, e.g., at the Japanese American nursing home, nurses told us that nearly all the patients express such a wish at some time or other during their stay. Other than those suffering severe physical or emotional anguish, however, extremely few people wish to die, whether or not they state that they fear death. What is there about life that they cherish? Diggory and Rothman (1961) described seven values destroyed by death, and they obtained ratings of the importance of these values from over 500 respondents. Shneidman administered the same questions in his *Psychology Today* study. (Shneidman also reports on the same items administered to 120 Harvard and Radcliff students.) Although the Diggory-Rothman sample was not limited to college students, about two-thirds were under 25 years old, two-thirds were unmarried, and one-fourth were

TABLE 3-4

Here are some reasons why people don't want to die. Tell me whether they are very important to you, important to you, or not important to you. (*Don't know* responses about 3%).

	B (%)	J (%)	M (%)	A (%)
(080) I am afraid of what might happen to my body after death.				
Very important	3	5	8	5
Important	6	11	9	11
Not important	91	84	83	84
(081) I could no longer care for my dependents.				
Very important	26	42	47	44
Important	26	33	29	29
Not important	48	25	24	26
(082) I am uncertain as to what might happen to me				
Very important	9	14	11	9
Important	16	19	21	19
Not important	75	66	68	72
(083) I could no longer have any experiences				
Very important	3	11	7	6
Important	9	26	27	23
Not important	88	63	66	70
(084) My death would cause grief to my relatives and friends				
Very important	19	14	38	29
Important	55	48	40	50
Not important	26	38	23	21
(085) All my plans and projects would come to an end.				
Very important	10	14	15	14
Important	24	43	34	22
Not important	66	44	51	64
(085) The process of dying might be painful.				
Very important	13	18	30	18
Important	41	38	27	36
Not important	46	44	43	46

Jewish. Diggory and Rothman also presented the values on a matched pair basis, the respondent being required to select the alternative felt to represent the greatest loss, while we had our respondents indicate whether they felt the value was "very important," "important," or "not-important." Results are, thus, not directly comparable to our study (see Table 3-4)

Our respondents were most concerned by the possibility of causing grief to their friends and relatives (based upon combining "very important" and "important.") Diggory and Rothman also found this to be the most important, but it ranked fifth for Shneidman, perhaps due to the different family roles of his subjects. Over half the Blacks and 75% each of our other groups also listed not being able to care for dependents as "important" or "very important," but this concern was ranked much lower by the other studies, depending as they did upon respondents not so likely to have dependents. However, Shaffer's (1970) study of just over 30 individuals who were concerned with making out their wills had results in keeping with ours. Hall (1915) expresses the feeling, "Often the last thought as the soul launches out to cross the bar is for others. There is often a tenacious clinging in thought of . . . a friend, and there is very rarely . . . any concern for the individual's future . . ." (p. 554).

Between one-fourth and one-third of each ethnic group felt that being uncertain as to what might happen to them was important or very important, ranking it fifth, while not being able to have any more experiences distressed well under one-third of our respondents to rank sixth. Shneidman's high-achievement sample placed it first by a wide margin, while Diggory and Rothman's intermediate group listed it fourth. And all studies agreed that what happened to the body after death was least important (see Table 3-5).

Clearly, concern over survivors ranks most highly as a reason for not wanting to die, while the fate of the physical body is obviously of minor importance. Fear of pain was also a major consideration. Somewhat unexpected in these results was the relatively low concern for the inability to continue with plans and projects or to have on-going experiences. If, as Kastenbaum and Aisenberg (1972) contend, cessation of experience is the one characteristic that differentiates death from other occurrences, these respondents certainly do not give the matter much status in their lives. Had we requested that the seven issues be rank-ordered, rather than rated, we could understand better the relegation of loss of experience to such a low level. The question we have, then, is not why the other reasons for not wishing to die were rated so highly, but why these two were not rated equally high. Why do two-thirds of these respondents state that loss of ability to have experiences is not important to them? Why do well over half make the same claim about the end of plans and projects?

TABLE 3-5

Comparison of importance of seven values lost by death, as ranked by respondents in three studies, based on lowest proportion of "Unimportant" rating.

	Kalish and Reynolds	Diggory and Rothman	Shneidman
My death would cause grief to my relatives and friends.	1	1	5
I could no longer care for my dependents.	2	5	3
The process of dying might be painful.	3	3	2
All my plans and projects would come to an end.	4	2	4
I am uncertain as to what might happen to me.	5	6	6
I could no longer have any experiences.	6	4	1
I am afraid of what might happen to my body after death.	7	7	7

Differences in sampling and methodology are described in the text.

One obvious answer is that many respondents do not actually believe that their death will result in the end of self-aware existence. Those who believe in a traditional Christian or Buddhist concept of after-life may not feel they need be concerned about these losses. Another explanation is simply that people are not that enthralled with life. This suggests the possibility that the elderly, who have presumably become disengaged to some extent with life, would care less about these matters than younger persons. Examination of the data does show that to be the case, but it can only explain away a portion of those who respond in that fashion.

We would opt for a different kind of explanation. When people think of death, they tend to think in terms of the loss of others, of pain, of financial difficulties. They seldom think about ceasing to have experiences, which inevitably constitute life itself. When philosophers and others have stated that people cannot conceptualize their own deaths, they are often referring to cessation, including cessation of experience. To contemplate this is to contemplate nothingness, absence, void—the task is overwhelming. It is to conceive of that which has never—and can never be—experienced. Therefore, the notion is not dealt with and it is not conceptualized as an important reason for not wishing to die. Shneidman's respondents being younger, more introspective, and more intellectually sophisticated, may have given more thought to this issue.

In our writing this report, we sometimes find ourselves focusing on statistics and theory, rather than exposing ourselves to the personal and existential meaning of pain, of loss, and of death. In this regard, we want to quote from the report of one of our research assistants who effectively combined the research demands of our project with her own desire to offer personal service.

"Mr. Z. was a friendly, gentle, gregarious individual in his early thirties whose physical appearance reminded me a great deal of another patient who had just died of leukemia. In all the time Mr. Z. spoke with me, he never once mentioned his illness by name—it was as though he had been afraid to say the word. On my second visit, he talked a lot about God and made frequent references to passages in the Bible, he spoke about faith and how one has to think of God as being *un Dios Posesiro*. He even read me a passage from the New Testament. I commented that I hadn't seen anyone with such fervent faith in a long time, especially a young Mexican man. I then asked him if he was Protestant. 'Yes, I'm a Seventh-Day Adventist.'

"My third visit. Mr. Z. recognized me and said hello. He told me he wasn't feeling well and was in pain, because some liquid had been drawn from his liver. The whole process was extremely painful, and Mr. Z. was very uncomfortable. He looked at me and said, 'I'd rather be . . .' and then he stopped, without completing the sentence. (Was he afraid that if he put the word *dead* at the end of his sentence, it might become a reality?)

"My fifth visit. Walking into Mr. Z.'s room I could see the anguish and pain he was going through. He restlessly changed from his back to his left side to his right side, all in vain. He was desperately fighting that pain. On top of his nightstand, beside his bed, I noticed a vase with red roses. Mr. Z. noticed me looking at his flowers: 'My wife brought them to me yesterday and look at them—they're all . . .all . . . dead.' He stared emptily, as if all hope for life were gone for himself as well as for his flowers.

"Never having seen anyone in such pain, I felt helpless and upset because I couldn't think of anything to do. I also looked at the roses in desperation. Then my eye caught sight of one rose that had been hidden. It was alive and in full bloom! 'Look!! You were too quick to judge. One is still alive!!' Mr. Z. looked over and smiled.

"My sixth visit. Mr. Z. was in such pain that he could hardly bear it. His only consolation was the news that he did not have cancer, but had a rare blood disease. The nurse had told him that he couldn't have any more medication and that he needed to relax. Then she left. 'Will you stay with me a while?' he asked. I nodded and he stared at me.

" 'Try to lie back and relax.' He tried, but he couldn't. He still kept fighting. In a final attempt, I told him, 'Lie back and hold my hand. Every time the pain comes, squeeze my hand as hard as you can.' He did. I sat with him for about thirty minutes before I felt the pressure on my hand slowly relax. He had fallen asleep."

(From the notes of Patricia Osuna Salazar)

Predicting the Future

We asked our respondents to look into their future for a few moments. How do they predict they will die? and when? Almost all of those who responded (many did not respond: B 37%, J 9%, M 34%, A 21%) predicted a natural death for themselves (about 90%), and median age at death of 75. (The 25%ile was 69 years of age, and the 75%ile was 82, with a range from 27 to over 100.) Over two-thirds of Shneidman's much younger group picked "an old age," but specific year of death was not provided. Significant differences (based on 't' tests) were found between the Blacks and each other ethnic group, with the former expecting to live longer. (A more detailed analysis is presented in Reynolds and Kalish, 1974.) Bengtson, Cuellar, and Ragan (1976), in their study of ethnicity and aging, also found that Blacks had longer subjective life expectancy than Mexican Americans or Anglos.

But how do they want to die? Relatively few have difficulty answering this one (under 7%), and all but a handful want to die a natural death. (We did find that 2% of the Blacks and 3% of the Anglos wanted to die by suicide, while about 25% of the Japanese and 7% of the Mexicans wanted to die in an accident.) And when? The median age was 80, with the 25%ile at 70 (virtually the same as for the expectation of death) and the 75%ile at 90. The range was from 40 to well beyond 100 again. And 66% of Shneidman's respondents also opted for "old age."

Although it is well-known that most people now die in hospitals and convalescent centers, many more of our respondents would prefer dying at home. Among the Blacks, the ratio was 2:1, and among the Mexicans, a little lower. However the Japanese and Anglos both preferred dying at home by better than 4:1.

We also asked how the person would spend his last six months, assuming he learned that he was dying from a terminal illness. Answers were coded by the interviewers, and they ranged over a number of categories. About one-fourth would make no change in life style (B 31%, J 25%, M 12%, A 36%), and another one-fifth would focus attention on their inner life (e.g., contemplate, pray). However about one-sixth would undergo a marked change in life style, such as traveling, satisfying hedonistic demands, essentially trying to soak up as many experiences as possible (B 16%, J 24%, M 11%, A 17%). Nearly 40% of the Mexicans and about half that proportion of the others would devote their remaining time to those they love. The categories described above were pre-established, based upon our pilot testing. However, the question was open-ended, and examination of the specific answers given by interviewees shows great diversity. Thus, devoting time to loved ones might mean taking a trip with the wife, returning to live with parents, or baby-sitting with grandchildren. Each of our categories encompassed numerous specific kinds of behavior.

How would these people die? A little more than one-third would fight death, rather than accepting it, with virtually no differences by ethnicity. Explanations varied greatly. A Black high school graduate said, "I believe if you're a Christian, you wouldn't fight—just get yourself ready to go. Ask forgiveness for your sins and put yourself in the hands of the Lord." Another Black woman interpreted the question somewhat differently: "If by fight, you mean seeking any medical aid available or through positive thinking and not giving up, then I would fight." A Mexican American woman made the differentiation, "If I was in the hospital and feeling very sick, I would just accept death. But if I was out in the world, I would fight it by enjoying life as long as I possibly could." Well over half the Blacks and Japanese, but somewhat under half the Mexicans and Anglos, would tell someone of their pain rather than enduring it in silence. One made the point that, "If it was the doctor, I would tell him of my pain. I think maybe I would tell my husband, but not my son" (who was still a child). A college graduate from the Japanese American community was more fatalistic: "If it's going to hurt, it's going to hurt. The doctor knows I'm hurting already and if there was a way to prevent it, he would prevent it." An Anglo American man was more demanding: "I would ask the doctor to give me some codeine or some other pain killer." Very similar proportions would refrain from encouraging their families to be with them, if it were inconvenient. A young Japanese American woman said, "No, I wouldn't ask them, but I would feel better if they did." A Mexican American woman of about the same age explained, "I would want my husband and my child there only—not the rest of my family. Not my parents—they would probably cry and have a lot of sympathy for me, but my husband, he'd be strong." And nearly 90% of the Mexican Americans, and over half the others, would call for a clergyman. Something has happened to customary ethnic stereotypes in these figures. The stoical Japanese Americans and the emotive Mexican Americans appear to reverse expected roles in terms of expressing their feelings of pain; the aggressive, competitive Anglos were no more likely to fight death than the more accepting Mexicans or Japanese. The highly familistic Mexican Americans do encourage their families to be with them, but not so the highly familistic Japanese Americans. Our point is certainly obvious: situational factors and competing demands often weigh more heavily than even well-established modal group characteristics.

Preparing for Death

In Riley's national survey, about 80% of the respondents had purchased life insurance, around one-third had made some funeral or cemetery arrangements, and about one-fourth had made out a will. Our percentages were similar, understandably, given the economic bias in our sample. Nearly 70% had some life insurance (B 84%, J 70%, M 52%, A 65%), and about one-fifth had wills (more Anglos and fewer Mexican Americans). Around one-fourth of the Blacks, Japanese, and Anglos (and half that many Mexicans) had a financial investment in a cemetery plot, while slightly more than half that proportion had made funeral arrangements. The overwhelming majority of Shneidman's respondents believed in having a will and making prior arrangements, but no data were provided as to whether they had actually done so.

Riley learned that about half his respondents had discussed "the uncertainty of life" with those closest to them. We avoided the euphemism, and received a lower affirmative response (B 27%, J 16%, M 33%, A 37%). Also about one-fourth of the entire sample (more Anglos and fewer Japanese) had arranged for someone to handle their affairs. Among the Japanese, such arrangements are handled automatically by persons filling roles designated by long custom. Nowadays the role expectations are less dependable, but the practical business of making individual arrangements has not yet caught up with the change.

Funerals

The polemics of those who favor or oppose today's funeral industry have been widely disseminated through books (e.g., Harmer, 1963; Mitford, 1963) and articles (Harmer, 1971; Raether, 1971). But what do people want for themselves? The modal cost for an adequate funeral, as stated in our study, was an even $1,000; this was the mode for each ethnicity as well as for the entire sample. However, the means for the ethnic groups varied considerably. The mean cost expected by the Blacks was $1,075, with 30% expecting to pay under $700; comparable figures for the Japanese were $1,948 and 9%. In between were the Mexicans ($1,209 and 29%) and Anglos ($1,179 and 31%). There were highly significant 't' tests of differences between the Japanese and each other ethnic group. Shneidman's young, well-educated liberal respondents felt funerals should cost under $300 (62%). (Recall that these interviews were conducted in 1970.)

The Japanese can expect to pay the most for their funerals because more of them anticipate that friends and family will share in the expenses (B 27%, J 43%, M 30%, A 27%). On the other hand, 92% of the Japanese (compared to between 79% and 89% of the others) rejected a big elaborate funeral, and 81% (compared to between 58% and 63%) wanted a funeral with only relatives and friends rather than many friends and acquaintances in attendance. For example, a Japanese American explained hesitatingly, "No . . . it's too . . . it takes away . . . I don't like something that's gaudy." Our observations indicate that, in spite of these expressed desires, fairly elaborate funerals are common for all these groups. About one-third of all respondents expected that a large percentage of their life insurance should go toward paying funeral expenses with a higher figure among Mexican Americans and a lower one among Anglos.

Most people want the clergyman presiding at the funeral to be selected by their family after their death, and most prefer that he be of their ethnic group (except that over half the Blacks are indifferent as are large proportions of the other groups). Similar figures were found for the selection of a funeral director of the ethnic group of the respondent; a slight majority of Blacks and Anglos were indifferent, while two-thirds of the Japanese and half the Mexicans preferred ethnic solidarity.

The desire for a wake varies greatly among the ethnic groups, with percentages pro and con being B 25% vs. 53%, J 41% vs. 46%, M 68% vs. 15%, A 22% vs. 72%. The preferred location for the wake is the funeral home, except for the Japanese Americans who wish to use the church, often a necessity for the large turnouts that attend their wakes. Somewhat under one-fourth (more Anglos and fewer Mexicans) want the wake in their own home.

On the other hand, two-thirds of the Blacks and three-fourths of the Japanese want the funeral in a church, while half the Mexican Americans and half the Anglos want the services in a funeral home (only 4% overall want to use their own home). One Mexican American explained she disliked funeral corteges that sped along the freeway and that she preferred using the cemetery chapel. And about half of each group feels that children under 10 should be permitted to attend their funeral.

Customs and rituals that pertain to disposal of the body after the ceremony are also of major concern. One in four Anglos and Blacks and one in three Mexicans and Japanese would object to an autopsy, suggesting a substantial resistance still remaining to physical violation of the remains. Feifel & Jones (1968) show 27% objecting. About 20% overall, fewer Black Americans and more Japanese Americans, object to embalming, perhaps related to the latter preference for cremation. Burial is preferred by nearly 20:1 over cremation for the Mexicans and Blacks, by about 3.5:1 among the Anglos. However, over half the Japanese prefer cremation, compared to one-third who desire burial. One-third of Shneidman's group wanted to be cremated and another third would request donation to medical school or science; only 22% desired burial.

Where the body/ashes are finally deposited is also important. Over half of each group selected Los Angeles, but the reasons for selection were more varied (17% preferred a location outside of Los Angeles, but within the United States; an additional 9% opted for another country). The reasons for the selected location also vary substantially as a result of ethnicity. Most frequently mentioned was that the community was where many family members lived (B 41%, J 27%, M 30%, A 10%), but the second most frequently-mentioned was that the respondent himself lived there now (between 19% and 24%). A birthplace was cited by about 15% (more Mexicans and Blacks, fewer Japanese and Anglos).

ANOTHER KIND OF ANALYSIS

Because our focus has been primarily upon differences among ethnic groups, we decided to investigate which variables showed no significant differences, either for the entire sample or between pairs of ethnicities. There were 32 items for which we found no significant differences (having eliminated items with very small Ns, those with continuous data, and second or later choices, a total of 19).

These items, we feel, represent the human condition, at least for persons residing in Los Angeles of low to moderate income and education. These are characteristics, feelings, beliefs, expectations, behavior, that people have regardless of social class.

The items on which our subcultures essentially agreed fall into several classes. The first class of responses deals with the familiarity of contact with death. The four groups were fairly similar in regard to knowing persons who had died from (a) accidents, (b) natural causes, (c) war-related incidents and (d) suicide. Neither was there a difference in the frequency of visiting a dying person, nor of having known someone who died under circumstances in which a decision was made to tell him or not.

A second category of response dealt with the acceptance of death. Around 60% of all respondents stated they would tend to accept their own death peacefully, and over three-fourths doubted that death would ever be eliminated. The resignation toward the ultimate (not the immediate!) inevitability of death is at least in part related to the belief that God has a hand in life and death. Around 60% of all respondents felt that accidental deaths showed God working among men. When they think of the elimination of human life from the earth, they tend to think in terms of nuclear-explosions or God's judgment. There is also consensus that the deaths of old people are less tragic than those of other ages.

But despite this contact with death and this recognition of it, there are ways in which impact of death is ignored or abridged by our respondents. Is this denial? or avoidance? practical-economic necessity? or transcendance? We cannot say. But fewer than 15% have made funeral arrangements, only some 25% are paying on a funeral plot, and upwards of 80% don't care particularly what happens to their body after they die. Revealingly, fewer than half could recall ever having dreamed about their own death or dying.

There seemed to be general agreement on some role behavior related to death. For example, physicians were handed the task of informing patients of a terminal condition by a majority of each ethnic group; family members were next most likely to be given this job. And these ideals corresponded closely to the reality of cases our respondents knew about. About 50% of the respondents in each group saw a relative as an appropriate person to turn to for comfort if a spouse died. And there were fairly uniform views toward people who threaten suicide. Roughly equal percentages in all groups felt such threateners want attention, are emotionally sick, need sympathy, and need professional help. There is consensus on the proper period of grieving for those in the role of the bereaved with approximately a third of each group choosing times within the "two weeks or less," "one to three months," and "six months or more" categories.

A few scattered items that showed no significant differences may be of interest. About 80% of all groups felt a person dying of cancer probably sensed it without being told. The groups were almost equally split as to whether or not the pain of dying is an unimportant factor (ca. 45%) in not wanting to die. Some 25-30% of each group would object to having an autopsy performed on their body.

To summarize, we found each of our groups to be well acquainted with death, in some ways accepting of it, but in other ways unable or unwilling to admit its impact or plan for its coming. They showed agreement on some role behaviors and role expectations. The overall impression is one of a practical and reasonable approach to the handling of death with perhaps a dash of avoidance when personal-emotional aspects are touched upon.

CONCLUDING COMMENTS

There seems little doubt that ethnic background is an important factor in attitudes, feelings, beliefs, and expectations that people have regarding dying, death, and bereavement. The survey results show this very clearly. We would also assume that these differences are translated into differing behavior in hospitals, at home, in health and social service agencies, and in the community. Indeed, other information that will be discussed in subsequent chapters support the assumption.

At the same time that our data show substantial ethnic differences, we are also aware that individual differences within ethnic groups are at least as great as, and often much greater than, differences between ethnic groups. We will come back to this point later.

4

The Role of Age

There is no escape from death, and it is the aging process that makes this so totally and, perhaps, frighteningly evident. In the contemporary world of hygienic nations, death is an imminent reality primarily for the old.

If death affects different age groups differentially in terms of its relentless statistics, we might assume—correctly as far as our data indicate—that different age groups perceive death differentially and react to it in terms of these perceptions. Inevitably, cross-sectional data leave something to be desired in determining age differences. We are confronted with trying to decide the degree to which differences result from the individuals having gotten older and the degree to which differences result from each age cohort having been exposed to unique life events.

To explicate briefly: Our 60 and over respondents were adults when the Depression occurred and were deeply affected by the economics and the World War that dominated the 1930-1945 period. Our 20-39 age group recall the Depression, if at all, as children, and were too young to fight in World War II or—with a few exceptions—in Korea. Thus differences between these two age cohorts in terms of attitudes toward the use of money or toward military involvement might well be the outcome of having been at a different point in their life cycle when a particular event occurred. Of greater relevance to this research, consider attitudes toward funerals. We find that older people are more likely to prefer a clergyman of their own ethnicity to officiate at their funeral. Is this because people become more involved with their own ethnic group as a result of getting older? Or were the elderly of today always more inclined to remain within their own ethnicity for personal services than the young? Is it an age-related change or an age-related difference? When today's young become older, will they resemble their grandparents? Or will they tend to adhere to their present views? Or do both forces participate in the results?

We would assume, based upon our own awareness of age-related differences, that older persons would be more familistic, more sentimental, more emotional, more romantic, more traditional. For the most part, the data confirm this view. However, again the problem arises: are the elderly more familistic because familism increases as people become older? Or because today's elderly were socialized to these values during their childhood and youth? Or because the contemporary social milieu is such that older persons are much more likely to have familistic values reinforced? Without longitudinal data, we can only surmise; even with longitudinal data, we would be hard-put to prove that we were measuring consistent trends rather than historical accidents.

When we talk about age groups in the subsequent discussion, we are referring to three breakdowns, 20-39, 40-59, and 60+ (Young, Middle-aged and Old); most of our statistical analyses use these groups. Only when the discussion refers to correlations were the ages based upon the actual number of years. Within and among the three age categories there are approximately equal numbers of men and women (See our sampling procedure and rationale in Chapter 2). Proportionately, older persons, especially older men, are over-represented in comparison with general population figures for Los Angeles county.

This chapter begins with a discussion of background factors in our age cohorts, with particular emphasis on religiousness; the second section will encompass reactions to the death and dying of others, including personal interactions with the dying and with people who are now dead, the funerals of others, and grief and bereavement; the third section describes the relationship of age to feelings about one's own death, including death preparations; and the final section is an integrative discussion, trying to place the relationship of age to death and dying into a meaningful frame of reference.

WHO ARE THEY?

Background Factors

Our basic data primarily confirm what is already known about the demography of aging. Thus we find an anticipated negative correlation between age and years of formal education ($r = -0.31$), and highly significant differences among our three age categories. These differences hold for both sexes and for all ethnic groups except for Anglos. The modal education for the youngest age cohort was some college; for the middle age group, high school graduation; for the elderly, grade school. Half the older respondents were born outside the United States, compared to less than one-fourth of the others. Of the oldest age group, about two-fifths were either widows (66%) or widowers (18%), with the Mexican Americans having by far the lowest proportion (27% versus 42-53% of the other three ethnic groups).

Age differences were related in some ways to the feelings of the respondent about the interview itself. Younger men were most likely to feel positively about it, while middle age men were most often negative. The interviewers felt that the older men were more evasive and less frank, but whether this was related to the stereotypes and expectations of the primarily middle age women interviewers cannot be determined.

The older an individual is, the more he feels himself to be religiously devout in comparison to others of his ethnic group (Y 9%, M 17%, O 27%). Results are consistent for both men and women and for all ethnic groups with two exceptions: results fall short of significance for Japanese Americans, and older Mexican Americans perceive themselves as devout less often than do the middle aged.

Two levels of explanation occur regarding the age-related differences in religious devotion, a finding that has been reported often on previous occasions (see Moberg, 1971a, 1971b, and Chapter 5 in this book). First, with age people may become religious, feeling that the end of life is more predictable or wishing to make peace with the God they have relatively ignored. Second, older persons may have maintained the same views they developed in their earlier years, while younger persons have begun to move somewhat away from these traditions. A third possibility is that the older respondents misperceived their relative devoutness in relationship to younger persons. We would adhere to some combination of the first two explanations, with particular emphasis upon the second.

Religious Factors

A substantial body of research supports the observations of most people to the effect that older persons adhere more closely to traditional religious views and practices than younger persons. With one or two exceptions, our data support these previous findings. We discuss the relationship of religion to death and dying more fully in another chapter; here our concern is only with the ways in which religious factors change with age.

To ask whether individuals become "more religious" as they get older is to ask for a simplistic answer to a complex question. Being "religious" is not merely one continuum, but many interacting concepts. Glock and Stark (1965) present five dimensions of religiousness which Moberg (1965, 1971) has reviewed in terms of their relationship to age differences. Although these dimensions are themselves complex, they will suit our present purposes.

Moberg found that religious feelings and religious beliefs are more traditional among older persons, that religious knowledge probably is higher among the elderly (although Fukuyama, 1961, found no age differences to speak of), that religious observances and use of ritual remains high in old age, but begin to diminish in the very old, and that the consequences of religion upon personal and social life are difficult to evaluate.

Our data basically confirm Moberg's conclusions. As indicated previously, older persons are significantly more likely to see themselves as relatively devout than other age groups. Not only were almost all relevant chi-squares significant, but the correlation of 0.30 between age and self-perceived relative devotion was highly statistically significant. Swenson (1967) also found older persons more in agreement with the statement "I am very religious (more than most people)."

Also, the older the individual, the more likely he was to consider his religious background as most important in influencing his attitudes toward death. Only 15% of the youngest group, compared to 24% and 38% of the older age groups, felt religion to be the most important factor. No other influence was more important to older people than religion, although the younger groups felt that the death of someone they knew had been more influential than their religious background. Although men and women responded quite similarly on this item, major ethnic differences were obvious. Of the older Blacks, 70% credited religion with being the dominant force, as opposed to 15% of the Japanese, 33% of the Mexicans, and 35% of the Anglos. Although all groups displayed the same general trend with age, the generation gaps were most conspicuous in the Black community.

Seven questions might be interpreted as measuring Glock's category of Religious Ideology and Moberg's category of Religious Beliefs. Respondents were asked about (1) accidents showing the hand of God at work; (2) fear of the uncertainty of what follows death; (3) the belief that persons living to be 90 must have been morally good people; (4) belief in life after death; (5 & 6) belief in heaven and hell; (7) the agent for destroying all human life, should such a catastrophe occur. The responses to the first two questions showed no age differences, but older persons did feel that the very old have a claim to some kind of moral superiority. We assume this meant that only the good are permitted to become old, although other interpretations are possible.

Older persons in our sample are significantly more likely to believe in life after death (Y 48%, M 48%, O 64%), and older women (but not men) believe that this life after death will be in heaven rather than some spirit form (e.g., return to earth in bodily form) or some naturalistic form (e.g., live on through children or works). The increased acceptance of afterlife with increasing age is often reported (e.g., Riley et al, 1968), and sex differences in religious values are also frequently reported. And of those who have considered the possibility that human life may be annihilated, more young and middle aged anticipate nuclear explosion (Y 45%, M 49%, O 27%), while fewer in these groups look to some supernatural event (Y 27%, M 20%, O 48%).

However, these differences do not appear in regard to belief in hell. Fewer older than younger people believe in hell, although the differences were negligible.

The evidence is fairly clear that older people are more likely to participate in religious observances and rituals than younger persons to the extent that their health and money permit. A variety of studies (see reviews in Moberg, 1971a, and Riley et al, 1968) show that church attendance, prayer and financial support and so forth do remain high or increase with age barring illness, disability, and financial and transportation problems. Religious shows on radio and television compensate those with reduced mobility for their lack of ability to get to church. Our data are consistent with these findings. The older the individual is, the more likely he is to turn to his clergyman for comfort following the loss of a loved one (Y 19%, M 24%, O 48%), or to call a clergyman when he knows someone who is planning to commit suicide (Y 11%, M 21%, O 23%). Other questions, although based upon small numbers of respondents, showed similar trends.

On balance, our data confirm in the death/bereavement setting what others have previously shown. The older an individual is, the more he turns to the traditional and the sacred to provide comfort during bereavement and to enable him to gain immortality. This occurs even though older people are no more likely to believe in hell than any other age group and are no more likely to want a clergyman called at their dying than any other age group. These inconsistent findings do not disappear, no matter how we shuffle the data.

Perhaps the most notable finding is the generational differences among the Blacks regarding the influence of religion upon their feelings concerning death. In view of the suggestions of Maurice Jackson (1972) that Negro spirituals reflect the desire for freedom and that death is often the only source of freedom, the impact of religion on death attitudes for a generation once removed from slavery is not surprising. The obvious and unanswered question is how the religious significance of death has been altered for newer generations. Are vestiges of the older rural Southern Black still remaining in the death-related feelings of the younger urban non-Southern Black or has he assimilated the views of his new community?

HOW DO THEY RELATE TO OTHERS

Interactions with the Dying

In almost every book that discusses the dying, mention is made of the need to relate personally and with warmth to the dying individual. While basic agreement can readily be found concerning the needs of the dying for warm human interaction, the ways in which the fact of imminent death should be brought into the relationship are the cause of considerable controversy. Share (1972) weighs the positions in the debate between what she terms the Protective Approach and the Open Approach, and she comes down on the side of the latter. Interestingly, physicians favor the Open Approach for themselves, but are more inclined to the Protective Approach for their patients (Feifel, et al, 1967).

The Open Approach of Share is comparable to the Open Awareness context described by Glaser & Strauss (1965). Both the dying person and those who have intimate contact with him, i.e., family members, and medical staff, are aware that death is reasonably predictable, and both know that the others know. They can then discuss death, health, and the future in a realistic setting. The alternatives—Protective Approach, according to Share, and Mutual Pretense or Closed Awareness, according to Glaser and Strauss—exclude the possibility of total honesty in the discussions, since either one or both parties are knowledgeable about the terminal conditions but are constrained from alluding to it. Their theme is that life dies shortly after hope, and that knowledge of impending death eliminates hope.

Although nearly 60% of the non-elderly sample approve of permitting the dying person to be aware of his condition, only slightly more than 40% of the oldest group approve. This is significant at the .01 level, and similar trends are found for both men (P.05) and for women (P.10); the correlation is 0.18. However, inspection of the individual ethnic groups shows that almost all of the age-related differences are found among the Japanese.

When the spotlight is turned on the respondent and he is asked if he would want to be informed about his coming death, nearly 75% are in agreement, and age differences virtually disappear, although— once again—the older Japanese are less likely to go along than the middle-aged and younger (P.05). We find the same inconsistencies, then, in our groups that Feifel and others found among physicians, i.e., a substantially higher level of protectiveness for others than for oneself. This occurred for each age group when seen as a whole, for each age group of males and females, and for each age group within the ethnic groups. It seems as though people are saying that "I know *I* can handle this, but I don't about those people." Christ (1961) found essentially the same results in a study of older psychiatric patients. Just under half felt the dying person should be told, while all wanted to be told themselves. When residents of retirement communities were asked whether they would wish to know if they had an incurable illness, over 80% replied in the affirmative (Mathieu, 1975).

Yet 82% of all respondents believe that a person dying of cancer senses that his death is coming, and there are no differences among age groups. On initial examination, it seems inconsistent for people to assume that the dying individual knows he is dying, to want to be told themselves if they are dying, but to wish to withhold this information from their friends. Although we are speaking in relative terms, the degree of protectiveness, especially among the older persons, is most evident. If, however, we consider that the process of informing is going to upset both the person doing the telling and the person hearing about himself, it would be comforting to feel that the individual already knows and, therefore, does not require formal explication.

Only a handful of persons have ever had to tell someone that he was about to die, barely 1% of the young and about 7.5% of the others (P<.02). Of the remainder, roughly half felt that they could not tell someone that he was dying.

No significant differences existed among age groups regarding the number of dying persons visited during the previous two years, but a significant correlation (0.16) between age and number of such persons visited was found. However, inspection of the data suggested that this correlation—admittedly small—was primarily based upon the lowered extent of contact among the young, since virtually no differences existed between the middle and older generations.

Younger people, who obviously have the least contact with the dying, are the most in favor of informing the dying (Y 59%, M 56%, O 41%). A case could be made that their inexperience is a causal factor in their wishing the dying to be informed, i.e., that they do not really understand death and that they are insensitive to the potential problems elicited by having the dying know of their own condition. Our own views differ considerably. We feel that younger persons tend to encourage open and honest relationships (they sometimes seem virtually compulsive about the matter), and that the subterfuges of the recent past, so evident in regard to sexual and other intimate relationships, are not acceptable to younger people today.

Nonetheless, the greater reluctance of the old to want to tell the dying, or to be told when dying, suggests that younger practitioners might be more cautious in discussing with these persons the nature of a terminal illness and imminent death. The older person may place greater value on the privacy of feelings involving death—he may prefer not to communicate or be communicated to, even though he is well aware that death is imminent. We would also speculate that younger people have been more effectively socialized to the assumption that knowledge and awareness of self are ultimate values, while their seniors may tend to adhere to a more fatalistic doctrine. The young may rush in where the elderly fear to tread.

The tragedy of a death cannot be punched on an IBM card, but a sense of the tragedy can be communicated statistically in some ways. Older people were relatively more likely to see a sudden death as more tragic than a slow death (Y 31%, M 36%, O 45%). The ideal death, as defined by many persons, is that of dying in action or dying while asleep of a sudden heart attack, and "never knowing what hit you." Older people are more likely to think in terms of the last opportunity to make contact with loved ones, to bring affairs together, and to reminisce a bit about life. A slow and painful death (which is not what the question asked about) is a different matter, but slowness, although often uncomfortable and frequently personally anxiety-provoking, does not need to be more painful than a sudden death. As a matter of fact, one researcher (Exton-Smith, 1961) has shown that only 14% of geriatric ward deaths are physically painful to the point of being highly distressing. Not all need be painful with powerful pain-suppressing drugs available to physicians, and with recent developments in terminal care now developing through the hospice movement.

The tragedy of the death of a man versus that of a woman showed all age groups opting for equality. However, the middle-aged saw the role of the man relatively more important vis-a-vis the woman than either the younger or the older. The same trends were found for both men and women, although we do find an intriguing cross-sex effect, with women more likely to pick the death of men as more tragic than the men see it themselves—and vice versa—at every age except middle-age (middle-age women opted less frequently for "equal tragedy" and, therefore, more often saw deaths of both men and women much more tragic than did men).

The removal of the elderly through death is obviously perceived as the least destructive to the social fabric. "One of the consequences of the devaluation of the old in modern society is the minimization of the disruption and moral shock death ordinarily brings about" (Blauner, 1966, in Neugarten, 1968, p. 532). "But when people die who are engaged in the vital functions of society . . . their importance cannot be easily reduced . . . they die with *unfinished business*" (Blauner's italics) (Blauner, 1966, p. 532).

The older person has lived out his allocated time. There is almost a magic about the way our feelings change from "he died prematurely" (about anyone dying prior to age 60) and "he lived his allotted years" (about anyone dying over the age of 70). Very few persons in our sample stated that an elderly person's death (we stipulated this to be around age 75) was most tragic, but over 70% did cite this age as least tragic, with no particular differences among the three age groups. Our 20-39 year olds felt that the death of children was most tragic, while the other two age groups mentioned the death of a young person as being the greatest tragedy. The trend that appears to permeate these findings is the selection of the next age group down, i.e., the age of one's children, as being most tragic.

Personal Contact with People Now Dead

Death is more salient and less frightening for the older person—our own data and those of several others (e.g., Christ, 1961; Kogan & Shelton, 1962) have established this fairly consistently. Why this occurs is less understood. One contributing factor is undoubtedly a recognition of the reality that older people are more likely to die than people of any other age, and since the greater proportion of the social life of most people is within their own age cohort, the healthy elderly of our sample are more likely to know someone who had died within the previous two years than the younger groups. This was statistically significant for the entire population, for both men and women, and for Japanese and Anglo, with the Blacks and Mexican Americans showing substantial trends but falling short of significance. And the correlation between age and the number of friends and acquaintances who had died recently was 0.25, confirming the other observations.

Some of the ethnic differences were conspicuous and meaningful. Blacks were more familiar with death at all ages, with many more Blacks having known five or more persons who had died and many fewer having known none (Anglos were the antithesis in both categories). These differences were even more noticeable among the young than among the middle-aged or older groups, i.e. over 30% of the younger Blacks had known five or more people who had died, compared to 16% of the Mexicans and only a little over 5% of the other groups.

Although older people are more likely to know people who had died, young people were most likely to have known people who had died from accidents, suicide or homicide.

Older persons are not only more likely to know people who have died, but they are also more likely to have attended funerals and to have visited cemeteries. These trends, however, were not consistent across ethnic groups, with older Blacks being only slightly more likely to have attended funerals than younger Blacks. Again we find a relatively higher participation of younger Blacks in death-related ceremonies and interactions than the younger of other groups. At this point, we feel the need to remind readers that "younger" refers to the age group 20-39 and not to teenagers or youth.

Although the middle-aged seem moderately willing to attend funerals (correlation with age is 0.28, and less than 30% had failed to attend at least one funeral in the previous two years) they are a little more upset at having intimate contact with the dead body at the funeral. They are least likely to be willing to touch the body (Y 57%, M 45%, O 55%) (a significant relationship) and least likely to kiss the body (Y 36%, M 25%, O 26%) (not a significant relationship). All in all, it is the young who claim to be most capable of touching or kissing the body. This trend is especially conspicuous among the Japanese where over half the young, but less than one-fifth of the old would willingly touch the body.

Grief and Bereavement

Since the older respondents are more relaxed about death and dying, are they similarly more relaxed about grief and mourning? The best answer that we can give to this is "Yes." We asked when the respondents would begin to worry that grieving behavior, such as crying or depression, had been going on too long. The older the respondent, the longer the permissible time (r = 0.12; chi square significant at .10 level). Whether the results have occurred through the experience garnered by older individuals in their actual confrontation of grief or whether they reflect a more casual attitude cannot be determined. We would, however, opt for the former. Having suffered loss of any sort is often much different than the anticipation of the loss, and younger persons might not fully appreciate the traumatic aspects.

On the other hand, evidence has accrued in the gerontological literature that younger persons have more ability to recuperate from depletion of physical resources because they have more reserves. This is probably reflected in psychological resiliency as well. The responses we found might reflect the recognition by the elderly that they lack this youthful ability to bounce back. This could also explain their greater reluctance to cry and express other overt emotion at a loss through death (see below). Although we wish to open up several optional considerations, we will still bow to the wisdom of age and assume that the determining factor is simply knowledge and experience.

The non-traditional views of younger persons apparently do not extend to their feelings concerning the propriety of mourning behavior. The interviewers asked about the proper length of mourning time prior to remarriage, the time at which to stop wearing black or other mourning symbols, to return to employment, and to return to dating. Age group responses were extremely similar, and, for three of the four criteria, the youngest age group had the smallest proportion stating that it was really unimportant.

Age does not predict whether the individual would feel constrained about expressing his grief in public. Although we might suspect that the older, more conservative mourner would be more inhibited from public expressions of emotion, no such trend emerged. Only when it came to willingness to cry at all did an age-related trend occur (Y 82%, M 75%, O 60%). Younger individuals are more willing to express their grief through tears than the elderly, although not more willing to do so in public. The trend is significant for both men and women, for both Japanese and Mexican, and it is consistent, but not significant, for Anglos. Among the Blacks, the old are least likely to cry, but it is the middle-aged group that appear most willing to give vent to their emotions. The overall correlation with age is 0.25.

Again, we can speculate as to the cause of this age-related trend. First, there is some possibility that responses were—to some degree—in terms of "what I think I should do" rather than of "what I would actually do."

But we must ask, more substantively, what are the elderly telling us? What are the young telling us? Are the elderly saying that they must protect themselves from constant emotional involvement in their inevitable losses? Kastenbaum has coined the term "bereavement overload," the phenomenon that occurs when a series of serious losses, especially deaths of significant others, take place in such rapid succession that recovery from one loss is wiped out through the occurrence of another loss. Although this can occur at any age, it is most probable at the end of the life span. The elderly woman who loses husband, brother, and uncle within a two-year period—not an improbable or unique circumstance—is a candidate for bereavement overload. She may well need to disengage from these emotional pains—or at least reduce their painfulness in the future by disengaging.

What we cannot determine is the degree to which these age-related differences have developed because of the fact that today's elderly were reared in a culture that disapproved of emotional expression (if so—why not age differential on *public* emotional expression?) or because the process of getting old and of suffering loss encourages an individual to build defenses against feeling and, therefore, against expression of feeling.

AND RELATING TO THEIR OWN DEATH

The awareness of our own death—a quality we seem to share with no other member of the animal kingdom—produces an amazing range of responses. These include fear and anxiety to the point of dread; they also include anticipation of rest and peace, of abiding with one's God or drifting in nothingness. Our eventual death is the cause of substantial planning, through insurance and wills and trusts, through contemplation of the significance of personal and social immortality, through concern over dependents, and through worry about disposal of the physical remains.

Older people are much closer, on a statistical probability basis, to their own deaths and should relate to death differently than do the younger or the middle-aged. However, whether their age is more important as a determining factor than their sex or ethnicity has not effectively been probed. In the following pages, we shall attempt a beginning.

Preparing for One's Own Death

Common sense dictates that older people are more likely to make preparations for their death than are young or middle-aged people, and the data confirm common sense. Funeral arrangements have been made with significantly greater frequency by older persons of both sexes and all ethnicities; the correlation with age was 0.47, one of the highest obtained for any item. Having made out a will ($r = 0.42$) and having paid, in full or in part, for cemetery space show the same linear trend.

Riley's national sample produced consistent results. He found that those over 60 were more likely to have made out a will. In these instances, controlling for education reduced but did not eliminate preparation for dying. Apparently both education and age are significant factors in these kinds of planning.

The older group has a higher proportion of individuals who have arranged for someone else to handle their affairs (Y 13%, M 27%, O 44%) in case of death, again a trend found for men, women, and all ethnic groups. Although unlike the findings of Riley (1963) there were no age trends as to whether the individual had seriously discussed the possibility of his coming death (the age groups were remarkably alike, each having slightly over 70% responding affirmatively), significant differences did appear in terms of whom they talked to about death. Of those few (N=11) who had talked with a clergyman, 6 were elderly; of the 39 who talked with friends, 23 were young; of the 66 who talked with a family member, 32 were middle-aged and 17 were elderly. What we find basically is that older people tend to discuss their death with family members and friends, but are more likely than other age groups to talk with a clergyman; middle-aged people talk only with family members, their spouses in most circumstances; and younger people are slightly more likely to talk with friends. Riley (1963), limiting his alternatives to professionals, also found clergymen selected more frequently than physicians.

Only in regard to insurance are the older less likely to have made preparations than another age group, the middle-aged in this case, once again confirming Riley's 1963 data (Y 61%, M 76%, O 66%). Two explanations probably interact to produce these results. First, a large proportion of our older respondents, exactly half, were not presently married and living with spouse (compared to

37% and 21% of the young and middle-aged), and very few of this age cohort had dependent children or other survivors for whom they would feel a high level of financial responsibility. Second, their incomes were, on the average, sufficiently limited that payment on life insurance would be prohibitively high; had they paid-up insurance, they might well have borrowed against the policy or cashed it in for day-to-day living expenses. In spite of this, nearly two-thirds of these people did carry some life insurance (Riley found 69%).

Throughout the centuries, people have thought about, worried about, and planned for their funeral services. Funerals and wakes were often community affairs that served not only to guarantee safe passage to the soul (or whatever essence the community perceived as passing), but also brought family members together and wove a network of relationships throughout the community. When the funeral cortege consisted of six pallbearers, selected from close friends and family, walking to the cemetery followed by a long line of mourners, the death was very much part of the social fabric of the community (see Osuna, 1970, and Reynolds, 1970). When the funeral cortege is a long line of limousines with a police escort speeding down the Los Angeles freeway system to a forty-mile-distant cemetery, its only majesty is that of disrupting normal traffic patterns (thanks to Fulton for the imagery).

Today's elderly can recall the more bucolic, more intimate funerals; today's young supposedly perceive the rituals as a giant potlatch to fill the pockets of a greedy funeral director. The elderly might wish an elaborate funeral to imprint their image upon the survivors forever; the young might wish a simple and inexpensive affair, providing the least drain upon family resources.

If that image is accurate, it was obscured within our data. We found no age trends at all regarding the desire for an elaborate funeral, except for a significant relationship (P <.02) among the Blacks, with more of the younger respondents wishing an expensive funeral than other age groups. Nor were age differences found in wanting many guests or few. Whatever slight trends did occur were in the direction of the younger people wishing the more expensive and better-attended event. Not even was there the anticipated age-related differences in desire for a wake; the three age groups were almost identical in their feelings about this matter.

Some age differences were evident. While younger people were more likely to expect their friends and relatives to share the costs of the funeral and burial (r = 0.20), older respondents expected to draw a large proportion of costs from their life insurance. This appears to represent the feelings of the old that they should retain independence and not be a burden upon their children, even in their death.

Older people are significantly more likely to object to autopsies (P <.02) and are more fearful as to what happens to their bodies after death (P<.02). However, it is the middle-aged who most wish burial and fear cremation (these overall results, however, are primarily due to the relative reluctance of some middle-aged Japanese to be cremated, although the Japanese on the whole strongly prefer cremation). Finally, no age differences regarding embalming were found, except a significant finding among the Japanese, with the elderly much more strongly opposed than other age groups. We would hypothesize that the elderly are much more likely to identify the person with his body. This may be the result of early teachings regarding the Resurrection. These traditions, ancient in Western culture, emphasize the importance of the dead body. They are explicit in Classical Greek tragedy and in contemporary embalming practices. Among the Japanese, a strong taboo has existed in regard to handling dead animals, so that tanners and butchers are both relegated to inferior status. Another possible explanation is that the elderly are more aware of their bodies because of increased medical problems. Gerontologists have noted that many elderly become intensely concerned with bodily function, and the term *body maintenance* is applied to the middle-aged and elderly concern with holding back the changes in hairlines, waistlines, and bustlines.

Trying to deal with the dissonance between our initial anticipations and our findings has led to one additional explanation. Our sampling was biased to exclude managerial and professional families. It may be among those groups that the young are moving away from funeral rituals. Our sample being drawn primarily from the lower half of the income curve and from people who live within their ethnic communities, the funeral ritual is still seen as filling an important function. Indeed, the potentially upwardly mobile young may see it as an opportunity to receive some of the deference in death that their ethnicity may prevent them from receiving in life.

To Cease to Be

LaRouchefeld wrote that "Man can look neither at the sun nor at his own death." Without a doubt, the task of staring at the glare of one's own death can be difficult and painful. Nonetheless it does occur. Admittedly we may be more capable of looking at the death of another and still more capable of contemplating the deaths of ten thousand anonymous others, but we have no alternative to looking someday upon our own dying and to anticipating our own death.

The elderly admit to thinking about death more often than the other age groups (Riley, 1963, obtained the same results). Among the elderly as a whole, among men and women, among Blacks, Japanese and Mexicans, twice as many elderly, proportionately, think of their death every day as do other age groups. Slightly fewer elderly than others say they think of death only about once a year or hardly ever or never. The middle-aged group claims to concern themselves least with thoughts of death.

Yet the older person is least likely to state that he is afraid of dying (Y 40%, M 26%, O 10%) and is most likely to claim he is able to face dying (Y 36%, M 52%, O 71%). The results are impressive, consistent, and overwhelming. The chi squares are all significant; the overall correlation is 0.32. They occur for males and females, and with two minor reversals, for all ethnic groups. A later study, also conducted in Los Angeles with representatives from Black, Mexican and Anglo American communities, confirmed the inverse relationship between age and fear of death (Bengtson et al., 1976).

A fascinating analysis by Riley (1963) based upon his national sample shows that older people do indicate more agreement with such statements as "Death always comes too soon," and "To die is to suffer." However, as soon as the factor of education is controlled, all age-related differences disappear. We have, to some degree, controlled for education through our sampling.

The reasons that death is more salient for the elderly are obvious. First, that which is nearer, on a probability basis, is more salient, and older people both expect and want to die sooner. Second, the evidence from one's own body and from the deaths of one's age peers is too great to disregard for the elderly, while the younger individuals receive fewer daily reminders.

If, in contrast, dying is less frightening for the elderly, this may also be traced to three sources. First, the increasingly prevalent forays upon physical and mental health that come with the aging process are distressing and depressing; these sap energy, induce confusion, lead to fear. The value of his life to the person living it is diminished. At the same time, the social fabric of our society has increasingly phased him out of its activities. The process of disengagement must fight to hold it at bay. Eventually, as the physical and psychological insults intensify, death becomes more acceptable. Our sample included very few sick and disabled elderly. Nonetheless, the inroads made by the variety of losses, e.g., health, friends, work role, physical mobility, income, may already have taken its toll.

The second explanation is more psychological. We would speculate that many people feel that the forces of life owe them a specific number of years. This is a reflection of what they see around them in terms of life expectancy in interaction with their own personality dynamics. At present, an American, Canadian, Japanese, or Western European can expect to live at least to his mid-sixties, assuming he lives through his first few weeks—women, a little longer, men, a little less. Given the expectation of some 65 to 70 years, an individual may feel cheated of his birthright if his death occurs before that time. He may feel he is on borrowed time if he lives much beyond 75 or 80, since he was not really entitled by the nature of his existence to live so long.

In claiming this latter explanation as a major contributor to the lowered fear of dying of the elderly and their greater willingness to die, we are admittedly being speculative. However, when, as we often do, we hear old people say they are ready to die, they are not saying they want to die but that they have lived what the life forces (God, nature, chance, eco-systems) entitle them to and they require no more.

Our third basis for assuming the validity of our data is the concept of anticipatory socialization. The rehearsal for widowhood is very evident among women, even young women (Kalish, 1971), and most certainly among older women. We would like to suggest that people also rehearse for their own dying, and that this increases in frequency and intensity with age. Older people readily admit to spending more time thinking about their own dying and planning for it. Each time a close friend or relative dies—or any younger person whose life has impinged upon us—we are confronted with a threatening reality that must be worked through. Defense mechanisms, of course, may be utilized, but, except for those whose defenses must become more rigid and more entrenched, we become increasingly capable of dealing with the deaths of others and thus with our own death as time progresses. In effect, having to work through the anxiety and threat of the deaths of others enables us to approach our own death with greater calm. As part of this working-through process, we wonder what it is like to die, we picture ourselves dying in a variety of fashions, we fantasize our own responses to a painful dying and to a non-painful dying. In spite of the potential anguish produced by these fantasies, they help us when we confront the reality of our own more limited futurity.

Indeed, all funeral directors have encountered the funeral follower, who seems to lavish attention upon the dead and his mourners, who is virtually compulsive in investigating all the details of each funeral and often communicates these details to anyone who will listen. He may be unconsciously—or perhaps even consciously—preparing for his own death. A group of elderly Japanese American men in rural California has been reported to attend funerals of those they know and those who are strangers, in a conscious effort to master their preparation for death. And perhaps—only perhaps, of course—we who write about death and you who read about it are participating also in the act of working through our own fears and uncertainties concerning our own death.

Other research is not much help on this matter, since most studies are done with highly specific populations, such as the mentally ill, the elderly, or college students. Kalish (1963), using an accidental sample of over 600, found no correlations between age and such factor analyzed variables as Lack of Death Concern or Death Anxiety. Templer, Ruff, and Frank (1971) found no correlations between a carefully validated fifteen-item scale of death anxiety and age within any of their four subsamples (upper-middle class apartment residents, state hospital aides, psychiatric patients, high school students) or for the entire sample. Templer questions this lack of relationship, in view of the " 'common sense' view that the closer a person approaches to the end of life, the more fearful of death he becomes." He then suggests the possibility that older persons use defense mechanisms more extensively. However, when he finds women displaying higher death anxiety than men, he does not propose that men are making greater use of defense mechanisms.

More recently, Kalish and Johnson (1972) reported on death fears of three generations of women within the same families, e.g., daughters, mothers, and maternal grandmothers. The grandmothers were significantly more accepting and less fearful of dying than their daughters who were, in turn, significantly more accepting and less fearful than the granddaughters. The elderly themselves believe that death is more disturbing to "people in general" than to their own age group (Kogan and Shelton, 1962).

In a similar project, when daughters, mothers, and grandmothers were asked to evaluate their own death anxiety and then to evaluate the death anxiety of the other two generations, each age group credited itself with less anxiety than it credited either of the other generations. However, the grandmothers rated themselves as more accepting of death than did either their daughters or granddaughters (Nehrke, 1974). Here again, is evidence of individuals considering themselves capable of dealing with their own dying, but having serious misgivings about the abilities of others.

Several investigators have reported the proportion of individuals who admitted fear of death or dying. Jeffers, Nichols, and Eisdorfer (1961) asked 260 community volunteers over 60 whether they feared dying; 10% answered affirmatively, while an additional 31% hedged their negative answers by admitting ambivalence or fear of pain. Their findings are extremely close to our own figures of 9.8% of the 60+ group stating fear of death or dying. Swenson (1959), using a more complicated scoring device, also arrived at the 10% figure for 210 respondents over age 60. Swenson ended up interpreting the responses of 45% of his sample as suggesting acceptance or even eagerness for death; another 44% were "evasive." We found over 70% to state acceptance, and only 20% to show uncertainty or a neutral position.

Studies of other age groups also seem to arrive at the 10% figure, although the data from our Los Angeles study shows 40% of the 20-39 year olds and 26% of the 40-59 year olds admitting to fear of death and dying. For example, Kalish (1963a, 1963b) studied both college students attending evening classes (mean age 27) and an accidental sample of Los Angeles residents; both groups indicated 10-15% were afraid of death (these figures are *not* in the cited articles, but are drawn from raw data).

Two other items throw light upon this matter. First, the young are most likely to admit to having had the unexplainable feeling that they were going to die (Y 26%, M 15%, O 15%) (specifically excluding dreams); second, the old dream significantly less often about death (chi squares significant and correlation 0.22). The first item supports the contention of the elderly that death is less frightening for them or else supports the contention that denial is higher among the elderly. The second item may be the result of the general reduction in dreams (or in dreams recalled) as a function of age, or it may result from the better ability of the older group to deal with their death concerns by thinking about them and coping with them during daytime conscious hours, thus avoiding the need to give heed to these feelings during sleep, since one often-assumed function of dreams is to continue to think of those matters that were not fully handled during the day.

Until some investigator can produce evidence of greater repression or other uses of defense mechanisms among the elderly, we will adhere to our assumption that these data may be taken at face value. Whatever defenses are being used are probably unrelated to age. We feel that both logic and parsimony preclude acceptance of the interpretation of these data as arising from denial or repression.

The age at which the younger repondents expect to die is significantly lower than the age at which the middle-aged expected to die; this is, in turn, lower than the age at which the elderly expect to die (correlation is 0.41). What was not expected was the neatness of the responses. The crude median for expected life for the youngest was 70; for the middle-aged it was 75; for the elderly, it was 80. Also surprising was the absolute lack of differentiation between the sexes, men anticipating exactly the same number of years ahead as women. Inevitably, part of the reason for the clean breakdown of responses was the tendency for people to cluster around the five-year marks, a majority of respondents expecting to live to 65, 70, 75, 80, 85, or 90, rather than the intervening years.

The age to which these persons desired to live did differ somewhat from their anticipated life expectancy. Both the younger and middle-aged stated 80 as a median preferred age, while the older respondents prolonged their own existence a bit more by selecting a median of 88 years (correlation is 0.24). Among men, the respective medians were 80, 80, and 90; among women, a little bit lower at 75, 75, and 85. These differences are somewhat deceiving, since not one person wanted to live to be 72 or 82, but the data do point up an intriguing anomaly. Women expect to live as long as men; the actuarial tables indicate that they will probably live longer; yet they do not desire to live as long. And these differences are quite consistent in all three age groups, so they are not reflecting the loneliness of the widow or the aspirations of younger women anticipating more equality of opportunity. (See also Reynolds and Kalish, 1974).

Compared to younger persons, the elderly were more likely to accept death peacefully than to fight death actively (Y 53%, M 65%, O 74%) (r = 0.21). These findings occurred for the entire sample, for men, and for Blacks; for women and the remaining ethnic groups the trends were identical but did not reach statistical significance.

Other questions that probed at the person's feelings about his own dying process did not turn up age differences. All age groups were equally likely to encourage their family to spend time with them, to call for a clergyman, to permit children to visit, and to remain silent in the face of pain. Surprisingly—for here we expected to find age trends—no differences occurred in regard to wanting to be told when one was dying. Between 69% and 73% of each age group did wish to be told.

Age differences were marked, however, as to how the individual would spend his last six months, assuming that he could predict his own death and that his health would permit activity. The modal response for the young was to express their concern for others; the modal response for the middle-aged was that they would not change their life style; the modal response for the elderly was withdrawal into prayer or contemplation or other inner-life involvement. (See Table 4-1) By combining these modal responses with the age-related trends, this one item appears to tap the implications of age roles amazingly well. Although the same trends were found for both men and women, the trends within ethnic groups were only partially consistent. However, the breakdown of age by ethnicity by six categories of item response makes analysis of ethnicity problematic.

TABLE 4-1

(037) If you were told you had a terminal
disease and six months to live,
how would you want to spend your
time until you died?

	Young (%)	Middle-Aged (%)	Old (%)
Marked change in life-style, self-related (travel, sex, drugs, experiences)	24	15	9
Withdrawal (read, contemplate, pray, inner-life centered)	14	14	37
Focus concern on others, be with loved ones	29	25	12
Complete projects, tie up loose ends	11	10	3
No change in life-style	17	29	31
Other/DK	5	6	8

Not many other studies on these issues have been found. However, Back compares elderly and youthful men in rural communities regarding their response to the question "If you knew

TABLE 4-2

Here are some reasons why people don't want to die. Tell me whether they are very important to you, important to you, or not important to you personally.

		Young (%)	Middle-Aged (%)	Old (%)
(080)	I am afraid of what might happen to my body after death.			
	Very important	3	4	10
	Important	10	6	13
	Not important	88	90	78
(081)	I could no longer care for my dependents.			
	Very important	49	48	19
	Important	33	25	30
	Not important	19	27	52
(082)	I am uncertain as to what might happen to me.			
	Very important	10	13	10
	Important	23	13	21
	Not important	67	75	69
(083)	I could no longer have any experiences.			
	Very important	11	6	3
	Important	25	24	14
	Not important	65	70	83
(084)	My death would cause grief to my friends and relatives.			
	Very important	24	30	20
	Important	57	43	43
	Not important	19	28	38
(085)	All my plans and projects would come to an end.			
	Very important	13	17	9
	Important	34	30	29
	Not important	53	53	63
(086)	The process of dying might be painful.			
	Very important	20	21	18
	Important	33	36	38
	Not important	47	43	45

you were going to die within 30 days, what would you do?" His older respondents, like ours, were less likely to indicate change in activities and were similarly less likely to show concern for others (reported in Kastenbaum, 1966).

Diggory and Rothman (1961) investigated what they termed values destroyed by death. We selected some of their items and, in spite of slight modifications, will be able to make comparisons between the two studies. The elderly are more likely to be afraid of what happens to their body after their death, both older men and older women being more likely than their younger counterparts to indicate this feeling. In the remaining six values potentially lost through death, three analyses led to significant chi squares. On each of these three, the youngest group showed the greatest concern, and the oldest group showed the least concern, although trends for sex and for ethnicity were not uniformly linear. (See Table 4-2)

The items that differentiated the old from the young seemed to represent three sources. First, the reduced concern for survivors is undoubtedly the logical outcome of the reduced impact their deaths would have upon survivors; the survivors of the elderly are primarily self-sufficient, while the survivors of the middle-aged and young are often greatly in need of help. Disengagement plays an obvious role for the elderly. Second, the reduced concern about ceasing to have experiences probably arises from the dynamics we have discussed previously, the feeling that one has had all of life that he is owed as part of his birthright. Also, the older individual has experienced more and is, in many ways, in a less effective position to continue with enjoyable experiences. And, third, the fear of what happens to the body following death is frequently noted by persons working with the elderly. Perhaps this concern is a vestige of the ancient tradition that the body must be intact in order to warrant heavenly approval, perhaps the lingering feeling that decay is immoral in some way, perhaps a dread of the disintegration of the flesh that conjures up images of grotesque ghostly apparitions. Whatever the origins, about one-fourth of the elderly consider this to be important, while less than half that proportion of the other age cohorts admit to its being bothersome. With illness and increasing age, the individual realizes how important body functioning is for life satisfaction. The young and middle-aged can take their bodies reasonably for granted much of the time. The elderly person cannot, and so he emphasizes this regnancy in all body-related responses and reactions.

AN ATTEMPT AT INTEGRATION

"Man cannot escape death—real or symbolic . . . He must accept . . . the fact that he has been condemned to death. Then he can start living" (Koestenbaum, 1971). For this discussion, we must specify two premises. First, we will accept responses at face value, without assuming denial, repression, or distortion, unless evidence of such is substantial. To the degree that we realize denial, repression, and distortion must exist, we will assume that it affects each of the age groups in a comparable fashion. Second, we believe that age-related differences may be caused by (a) each age cohort having been socialized during a different time in history, (b) age-related changes that occur inevitably, perhaps caused by illness and physical changes, (c) age-related changes that occur because of social conditions, based upon altered roles and altered self-concept, (d) any two or all three factors in varying proportions.

The Elderly

All the evidence indicates that the elderly encounter death more. Thus nearly two out of three older women and over one out of six older men have lost their spouse through death, and others undoubtedly have also lost a spouse, but subsequently remarried. Older persons are more likely to have known one or more persons who have died recently, are more likely to have gone to one or to several funerals, are more likely to have visited someone's grave, and are more likely to have made out a will and arranged for funeral ceremonies and cemetery purchase. In every sense, except for having life insurance which is the understandable province of the middle-aged, the older person has had greater contact with death.

Furthermore, when he is asked how much he thinks about death and dying, he admits to considerably more preoccupation than do his younger confreres. Nonetheless, he is least likely to admit being frightened or terrified of death and dying, and is most likely to indicate acceptance of death. Are older persons using denial to cope with this omnipresent spectre of death that is so frightening? We think they are being honest.

Our respondents supply us with additional evidence. Older people are significantly more likely to say they will accept death peacefully than to fight against it; they are less worried about dependents than are the young (having fewer people who do need them); they are less concerned about cessation of experiences, perhaps feeling that they have had their share and that further experiences are bought at the price of physical and psychological pain. It would appear that their entire affective response pattern regarding death has been reduced. Lacking longitudinal data, we cannot ascertain whether these feelings are the continuation into the later years of attitudes held at earlier times in life or whether the awareness of being old is the major basis.

Nonetheless, these people are not in a hurry to die. They are less likely than the middle-aged or the young to espouse the idea that people should be permitted to die. And they are most likely to worry about what happens to their body after they die. In addition, they perceive sudden (compared to slow) deaths and accidental deaths as more tragic than do their youngers.

The old have had much more experience with death and dying; they think much more about it; they appear more ready to die, yet they do not feel death should be precipitated or occur without the opportunity to deal a little more with life. As a group they do not seem to be in despair but they do appear to be experiencing disengagement, withdrawal, and reduction of involvement with life.

One vital, vigorous, 92-year-old man expressed the feelings of many others. After forty successful years as a teacher, he spent another quarter century developing new breeds of flowers. Now, he stated, he was bored with that; he also feared the changing political arena and the changing neighborhood. No one in his family needed him, and he felt he was physically and financially unable to have new experiences (he had already done a good bit of living in his 92 years). He was able to express his total lack of interest in living to reach one hundred years of age. He did not even wish to live to see what he felt was the culmination of the present disruptions in the social order. With great calmness, he said that he was totally ready to die. I believed him. Yet I also believe that he will do nothing to expedite death and that his readiness to die will only have one effect upon him: he will not re-engage in new lines of activities but instead will pursue only those activities and relationships now on-going. We cite this man as a prototype. (Incidentally, his verbalized solution to his life situation was to spend a "few more years with my flowers.")

The social-interactional world socializes us to reduce the focus upon inner self found in infancy by rewarding and reinforcing attachments with people, objects, and events. Then, in the late years and especially in the terminal stages, pressures for reducing attachments brought about by society again returns the individual to his inner focus, aided and abetted by aches and pains and reduced futurity. As old attachments diminish in number and intensity, re-engagement with matters directly pertaining to self are permitted. Ironically, then, the elderly are frequently chastized for self-centered behavior, which is often the only kind of behavior left to them.

Although we believe that the reduced fear of death and dying results from the factors discussed above, another possibility must be considered. The elderly are more religious, and we find that religiousness is also related to thinking more and worrying less about death. When we compare the relatively devout elderly with the less devout elderly on (1) frequency of thinking about death, (2) informing the dying, (3) willingness to accept death rather than fight it, and (4) fear of death, we find no significant chi squares. Since our testing of religiousness upon these four variables provide no significance with age held constant, we can tentatively assume that age is predictive of differences on these issues over and above differences in religiousness.

The Middle-aged

On most variables in which meaningful trends appeared, the middle-aged were safely ensconced between the young and the old, but one trend did emerge based on a handful of variables in which the 40-59 year olds were at one end of the continuum. First, the middle-aged were slightly more negative about the interview itself, and relatively more of them admitted personal anxieties, although differences in both situations were small. They were more likely to admit being unable to tell a person that he was dying (but, again, the differences were not statistically significant), and they were more reluctant to either touch or kiss the body (the latter was not significant). They also thought the least frequently about their death or dying.

Perhaps this is—in regard to death—the awkward in-between age. Kalish and Johnson (1972) found that, although the middle-aged women were intermediate in terms of fear of death, they indicated greater dislike of the elderly and greater concern about becoming old than either their daughters or their mothers. Similarly, Shanas (1962) showed that old people suffering from chronic disease are more likely to consider themselves in good health than are those persons approaching their later years who objectively have better health.

The middle-aged see their parents grow old, and they recognize their own infirmities and changes. Erikson (1963) writes about the development crisis of generativity (e.g., productivity, creativity) versus stagnation, but he is probably addressing himself to a somewhat younger population. Consistent with Erikson's theory, we noted responses to two questions asking whether specified reasons for not dying were important or not. The middle-aged, more than the young or the old, felt that the grief caused to friends and relatives and the end of projects and plans were "very important." (The latter comparison was statistically significant, but the former was not.)

Nonetheless, we would speculate that the middle-aged have not yet had the experience with death that forces them to, in Koestenbaum's terms, accept the fact that they have been condemned to death. At the same time, they recognize that they can deny the inevitable only a short time more. They are in the early stages described by Ross (1969), i.e., denial and anger, since their death produces greater loss for them and for society.

Young Adults

The young are, by and large, the opposite of the old. Erikson notes their developmental crisis as being intimacy versus self-absorption. When asked the outcome of their being close to death (for those who indicated that they had been), the young were most likely to mention that the experience brought them closer to others and made them appreciate life more. Similarly, with only six months to live, they would display their concern for other people and would markedly change their life style.

The young adults have had the least contact with death, with the dying, with funerals—with about all that goes with death except for homicide. They were less likely to feel negative and more likely to feel positive about the interview (but differences were small); they were most likely to feel that the dying should be informed of their condition; they were the most agreeable to children visiting the dying (again differences were small). At the same time, they admit to being more afraid of death and dying; they dream about death more than the others; they are more desirous of dying quickly (which reduces the affective load of the death encounter, as well as the physical and emotional pain and financial cost); and they would be more likely to fight death than to accept it peacefully.

On the one hand, the young adults would have more to lose than their middle-aged and elderly counterparts, since they had not yet received the number of years of life, of experiences, and of relationships to which we so often feel entitled. Their concerns regarding death are more people-centered than religion-centered; they turn more to family than to clergy; they want to impinge actively upon their environment, rather than having their environment move them. At the same time, they display an openness, a willingness to discuss death and bereavement, a belief in the importance of communicating with others (although they were no more eager to be informed about their own dying than were the other age groups).

And Then . . .

Building an elaborate developmental theory from these kinds of data would be inappropriate. Although Erikson's formulations appear to have some meaning, our questionnaire was not geared to testing the concept of development crises, and all we can do is attempt to integrate them into our conceptual framework.

In facing death, as in so much other behavior, the young and the old differ in (1) the degree to which they integrate their formal religious training into their lives; (2) the degree to which they have had existential experience with the phenomena of death and dying; (3) the degree to which they approach the problems with a primarily external or internal focus of activity; and we believe, albeit recognizing its controversial nature (4) the degree to which they have accepted the idea that they have been appointed to die.

5

Sex, Education, and Religiousness

Although we found that age and ethnicity were the most fruitful variables with respect to making meaningful analysis of our data, sex, education, and religion were also evaluated, and these findings added further dimensions to our understanding. Our organizing themes of familistic and individualistic, pragmatic and sentimental, intellectualistic and emotional, were all applicable in the following discussions.

SEX

Describing the Sample

Neither education, age, nor religiousness differentiated men from women in our study. Not only did our measures of self-perceived relative devoutness show virtually identical responses for both sexes (both across all ethnicities and within each ethnicity), but other questions related to religious feelings similarly showed no sex differences, e.g., belief in afterlife or belief in hell. Moberg (1971), in summarizing studies on sex differences, states that, "Study after study has revealed the greater tendency of females than of males in the American cultural milieu to be church members, to attend church, to engage in private devotional behavior, and to maintain traditional or orthodox religious beliefs" (p. 577).

What would comprise an adequate explanation for the lack of similar findings within our samples? Only in terms of increased willingness to contact a clergyman for the dying do women display greater religiousness than men. Several interpretations are possible.

First, perhaps because of the nature of our criterion questions concerning relative devoutness, men, with or without awareness, tended to compare themselves with other men, while women compared themselves with other women. Second, men and women express religiousness in different fashions, with women more involved in rituals and formal observances but not necessarily more devout. A familiar comment often made by men, is "I may not go to church as much as she does, but I'm just as good a Christian (or whatever) as she is."

Interactions with the Dying and the Dead

Sex differences in frequency of contact with those who have died were not found, except for Anglo women who were less likely to have attended recent funerals and paid recent visits to grave sites than Anglo men. Even sex-related differences on items having to do with the dying were minor. Women were more likely to believe that persons dying of cancer were aware of their impending death (P <.01, r = 0.36) and they were more likely to have known someone who had died under such circumstances.

When asked whether they had ever told anyone that he was dying, 3.7% of the women, as opposed to 7.0% of the men, responded affirmatively. The result was not significant (P <.20), but did appear consistent with the highly significant difference between women and men when asked if they felt capable of informing a person of his coming death. In addition to the significant chi square, the correlation was 0.30 between being male and feeling able to engage in such activity.

Another intriguing trend appeared that, although falling far short of significance, seemed to call for later follow-up. Women were more likely than men to feel that the death of a man was more tragic than the death of a woman; men were more likely than women to feel the death of a woman was more tragic than the death of a man. Although the differences were small, we felt that future investigators should take note of this trend; perhaps each is deeply concerned by the potential loss of support figures.

The traditional sex roles did appear in feelings about the mourning process. Women do not feel that they must control their emotions and so were more able to cry (not only were both chi squares significant, but correlations were 0.19 and 0.35). They also see the grieving process as requiring more time, and were more willing to let people wear black longer (P <.10, r = 0.16), to remain away from work longer (P <.02), and to grieve longer without worrying that the process was going on for too long (r = 0.20). Since the nature of the questions required that each person respond in terms of his own sex, we believe that these women are saying that they, compared to men, require more time for recovery from loss and, also, are more bound by propriety, e.g., they must wear black to signify their unavailability to other men and their faithfulness to the memory of their spouses. If role expectations for the two sexes become more similar, differences such as these may diminish. The only other statistically significant finding was that women selected death in war as most tragic, while men chose death from accidents or homicide. But what struck us about these data was not the findings that differentiated men and women, but how similar men and women were in their responses.

Their Own Death Preparations

Men have obviously been more engaged in the practical matters of preparing for death, such as having life insurance (P <.05, r = 0.17) and making out wills (P <.10, r = 0.15). The most parsimonious explanation, of course, has nothing to do with personality, values, or attitudes, but is merely a reflection of earning power, financial responsibilities in marriage, and traditional sex roles. Women were also more likely to opt for a less expensive funeral (P <.10), but we cannot determine whether this reflects a lower self-worth or a less realistic awareness of the cost of funerals (30% of the women and 20% of the men felt that an adequate funeral would cost about $700 or less).

A few sex-related differences were found in the mechanics of the funeral, but these displayed a pattern that we did not find elsewhere in the study, i.e., the significance levels (ranging from 0.001 to 0.10) were a function of the fairly substantial number of men indicating indifference or being undecided. Thus more men than women did not know or were undecided as to whether they (a) wanted many or few people attending their funeral (21% vs. 12%), (b) whether their funeral should include an open casket or closed casket (32% vs. 18%), (c) whether they wanted burial or cremation (10% vs. 4%), (d) whether they would want to have a wake (19% vs. 11%), and (3) whether or not young children should be able to attend the funeral (22% vs. 14%).

The greater indifference of men to the death rituals may be given several alternative interpretations. First, it can be seen as evidence of greater denial since lack of decision might mean less willingness to even make an attempt to cope with these obvious (to others, at least) pressures. Second, the greater indifference might arise because men find the pros and cons more nearly in balance, so that whichever alternative eventuated, it would be equally all right (or equally wrong) from their point of view. Third, the men may simply care less, be less involved, than the women. Remaining consistent with our principle that people should be taken at their word, unless strong evidence to the contrary is available, we will accept the third interpretation of the data. This is also consistent with the hypothesis that men are essentially more intellectualistic and secular, while women are more emotive and more involved with traditional ritual.

And Their Own Death Encounter

Previous studies of sex differences have been, for the most part, restricted to limited populations. Thus Rhudick & Dibner (1961), Christ (1961), and Jeffers et al. (1961) all focussed upon the elderly. Middleton (1936), Diggory & Rothman (1961), and Kahana and Kahana (1972) and Pandey and Templer (1972) attended to college students.

Many of the other studies evaluated death anxiety, using a variety of measures but usually involving some kind of direct questionnaire. Templer, Ruff, and Franks (1971), using Templer's 15-item death anxiety scale (Templer, 1970), found consistently higher anxiety scores for women in three settings with a substantial range of social class and age. Kalish, with his accidental sample, also reported supportive findings (1963a). Templer and Pandey (1972), studying a bi-racial sample, found no sex differences for either Black or Anglo university students. Handal (1969) found no differences in death anxiety between men and women graduate students. Dickstein (1972) also found no differences on a Death Concern scale between college men and women.

Our present study does not effectively measure death anxiety, although we did pose the following query: "Some people say they are afraid to die and others say they are not. How do you feel?" Responses were open-ended, and the interviewers coded them on the spot, while frequently recording explanatory comments. We found no sex differences for either the entire group or within any of the individual ethnic groups (See Table 5-1).

Our other evidence is sketchy but could be used to support the idea that women are more anxious about death than men. Women think more about death than men, and they are more likely to have had the unexplainable feeling that they were about to die. At the same time, women expect to accept death passively rather than fight it actively.

One way in which traditional sex roles are expressed was found in each of the ethnic groups. We had asked, "If you were told that you had a terminal disease and six months to live, how would you want to spend your time until you died?" Table 5-2 suggests that the approach to death elicits social and nurturant responses from women and action and work responses from men (the familistic and ceremonial orientation versus individualistic and secular); similarly, the women seek passive ways to finish their lives, while men seek the active.

In summary, we find some substantiation of traditional sex

roles in these data and some lack of substantiation where we might have expected otherwise; at no time do the data suggest the opposite of expectations. Men are more likely to be pragmatic, individualistic, and intellectualistic; women appear more sentimental, familistic, and affective.

TABLE 5-1

SELECTED VARIABLES BY SEX

		Men (%)	Women (%)
(088)	Some people say they are afraid to die and others say they are not. How do you feel?		
	Afraid/terrified	27	26
x^2 — not significant	Neither afraid nor unafraid	22	16
r — not significant	Unafraid/eager	47	55
	Other	3	2
(024)	About how often do you think about your own death?		
	Daily	14	21
	At least weekly	10	10
x^2 — significant, 0.02	At least monthly	13	17
r — 0.17, significant	At least yearly	12	20
	Hardly ever	27	18
	Never	24	15
(132)	Other than during dreams, have you ever had the unexplainable feeling that you were about to die?		
x^2 — significant, 0.10	Yes	15	23
	No	85	77
(039)	Would you tend to accept death peacefully or fight death actively?		
x^2 — significant, 0.10	Accept	59	68
	Fight	41	30
	Other	1	2
(165)	Where would you like to die?		
	At home	55	60
x^2 — significant, 0.001	Hospital	17	26
	Other	27	14

TABLE 5-2

TERMINAL ACTIVITIES BY SEX

	Men (%)	Women (%)
(037 & 038)		
If you were told that you had a terminal disease and six months to live, how would you want to spend your time until you died? (First and second choices combined.)		
Marked change in life-style (e.g. travel, drugs, experience)	35	17
Withdrawal (e.g. read, contemplate, pray, inner-life centered)	29	44
Focus concern on others, especially loved ones	45	67
Complete projects, tie up loose ends	40	20
No change	39	40
Other	12	14

And Therefore . . .

We would have expected more sex differences to emerge from our data. The differences we did find paralleled stereotyped sex-role characteristics, with males appearing more pragmatic, controlled, aggressive, and individualistic; and females being more sentimental, emotional, passive, and familistic. Women, although they felt that the dying person senses his impending death, were still less able to tell him about his death. They were freer in their grief and more aware that grief takes time. Women had more concrete plans for funerals and related rituals, while men were more likely to have arranged for the more practical matters of finances and care. If these differences seem to resemble the middle class Anglo value system, it may be because it was in the Anglo population that we found the greatest differentiation in response according to sex (of the chi squares between Anglo males and females, 17% were significant, compared to 6-7% for the other three groups).

EDUCATION

Education, either in and of itself or as a reflection of social class, is undoubtedly a major determinant of values, attitudes, expectations, and behavior. Numerous studies have also found education closely related to death attitudes and our results provide moderate verification for these. Although we did not find education as pervasive a determinant as Riley did in his research, perhaps because our sampling was biased in the direction of under-representing more highly educated people, a fair number of our variables were related to education, and there was considerable consistency between our chi squares (based on four levels of education, e.g., grade school, high school, high school graduation, and college) and our correlations (based on five levels of education).

Education is related both to age and to ethnicity. Mexican Americans, as a group, and the elderly, as a group, have less education than other ethnic and age groups. The mean educational level, in number of years, for the four ethnic groups was otherwise quite similar (B 10.6, J 12.4, M 6.5, A 11.1). The heavy recent immigration from rural Mexico precludes the logic of going further than we did in controlling for education, since it would have provided too highly biased a sample of the other ethnic groups.

Education is often believed to lead to more stress upon intellectual reactions to events, upon scientific thinking, and upon pragmatic approaches. There is little in our findings to contradict these frequent assumptions.

Interactions with the Dying and the Dead

The most intimate level of physical contact with the dead person, touching and kissing the body, is much more acceptable to those of less education; similarly, they appear most able to express their emotions openly (see Table 5-3). In the same vein, less educated persons anticipated longer periods of mourning as necessary before returning to normal social activities (P <.001); they also felt that remarriage (P <.05), ceasing to wear black (P <.001, r = 0.29), and returning to dating (P <.001) should be postponed relatively longer than those with more formal education.

Each of the cited issues suggests that the role of education is to reduce the overt expression of emotionality and to attend pragmatically to the world around. One exception was found: there was no relationship between education and the length of time following loss that the mourner could remain away from work. Work is a necessity for those with less education, if they are to exist. Missing work is a luxury that cannot be afforded for long.

As they are sentimental in relating to the death, those with less education are protective when relating to the dying. They are less likely to believe the dying person should be informed (P <.001, r = 0.28) or that they could personally tell someone he was dying (P <.001, r = 0.34). Again their feelings seem to dictate their way of handling the problem.

To some extent, the lower educational levels of the Mexican Americans contributed to the relationships discussed above. However, the general trends extended beyond this one ethnic group. Age differences are also involved, but it was difficult to separate statistically the role of age from that of education.

Encounter with One's Own Death

Again the more educated were more intellectual and more pragmatic. College persons were less likely to call a clergyman when death was imminent (P <.001, r = 0.34); they would not expect family members to attend them, if inconvenient (P <.01, r = 0.23); and they were much more likely to want to know when they were dying (P <.001, r = 0.34). Here the elements of a familistic versus individualistic orientation is suggested. Education in the United States is probably most effective in socializing persons away from the traditional familistic approach and toward individualism (not in the sense of "rugged," but in the sense of "self"). Indeed, the contemporary search for community, through communes and other relationships, is often explicitly anti-intellectual and hostile toward contemporary formal educational institutions.

When asked how they would spend their last six months, persons with less education were more inclined to mention prayer or contemplation or other inner-centered activity; they also stated less desire for marked change but also less desire for no change. Concern for others was relatively more prominent among those with less education. (They were also less likely to wish to die at home, which does seem to conflict with other findings.) At this juncture in their lives, the more educated want to continue to live as before, or even more, to cram into their remaining months as much living as possible; the less educated seek a relationship with their loved ones and with their God.

TABLE 5-3

RELATIONSHIP OF EDUCATION TO SELECTED VARIABLES

	Significance level of x^2	Correlation
(047) Would you be likely to touch the body at any of the funeral services?	P<0.01	r=0.25
(048) Would you be likely to kiss the body at any of the funeral services?	P<0.01	r=-0.24
(044) Would you worry if you couldn't cry?	P<0.01	r=0.27
(045) Would you try very hard to control the way you showed your emotions in public?	P<0.01	r=-0.24
(046) Would you let yourself go and cry yourself out (in public or private or both)?	P<0.10	r=0.03

In spite of their apparent pragmatism, those attending college were most afraid of death, while those not going beyond grade school were least afraid (P <.01). (Results from the 1975 National Council on the Aging survey were consistent.) These results were not due to ethnicity, but they may reflect age differences. We did a further analysis of fear of death only among the elderly, and within that segment of the sample, education was not significantly related to fear of death. Nonetheless, we are forced to conclude that education certainly does not appear to ameliorate fear of death and may even encourage it.

A secularized pragmatism follows the better educated person to the grave. He probably does not wish a wake (P <.001, r = 0.23) or an open casket (P <.02). He prefers not to be embalmed (P <.10, r = 0.16), and does not wish a high proportion of his life insurance to be applied to funeral costs (P <.001, r = 0.19). College people were also most likely to prefer their own home for the funeral service, and least likely to wish the service to take place in a funeral home, but they also showed the highest proportion of indifference to the issue. The relationship of education to wanting a large funeral was more complex: although grade school persons were most favorable, those having attended college were second (P <.01).

Preparation for Death

Differences among educational groups in preparing for death were not as substantial as might be anticipated. Perhaps those with less education (also tending to have lower incomes) did not make certain preparations simply for reasons of finance or awareness. We found that those attending grade school were least likely to have life insurance, while high school graduates were most likely to do so (P <.001), and there was a barely significant trend for the better educated to have made arrangements to donate their bodies to medical programs (P <.05). Similarly, a trend was observed for the better educated to be least likely to have made funeral arrangements (P <.05). In our view, the inverse relationship between education and having made funeral arrangements is in part a function of ideology and in part a function of age; the greater propensity for the better educated to donate their bodies probably reflects both ideology and awareness; and the curvilinear relationship for education and life insurance is a function of income and age, i.e., the drop-off for college people resulted from age differences, while the straightline function for the first three educational groups is a direct outcome of discretionary income, a correlate of education.

Ideology

People with more formal education, who also tend to be younger, are more likely to take an individualistic, secular view of social issues, rather than a familistic, sacred position. Since they feel that both the individual and the society function better if some persons are permitted to design their own deaths, they are more likely to believe that—under certain conditions—people should be permitted to die (P <.001, r = 0.24). Those with grade school education, more often elderly and more often Mexican American, are less willing to have a human being make the decision they feel should arise from divine authority. Similarly, the better educated accept the notion of will-to-live and will-to-die (P <.001, r = 0.42), also suggesting the power of individual will to compete with or coexist alongside divine will.

The scientific, as opposed to the traditionally religious, is again shown by the tendency of the better educated to disagree that those living to be 90 must have been morally good (P <.001, r = 0.34) or that accidental deaths show the hand of God (P <.05). The theme that God, not man, intervenes in death-related issues is evident; so is the theme that God is pervasive and that He rewards the good. If an individual has the ability to extend his life through his own will, he might be able to overcome God's will as well as overcoming the natural law that God displays through accidents and illness.

A Summing Up

Education appears related to a more pragmatic, secular, rationalistic, and individualistic approach to death and grieving. For example, with increasing education fewer people would encourage their family to spend time with them if they were dying, fewer would call for a clergyman, more felt they would try to control their emotions at a time of grief, more felt that death could be hastened or slowed by will, more could communicate with the dying and more would encourage such communication, and more felt that people who wish to die would be permitted to do so. Again, education, religiousness, and age are interrelated in such fashion that we cannot extract each one for separate examination, but need to view them in interaction for the most part.

RELIGION

"The wages of sin is death" (Romans VI:23). More than any other institution, the church holds sway in the realm of death. The physician may attempt to cure or alleviate; the family may offer love and sustenance; the university professor may philosophize; the funeral director may organize and comfort; but it is the clergyman who provides the rites of passage from this life into whatever comes next and who supplies the basic and authoritative words of solace and explanation to the dying and the bereaved. The majority of people in the United States and Canada believe in a traditional Judaic-Christian God, a life after death, and a hell (Gallup polls, various dates).

Background Factors

The literature is well supplied with studies comparing death attitudes of various religious groupings with each other (e.g., Gorer, 1965; Chenard, 1972; Kalish, 1963a, 1963b; Vernon, 1970; Diggory & Rothman, 1961). Unfortunately, we had no way to replicate these earlier investigations, since religious affiliation was too strongly tied to ethnicity in our sample. Just over half of the Black Americans were Baptist, with an additional one-third belonging to other Protestant denominations and 6% being Catholic; 90% of the Mexican Americans were Roman Catholic while 8% were Protestant; over half the Japanese Americans were Buddhist with an additional 15% being Methodist; and the Anglo respondents were 17% Roman Catholic, 20% Baptist, and 45% other Protestant. We could have made comparisons within ethnicities and between major religious groups, i.e., between Catholic and Protestant Anglos, but we felt that the numbers did not warrant pursuing the issue.

Religiousness can be evaluated in many ways. However, a multicultural study adds considerably to the difficulty of obtaining measures of religiousness that have the same meaning for all groups; e.g., belief in a heavenly life following the earthly one is not a significant part of either traditional Judaism nor of many Buddhist sects; the concept of God as such is lacking in some Buddhist sects, but Jodoshinshu Buddhists worship Amida Butsu much as Christians worship God.

We therefore selected an approach that would not have an initial built-in bias. Each individual was asked to compare himself with other members of his religious group. Specifically, he responded to the question, "Compared to most_____, do you feel you are more, about the same, or less devout?" The blank was to be filled in by the interviewer with whatever religious affiliation the individual had previously indicated. The response to this item was our first measure of religiousness. To supplement this, we also used a question asking about the existence of some form of life after death.

Nearly half the Anglos and over half the other groups considered themselves "about the same" (B 64%, J 52%, M 50%, A 46%). One out of six Black Americans perceives himself as less devout than his denominational peers, while slightly more than twice that proportion of the other ethnicities make the same claim (B 16%, J 36%, M 33%, A 36%).

Roughly half the entire sample definitely believed in some form of life after death (B 59%, J 47%, M 40%, A 66%). The rest either did not believe in an afterlife or were uncertain about it. That the predominently Catholic Mexican Americans show such a low degree of acceptance concerned us. We tested matched pairs of respondents receiving the questionnaire in English and in Spanish, to determine whether any translation problems may have led to this unexpected finding, but there were no significant differences between the two. Perhaps they perceived the question as pertaining to some kind of imminent bodily resurrection.

About two-thirds of the Black, Mexican, and Anglo respondents who did believe in life after death described some form of heavenly paradise, but over 40% of a comparable group of Japanese mentioned return to earth in spirit form in some fashion. And nearly three-fourths of all respondents, but fewer Japanese Americans, agreed that they wished there were life after death (B 80%, J 51%, M 69%, A 88%).

An intensive interview study conducted in Tokyo found that 55 of the 100 respondents believed that a man's spirit lives on after death (Dore, 1958). Of these same urban dwellers, 39% implied that they believed the spirits of dead relatives know about family events, are concerned about them, and can provide help in these matters. These spirits, called *kami* or *hotokesama*, are fed and communicated with at the family shrine. The line between belief that the dead person's influence continues to be felt in behavior and in the on-going respect from family members is difficult to draw (see Hearn, reprinted in 1956). Rather than focusing upon the clarity of the concept, the Japanese family members will emphasize the appropriateness of the feeling. Although we recognize the risks in drawing too many parallels between urban Japanese in the 1950's and urban Japanese Americans in the 1970's, we feel that the data mentioned in the previous paragraph evolve from the same cultural origins that led to the findings of Dore and Hearn.

Only those who stipulated their belief in something approximating heaven were queried further. Of these (about 30% of the entire sample) a great majority of all groups felt that those in heaven watched over those on earth, except for Blacks, among whom three out of five persons believed those in heaven had no concern for earth. Similarly, a great majority believed in hell, except for Japanese: only a handful of Japanese Americans accept the notion of a literal hell.

For the remainder of our analysis, we used the measure of self-rated relative religiousness as our primary tool. It was part of our correlation matrix, and we ran chi square tests of significance relating religiousness to almost every other item on the interview schedule. To supplement this, we used the question about belief in an afterlife constructed to minimize ethnic differences, in the correlation matrix.

The two measures correlate 0.25 with each other, showing that they were tapping related but far from identical factors.

Religiousness is closely related to age (chi square and correlation were both highly significant) and to marital status. Fewer of the devout have never married and more are widowed (a function of age). Interestingly, our measures of religiousness are answered almost identically by men and women, contrary to observations and findings of most investigators.

Death-Related Religious Ideology

Although death is often, perhaps usually, perceived as a natural and biological event, occurring as an inevitable point of termination in the human life cycle, even seemingly rational persons endow death and dying with various mystiques. Among the 47 tribes for which Simmons (1945) could find information, 17 regarded death as unnatural (i.e., the outcome of hexes, witches, supernatural interventions), while in 26 others death as a natural event was only partially accepted. This type of mysticism was evident among our respondents. Excluding from our count those who did not take a position, slightly under two-thirds agreed with the statement, "Accidental deaths show the hand of God working among men" (B 63%, J 63%, M 71%, A 56%). Apparently our more religious respondents think along these lines also, since the correlation between belief in afterlife and agreeing that accidental deaths show the hand of God at work was much higher than with relative devoutness (see Table 5-4).

Approximately 40% also backed the statement, "Most people who live to be 90 years old must have been morally good people" (B 40%, J 43%, M 40%, A 20%). The relationship between responses to this item and religiousness was in the expected direction, but not significant.

One possible interpretation of these items is that death is perceived, at least to some extent, as a punishment, the wages of sin, while long life is looked upon as a reward for virtue. The correlations of these two items with each other was 0.37. Simmons also reports that longevity is often seen as a just reward for having led "a good moral life" (1945, p. 221). An alternative interpretation is that God's working is a way to explain why an event occurred to someone at a specific time: it is part of God's plan and is unrelated to reward or punishment. Much as the Azande use witchcraft and sorcery to explain otherwise inexplicable events (Evans-Pritchard, 1937), our respondents have turned to God's design to explain unexpected and presumably premature death and its converse, unexpected lengthy life.

In a related matter, around 60% of the Black, Mexican and Anglo Americans and 42% of the Japanese Americans answered

TABLE 5-4

CORRELATION OF STATEMENT WITH SELF-ASSESSMENT
OF DEGREE OF RELIGIOUS DEVOUTNESS
AND BELIEF IN AFTER-LIFE

		Religious Devoutness (%)	Belief in Afterlife (%)
(097)	Accidental deaths show the hand of God working among men.	0.11*	0.41***
(098)	Most people who live to be 90 years old must have been morally good people.	0.13*	0.05
(088)	Some people say they are afraid to die and others say they are not. How do you feel?	-0.10	0.13*
(024)	About how often do you think about your own death?	0.12*	0.21***
(101)	Have you made out a will?	0.23***	0.25***
(103)	Have you made funeral arrangements?	0.07	0.16**
(041)	Would you encourage your family to spend time with you even if it was a little inconvenient for them?	0.27***	0.17**

*$P<0.05$
**$P<0.01$
***$P<0.001$

affirmatively the question, "Have you ever seriously considered that all human life might be eliminated from the earth?" The less devout are most likely to have considered this possibility, while those rating themselves as average in devotion are least likely to have contemplated such an ending. Of those who were positive in their responses, the less devout referred to nuclear explosions or ecological disasters as destroying the earth. The more devout individuals turn to cosmic and supernatural events, e.g., God bringing the world to an end (B 36%, M 41%, J 11%, A 25%).

Perhaps these data are the outgrowth of totally separate sets of forces, one working upon the traditionally religious and one working upon the secular, but neither having much impact upon the intermediate group. This would be consistent with their orientations: the secular, being person-centered, place people as the focal point of decisions and events and attribute the causes of disaster to people as well. The religious are God-centered, assume God has ultimate responsibility, and tend to feel that a catastrophe of this magnitude would probably arise from divine intervention.

Interactions with the Dying and the Dead

Those who rate themselves as more devout than average also appear to have more contact with the dying and the dead. They have attended more funerals and more funerals recently; they have visited the gravesites of friends and family members more frequently; and they have called upon dying friends and relatives more often. Since the more religious are also older, it is difficult to ascertain the degree to which these death contacts are due to the dying off of age cohorts and older friends and relatives and how much arose from religious feelings that prompted or enabled a more comfortable feeling regarding death and the dying.

The Personal Encounter with Death and Dying

Does a Christian (or Jewish or Buddhist or ...) belief and affiliation enable a person to die a better death? Does acceptance of religious ideology preaching salvation (or reincarnation or ...) permit the dying process to rest a little more lightly? This issue has been hotly debated among theologians and clergymen, among college students and housewives and laborers.

Elisabeth Kübler-Ross, in her excellent treatise on the dying process, observed dying patients, comforted them, and enabled them to serve as teachers to the living. Her now well-known project was actually initiated because of the desire of several theological students to understand at a more personal level what death meant. Yet she says, "Religious patients seemed to differ little from those without a religion. The difference may be hard to determine, since we have not clearly defined what we mean by a religious person. ... we found very few truly religious people with an intrinsic faith. Those few have been helped by their faith and are best comparable with those few patients who were true atheists. The majority of patients were in between, with some form of religious belief but not enough to relieve them of conflict and fear" (Ross, 1969, p. 237).

Earlier research (Kalish, 1963b; Hinton, 1963) has borne out Ross' surmise. Kalish found a curvilinear relationship between church attendance and several factor-analyzed variables that were related to death and dying. In each instance, the regular church attenders were the least afraid of death, while the non-attenders were close behind, with those who attended erratically being the most fearful of death and dying.

Hinton, in evaluating the fear of death of dying persons, found that about 20% of regular church attenders and 25% of non-attenders were apprehensive or anxious concerning their coming death, but those who professed a religious faith that they did not act upon were twice as likely to be fearful.

Several studies have found fear of death inversely related to religiousness. Martin and Wrightsman (1965) surveyed 58 middle-aged adult respondents in Tennessee, learning that death fear was greater among those who did not attend church, did not pray, and did not read the Bible. Swenson found that religious belief and religious activities were predictive of lower death fears in an elderly sample (1959, 1961). And Jeffers, Nichols and Eisdorfer (1961), also working with persons over 60, found highly significant relationships between fear of death and less belief in afterlife, less frequent reading of the Bible, and less frequent reference to death with religious connotation. When Templer examined the relationship between his Death Anxiety Scale and religiousness of college students attending an interdenominational religious retreat, he found significantly less anxiety among the more religious students. He hypothesized that these relationships do not occur unless the persons studied perceive religion as having importance (1972).

Feifel (1956), on the other hand, suggests that people use religion to ward off fear of death. Therefore, there is either no difference in regard to death fears as a function of religious feelings or, perhaps, the religious actually fear death more. Christ (1961) and Kalish (1963a) also found no relationship between death fear and religious beliefs, although the latter study investigated both religious affiliation and belief in God.

Our present study does not have information regarding church attendance, belief in God, or involvement in religious activities. Based upon the self-evaluated relative devoutness question, however, we obtained a highly significant difference in death fear as a function of religiousness (although the correlation between belief in afterlife and fear of death was low). The more devout definitely claim to be more accepting of death and dying and less fearful. Since the devout are disproportionately elderly, we analyzed the responses only of those over age 60. Our chi square analysis of this relationship was not significant, although this time we found the trend that those high and those low in devotion reported lower fear of death than the intermediate group, even when limited to the elderly respondents.

The argument has been raised that religious persons feel more obligated to report themselves as being unafraid of death than non-religious individuals. Our own observations (we have no data) cause us to doubt this. We feel that there is a tendency among persons of all degrees of religiousness to feel their faith helps them deal effectively with death. Therefore, although we do not deny the operation of distortion on this issue, we believe the degree of distortion is probably unrelated to religiousness.

The devout not only display less fear of death, but, again like the elderly, they admit to thinking more frequently of death in general and their own death in particular. Although the chi square was *not* significant in this instance, the trends were extremely consistent, and the correlation with belief in afterlife (r=0.21) was highly significant. Religious devotion is also related to having made out a will and having made funeral arrangements (see Table 5-4). The more devout are also more likely to have paid for a cemetery plot and to have arranged for someone to handle their affairs in case of death. Again, we are not certain whether these arrangements are the outgrowth of the greater age of those who are devout or of their greater willingness to recognize the need to deal with the coming death. We would suspect both forces are at play.

In our discussion of the relationship between death attitudes and age, we made the point that theorists are too likely to attribute repression and denial to responses when the results are in opposition to the theorists' biases. It is our assumption at this point that, if repression and denial do exist in the ways people answer our questions (and we assume that they do exist), such influences are constant across all our groups. Therefore, if the more religious or the older respondents state that they fear death less, we will accept their word at face value.

Who fears death the most? Our answer must be: those who lack a reasonably firm acceptance of some coherent life system that tries to make death understandable and that tries to make life meaningful. We feel, therefore, with Kubler-Ross, that the firmly devout and the true non-believers can cope with death more effectively than those whose views are vague or ambivalent.

Contrasting Roles: The Clergyman and the Physician

Although many professions are involved with death and dying, e.g., cemetery manager, florist, social worker, hospital administrator, life insurance salesman, the three that come most readily to mind are the clergyman, the physician/nurse, and the funeral director. Numerous studies of physicians and nurses have been conducted, to the point that one irritated urologist told the authors that he was "sick and tired of you behavioral scientists, who have none of our responsibilities and pressures, walking in off the street and telling us how to treat our patients." The urologist had a valid point. Somehow physicians seem to end up the villains in a great many behavioral research studies. Nurses fare only somewhat better.

Strangely, very little research has been published regarding the feelings that clergymen have toward death and bereavement. Perhaps there are subtle reasons for this, but we assume that much of the explanation arises from the simple fact that there are many more research-oriented psychologists, sociologists, and psychiatrists around health care facilities than around religious facilities.

In spite of the importance of the church and of religion for many people, they tend to turn to friends and family members more frequently for comfort and satisfaction. Given the death of a spouse, just over half of each group would turn to a relative—a child, a parent, a brother, or a sister for the most part—for comfort. Nonetheless, roughly 30% would seek solace from their clergyman. (One person selected "Physician" and five would turn to the funeral director—all six are Black or Anglo). As might be expected, the devout are more likely to turn to religion for comfort when in mourning and are more likely to call a clergyman in case of impending death (correlation with belief in afterlife of 0.19). In addition, religiousness relates to the wish for a life after death with significant chi square and significant correlation (r = 0.44).

Nearly 90% of the Mexican Americans and well over half of the others would call a clergyman in case they know their own death was likely within two weeks, but only a few have discussed their eventual death with the clergy, while many more have talked with family members and, on occasion, friends. Informing the dying person is rarely seen as the clergyman's role, and the church is seldom seen as the proper place for the wake except by the Japanese (B 27%, J 50%, M 21%, A 15%) and then not for religious reasons but because the large scale turnout at many Japanese American funerals can be handled by neither of the two Japanese-owned funeral homes.

The implications of these data appear to be that the family is the first line of comfort and support, with the clergyman (and, perhaps, God and prayer) second; the physician, the funeral director, and even the policeman (who is most frequently called upon to intervene in case of suicide) all have designated roles. Of those who feel the dying patient should be informed about his condition, twice as many designate the physician for the task as all other persons combined. For the 90 individuals who were aware of someone who was dying under related circumstances, 67 stated that the dying person was informed by his physician. However, only one person in the entire sample would turn to a physician for comfort in case of the death of a spouse; only 20% would contact a physician in case they knew of someone about to attempt suicide—and almost all stipulated a psychiatrist; none had discussed their own death with either a physician or a psychotherapist. And—of those who specified—slightly over one-fifth preferred dying in a hospital, compared to nearly three times that number who wanted to die at home.

We interpret our results as indicating a strong religious overtone running through all of our ethnic groups, albeit the Japanese Americans appear most pragmatic (which is consistent with other interpretations of Japanese Buddhism), and the Mexicans most traditional and emotive. Certain cautions must be applied to survey data-reporting. For example, more people think the world might end from nuclear explosion than from divine intervention, but these people are not necessarily non-religious. Likewise, more people would seek comfort for their bereavement from family members than from clergymen, but these people may not be ignoring their churches.

Our research did not focus upon religiousness, and we cannot claim that our data have explicitly established that religious rituals or ideologies, dependence on the clergy, or belief in God or afterlife, are cogent in determining the ways in which individuals will cope with their own death encounters and the loss of others through death. We do not hesitate to state, however, that we find the most parsimonious explanation of our data indicates a role for the church and the clergy that ranges from moderate to very important.

6

Black Americans

In the rich folk literature of Black Americans, in their songs and poetry, in their contemporary writings of anger and violence and scorn, death is omnipresent. In the behavioral and social scientific studies, in the ethnographies, in the careful compilations of numbers, death is absent. We can only posit that if Blacks had written their own history and their own anthropology, death might have been more discussed.

The history and culture of Black Americans have certainly not avoided academic scrutiny, albeit as seen through White-tinted glasses. The substantial amounts of information, misinformation, and misinterpreted information makes it both simple and immensely difficult to write this chapter. With Mexican American and Japanese American communities we had access only to limited stores of writing from which to draw. Writing on and writing by Black Americans is so voluminous that we cannot hope to do more than scratch the surface. Despite all this writing, there is so little of the academic kind of writing about the meaning of death to the contemporary Black American as it compares to that for other Americans that we begin almost at the beginning.

The attitudes and behaviors of Black Americans in regard to death cannot be adequately understood without reference to the accompanying persistent historical presence of violent death. Struggle, violence, suppressed and exploded aggression have followed the Black American since the earliest years of slavery. A preoccupation with violence and death is apparent in the historical and folklore from the past and in the psychoethnographies (Kardiner and Ovesey, 1951; Hendin, 1969; Grier and Cobbs, 1968), newspapers, art forms,

94

and even ghetto children's essays (Joseph, 1969) of the present. Similarly, we found that death is difficult to conceal and ignore in the Black communities of Los Angeles.

One student's account of the grim reality of sudden death in the ghetto follows:

> Death in my own home ghetto is all too sudden and very seldom peaceful. A teenager was once walking through a housing project on his way home. Suddenly, without warning, a bullet shattered his skull. A man has crawled down a street and died as his fellow citizens stumbled over his body. Children playing in vacant lots and fields have found the bodies of dead men and women, mutilated and left to rot. Death is common and violent in a class of people held prisoner by the invisible chains of racism. (Carter, 1971, p. 269)

Does this attention to violent death reflect the objectively-viewed reality? We would have respond with "No, but . . .." "No" because only a small proportion of Black Americans are directly involved with violent death and because fewer Black Americans are victims of suicide. ". . . but" because of the relatively high rate of homicidal deaths in the Black community of Los Angeles and because more Black American respondents knew people who had died in accidents or in war. The "but" is also necessary because the media, including the Black dominated media, play up the sensational aspects of that violence which does occur.

HISTORICAL ROOTS

Herskovits (1941) has argued that the roots of Black American culture survived the transplant from Africa to America. He enumerated many parallel customs and perspectives in African and Afro-American settings, attributing them to the survival of fundamental African cultures despite the dehumanizing effects of slavery and the subtler dehumanizing racism of modern America. More recently, Lomax (1970) has found similar surviving parallels in Afro-American musical systems.

On the other hand, Kardiner and Ovesey (1951), following Frazier (1949), argue that "The most conspicuous feature of the Negro in America is *that his aboriginal culture was smashed*, be it by design or accident" (p. 39, emphasis theirs). Hammerz (1970) offers a concise summary of the culture survival vs. culture demolishment theories (or, as he calls them, the "Africanist" and the "slavery" explanations), as they apply to Black family structure and adds a third which he describes as "now probably dominant" (p. 314), that the Black family structure is a response to the employment difficulties encountered by Black men.

An alternative explanation, seldom acknowledged, is that the family structure of the Black community is seriously affected by the lack of available Black men (Jackson, 1971). The 1970 Census establishes that, nationally, there are fewer than 91 Black males for every 100 Black females, all ages combined. The figures for California are 95:100. As is well known, educational differences between Black men and Black women are negligible, and the former out-earn the latter by substantial amounts in every educational category. Moreover, the higher the male-female ratio in a given state in the United States, the lower the proportion of families headed by females (Jackson, 1971). Thus, the difficulty in family structure may not be so much inadequate sex roles or male employment opportunities among the Blacks or the problems of the Black man in relationship to the Black woman but simply the long history of insufficient Black men available as husbands and the low income of all Black wage earners.

Blauner (1970) has made an attempt to distinguish between *cultural* characteristics which are unique to Black consciousness and rooted in the exclusively Black historico-political experience, and *social class characteristics* shared by low-income peoples in general. In this way, he brings a new sort of explanation to the understanding of Black Americans. They are not to be seen simply as New World Africans, nor are they only Black imitations of Anglos, nor yet are they merely molded plastic tokens stamped by an economic environment, but, in his view, they are eminently culture carriers of a unique perspective born of slavery, the American South, and Emancipation.

In this view, Black Americans may be evolving new kinds of family structures, perhaps as viable as traditional models and undoubtedly more attuned to the changing nature of American families in general. Implications of this view for the impact of death and dying upon the Black family (or, indeed, any family) must be considered.

If ideologies of death are, in a sense, projections of basic world-view perspectives, as we believe, then we might explain Black American perspectives by means of one or more of four conceptual frameworks. First, as Herskovitz has pointed out, death-related rituals and behavior may be forms of African survival; Herskovitz has discussed this at some length in *The Myth of the Negro Past* (1941). Second, Black American responses to death might be primarily determined by the imprint of the dominant culture within which they have spent the past three centuries. Third, their reactions may represent the value system of the socioeconomic status group within which Black Americans are disproportionately found. And, fourth, there may be themes unique to being part of Black America, understandable in terms of Blauner's conceptions.

We have made an attempt to relate the study's findings to each of the conceptual frameworks, but our emphasis is primarily descriptive. Nonetheless, we ask readers to keep in mind—for all three ethnographic descriptions—these four explanations.

BACKGROUND

The initial impetus for the rapid migration of Black Americans to Southern California was World War II. This growing urban area needed labor, and war-induced mobility provided many Blacks with a new awareness of the world outside the rural South and a few Northeast and Middle West cities. Of our Black respondents, 32% were born east of the Mississippi, primarily in the Southeast; 58% were born west of the Mississippi, primarily in Texas and Oklahoma. Only 10% of the respondents were born in California and only 5% in Los Angeles, and Black Americans indicated the shortest average residence in California (B 20, J 30, M 25, A 25).

The importance of religion among the Black Americans will be touched upon both in this chapter and elsewhere in this volume. Most respondents, as might be expected, were Protestant (86%), with slightly over half of the total sample being Baptist; a few were Catholic and a few were Other or without religious association. These percentages correspond to the 1960 Census data (Current Population Reports Series P-20, #79, 2/2/58) in which non-Whites were roughly 87% Protestant and slightly over 60% Baptist.

To a significant degree, Black Americans perceived themselves as more religious than others of their own ethnicity rather than less religious (B 20% vs. 16%, J 12% vs. 35%, M 18% vs. 33%, A 18% vs. 36%). Older persons, especially older women, saw themselves as relatively more devout than young.

Other demographic differences also were found. Thus the relatively high percentage of widowed, divorced, and separated Black Americans (37%) was approached only by that of the Anglos (24%), with women being significantly more likely than men to report being widowed or separated. In a similar vein, Black American women were less likely than women of other groups to refer to themselves as housewives (about one-third of the Black women as opposed to over half of the Japanese- and Anglo-American women and nearly all of the Mexican American women), and more likely to be categorized as unskilled workers (in 1969, 20% of employed Black women were household workers, based upon nationwide statistics—Jackson, 1971). Our data are consistent with other writings, and there does appear to be ample evidence that domestic units in Black communities are relatively likely to have women heads of households. In Los Angeles County, the ratio of male-to-female heads of household was nearly 8:1 for Whites, but less than 2.5:1 for Blacks (General Population Characteristics, California, 1970 Census for Population, Table 36).

Another aspect of the Black experience is the ethnic constitution of their neighborhood. More Black Americans than others estimated that at least 75% of the people on their block were of similar ethnicity (B 87%, J 11%, M 64%, A 51%). When they leave their jobs, the Blacks are most likely of all the groups in this project to return to a community of high ethnic density.

EXPECTATIONS REGARDING DEATH

The expectations of a community are expressed not only through their overt statements regarding what they desire and what they anticipate but also through their arts and their institutions. We had available to us both life expectancy data (unfortunately based upon national rather than Los Angeles norms), which we could compare with our interview responses and also with selected references in Black American literature.

The life expectancy from birth for Black Americans increased 15 years between 1900 and 1931, with a similar increase between 1931 and 1967. But the expectations of our Black American respondents and their desires for longevity have advanced even beyond these gains. (See Reynolds and Kalish, 1973, for fuller discussion.)

As might be assumed, Black Americans who are younger tend both to expect and to wish more future years than their elders. However, compared to the other groups, Black Americans as a whole expect to live longest and would like to live longest. Such expectations certainly are not in keeping with actuarial life expectancy tables which indicate that, based upon their present age, these Black American respondents could expect to live an average of 77 years as compared to 80 years for Caucasian Americans. In view of our sampling biases, however, both figures might be a little high.

Not only do these statistics have implications for the length of time these respondents can expect to live, they already reflect a very direct influence on the personal lives of the members of this subcultural group. For example, a Black American child born in 1900 could expect his 20-year-old mother to live for about another 37 years. The 20-year-olds in our sample (born around 1950 to then-20-year-old mothers) can expect their mothers to be alive for about another 47 years (nearly 10 more years than could their grandparents). One becomes increasingly old before he is likely to experience the death of a parent, an event that probably provokes more active thoughts and plans regarding one's own death than virtually any other. Kardiner and Ovesey (1951) noted the frequency and psychological impact of early parental death on the lower-class Blacks they interviewed.

United States data for non-Whites between 1950 and 1967 show increased death rates due to malignant neoplasms, suicide, and diabetes, and decreased death rates caused by pneumonia and influenza, tuberculosis, accidents, and major cardiovascular-renal diseases. Although non-White mortality has been reduced in such areas as pneumonia, tuberculosis, and accidents, these reductions are mirrored in the rates among Whites, so that the ratio of deaths of non-Whites to Whites from these causes has not changed. In 1964 the death rates for tuberculosis, for syphilis, and for high blood pressure among Black Americans far exceeded rates for Whites.

Many factors conspire to produce these racial differences in life expectancy. Black Americans are plagued by early nutritional deficits, inadequate health care and health care facilities, and poor health conditions. Health educators, at least until very recently, have not reached effectively into these communities; building inspectors and sanitation workers shut their eyes to code violations. In addition,

> ... The Negro is selected to die sooner because of subtler causes, such as having to spend a higher proportion of his income on housing, leaving less for food and medical care, or for being forced to live in less advantageous sections of the community, regardless of income. In addition, of course, are his lesser job opportunities and more limited access to the type of information and education that provides the sort of knowledge and understanding that extends life (Kalish, 1965, p. 89).

But neither their wishes nor their overtly expressed expectations for a long life seem to reflect awareness of these mortality statistics. Several ways of interpreting these data suggest themselves, from the possibility that Black Americans have developed a stronger will-to-live to the notion that their fears of death or enjoyment of life induce them to postpone, in their fantasies, the inevitable.

The picture of the Black Americans as most optimistic and most eager can be further substantiated. We looked separately at all persons who expected to or wished to live to be 98 years or older. Expecting to live to be 98, for all except a handful, is a fantasy, albeit a fantasy touched with exuberance and vitality: wanting to live to be 98 or older should signify if not enjoyment of life, at least a satisfaction with the way one is coping with life. More Black men and Black women *expected* to be alive close to or beyond the century mark than any other group (except for one reversal) (B 22%/33%, J 6%/0%, M 4%/8%, A 9%/14%). Even more remarkable were the sex differences in the *wishes* of Blacks to live beyond their 98th birthday (B 52%/39%, J 25%/0%, M 9%/7%, A 16%/16%).

Given the pressures and the prejudices, the stresses and the discrimination that Black Americans face, their desire to attain a relatively long life, especially in the face of their actuarial life expectancies, is remarkable. While one might patronize these views as unrealistic, to expect to live longer than your allocated time and to wish to life still longer would appear to reflect optimism and hope, particularly when the surrounding world works toward destruction of the hopes. In these data, we find both a resiliency and an appreciation of life, undoubtedly supported by religious faith.

An on-going study by Kastenbaum, based upon interviews with 100 elderly Black men and women, underlines these interpretations. Although by virtue of having been restricted to the elderly Kastenbaum admits a biased sampling, he states that the tendency of elderly Blacks to suicide is absolutely minimal, and that they express an unusually high regard for living. Both men and women attribute much of their desire to live to their faith in God, although the men are more likely to acknowledge the usefulness of social security checks as well. "Our impression is that maintaining life has required so much energy, endurance, and resourcefulness that they would not think of letting go just because things might get tough in one way or another" (Kastenbaum, personal communication, 1972).

Another piece that fits this puzzle is the low suicide rate of Black Americans, both in Los Angeles and nationally. Not only did this emerge in our data, but Swanson and Harter (1971), in interviewing 20 older Black men and women, summarized their findings by stating, ". . . they have never considered that life might not be worth living, nor can they conceive of a situation or problem with which they, themselves, or with the help of the Lord, cannot cope" (p. 216). Similarly, another study conducted in Detroit shows that Black men and women, substantially more than Anglos, believed that people should live as long as they can, and that helplessness, but not pain and suffering, would justify dying (Koenig, Goldner, Kresojevich, and Lockwood, 1971). Our own results also showed Black Americans as more likely than Anglos to disapprove of allowing people who want to die to do so. However differences are slight and both Japanese and Mexican Americans disapprove more than either Black or Anglo Americans (B 47%, J 51%, M 69%, A 39%). The reasons given in the Los Angeles study did not support those from Detroit. However, since the latter draw from a low-income, hospital population, they were not fully comparable. Nonetheless, the basic premise appears to hold true: whether it is their religiousness or their survival of ordeal, Black Americans express a high acceptance of life.

Expectations Mirrored in Literary Materials

We mentioned above the way in which the arts mirror the reality, albeit the mirror often becomes distorted. The arts of Mexican Americans and of Japanese Americans are still too young to incorporate in this presentation (we refer, of course, to the development of an artistic tradition that is neither an emulation of the parent culture nor an acceptance of mainstream America). The Black Americans, however, have had many artists who focused their efforts upon their own people. In our consideration of Black literature and art, we made an effort to draw a random sample of works, but rather selected readily available collections from Black literature and poetry (*Black Voices*, Chapman, ed., 1968), plays (*New Plays from the Black Theatre*, Bullins, ed., 1969), folktales (*American Negro Folktales*, Dorson, ed., 1956, and *Mules and Men*, Huston, 1935) and narrative folklore (*Deep Down in the Jungle*, Abrahams, 1963).

The most striking feature we found in the selections from literature and the theatre is the centrality of death themes. On the average, about every fourth page in the literature collection and every second page in the collection of plays contain some clear reference to death. And the deaths are most often sudden and violent—killings, auto accidents, suicides. The literary figures are frequently references to death: "I exist like death" (Bullings, 1969, p. 228), "Lord Death" (Chapman, 1968, p. 384), and "bitter forms of endless dead" (Chapman, 1968, p. 361) are examples. In these works there is no hesitation to refer to death in its stark immediacy. Death's impact underlies the main themes of many stories and poems and all of the plays. For some, like James Baldwin, sudden death is regnant in the minds of Black Americans. The Black (like Bigger Thomas) must struggle with the impulse to die violently in rebellion against but simultaneously in acquiesence to American society . . ." he *wants* to die because he glories in his hatred and prefers, like Lucifer, rather to rule in hell than to serve in heaven.

"For, bearing in mind the premise on which the life of such a man is based, *i.e.*, that black is the color of damnation, this is his only possible end. It is the only death which will allow him a kind of dignity or even, however, horribly, a kind of beauty" (James Baldwin, *Notes of a Native Son*, 1955, reprinted in Chapman, 1968, p. 603).

Abrahams (1963) sees another root of the violent and self-destructive themes in some of the narrative tales of young men. He quotes from the story of Stack, the heroic image of the young men of an Eastern U.S. ghetto, " 'Got a tombstone disposition and a graveyard mind, I'm a mean mother fucker and I don't mind dying' " (p. 78). Abrahams sees this attitude as a consequence of the young men's conflicts engendered by ambivalent feelings toward women (see also Hannerz, 1970). Women, femininity, and family chains must be rejected, but they are at the same time attractive and potentially nurturant. The guilt and conflict in the male leads to the desire to die, but suicide reflects weakness. So the hero in these stories sets up a situation in which others have the opportunity to kill him. He punishes himself through another's violence.

Seiden (1970) argues that such "suicides" are common among ghetto youths although, of course, they are technically reported as homicides. But the cause of these "victim-precipitated homicides" is not frustration over females, Seiden feels, but anger at the social system that encourages failure and the wish to die in an honorable explosion of rage and destruction rather than to admit an inability to survive and to die passively as Anglos are perceived to do. Certainly, our data do not clearly refute Seiden's hypothesis. A significant proportion of our Black Americans do see (accurately) suicide as an Anglo's alternative. And both suicide and homicide rates for Black American males in Los Angeles County in 1970 peak in the 20-40 year age group, just as Seiden predicts they should, since both are expressions of similar frustrations. But the Black American respondents are more likely to see a person who kills himself as crazy (40%) or upset (28%), rather than cowardly (7%), and Blacks do not attribute cowardice to suicides more frequently than others.

Again, we do not have the data to select from these alternative understandings of violent death themes in Black literature and narrative, whether it is the society's hatred internalized, as Baldwin suggests, or the sex role feelings, as Abrahams argues, or the frustration of helpless rage postulated by Seiden, or all of these or none. We must leave this to those who wish to untangle the complicated problem of death-as-the-wages-of-sin or death-as-the-wages-of-racism. But the theme is well represented in the works of contemporary Black artists and the emphasis is on death as destruction accompanied by anger and indignation, as opposed to death as loss with associated nostalgic sadness, as in the themes underlying both Mexican and Mexican American works. Death's theme of tragedy seems to crosscut all the groups, but the nature of the tragedy varies.

Generally speaking, the traditional Black folklore seems to contain fewer references to killings and violent death, although these themes are by no means absent. But another death-related theme turns up with even greater frequency in this medium. It is the concern with ghosts and "hants" and their control. Elaborate ritualistic behavior seems to be the most effective means of handling these frightening and dangerous contacts (see Dorson, 1956, pp. 212-236, and Huston, 1935, pp. 229-304). Among Black American respondents, 55% had personally experienced contact with someone after that person's death, but the experience was by no means necessarily a frightening one. Only 31% of the Black American respondents who had such contact reported the experience to be unpleasant or fearful (J 19%, M 36%, A 13%).

Death has provided Black Americans with a reference point for existence. From the shipboard horrors of slaving ships to the slavery era to the ghetto of modern America, death was compared with life and, not infrequently, death was preferred. It is not surprising, then, to find clear reference to this measuring stick in the arts of Black American people. As the words of one spiritual put it, "Before I'd be a slave, I'd be buried in my grave, and go home to my Lord and be free," again, sounding the themes of freedom and returning home along with the religious theme. Maurice Jackson (1972) has brought out the importance of the secular message of freedom underlying the sacred references to God.

Encounter With Death: Of Self, Of Others

To be Black in America is to be part of a history told in terms of contact with death and coping with death. The theme of death permeates early spirituals and later novels, and the encounter with death is personal. For the Black in slavery times, death or other forms of personal loss could come at any time, at any age, randomly, and often at the whim of someone else.

Our Black American respondents revealed this history as they expressed their experience and feelings. They had more contact with those who had died during the previous two years than respondents in other groups. More Black Americans had known at least eight individuals who had died during this period, while fewer had known none at all (B 25%/10%, J 15%/17%, M 9%/19%, A 8%/25%).

These Black Americans also had significantly more contact with victims of homicide, accidents, and wartime death than other groups (all comparisons between ethnic pairs were statistically significant except for one). Nine of the 15 persons reporting having known a homicide victim were in the 20-39-year-old group of Blacks. This is also the group with the highest homicide rate in Los Angeles County (1970 statistics).

The Los Angeles Sentinel, the Black newspaper with the largest local circulation, reported significantly more homicides than did its Spanish-language or Japanese-language counterparts (Reynolds and Kalish, 1976). With recent research suggesting that exposure to violence may trigger more violence, with the substantial amount of publicity given to Black victims of homicide—whether the death was caused by criminal, policeman, storekeeper, or spouse—and with our data showing that acquaintanceship with homicide victims is found largely in our subsample of younger Blacks (which is an accurate reflection of the area's homicide statistics—six to seven times that of Mexican American and Anglo rates and forty times that of Japanese American rates), consideration should be given to the possibility that the media may have influence upon this behavior.

Before making conclusions too quickly, however, we also need to be aware that suicides are relatively infrequent in the Black community (rates are three-fifths those of Anglos for Los Angeles County, 1970), are especially infrequent (relatively) among older Blacks, and yet are also highly publicized in the media. How would the media stimulate violence in the form of homicide and yet seem to have no effect upon suicide rates? Obviously the picture is a complex one.

So much attention has been given in newspapers and on television to minority group members as perpetrators of homicide and other crimes of violence that there has been little space left to contemplate the effects upon those who are in close physical or social proximity to the victims. What is the effect upon Blacks, especially young Blacks, of having the most extensive contact with victims of homicide? With victims of accidents and of war-connected deaths?

Yet Blacks do not report thinking or dreaming about their own death more than the other groups. Nor do they report having the unexplainable feeling that they or someone else are about to die (in our data these latter feelings seem strongly associated with low levels of education rather than subculture). Nor have they experienced or felt the presence of someone after he died significantly more than the other groups (within the Black sample such experiences are more likely to be reported by older persons, especially older males, and by the more poorly educated). Nor were they more likely to report having felt close to death themselves. Thus the relatively greater contact with violent death may not be sufficient to affect a population sampling such as ours, although it may well have influenced certain individuals.

If visits with the dying are not exactly everyday occurrences for the Black Americans, neither are they uncommon. Although the majority of each ethnic group had not visited or spoken with a dying person during the previous two years (B 65%, J 58%, M 60%, A 68%), about one in six of each group had visited at least two such persons. Well over half the Black Americans believed that the dying person should be informed of his condition in some way (B 60%, J 49%, M 37%, A 71%), and two-thirds of these acknowledge the physician as the most appropriate bearer of tidings.

As with all four ethnic groups, substantially more Black Americans would wish to learn of their own impending death (71%) than feel others should be told (49%) or feel capable of telling another of his own death himself (7% had provided such information, plus 51% of the remainder who thought they could do so). Since over 80% believed that a person dying of cancer probably knows of his status—and even a higher percentage of Black women believe this—the need for communication from others is substantially diminished.

In view of the health statistics and the review of Black literature, greater death fear and more pervasive awareness of death might be hypothesized for Black Americans. If this has indeed occurred, our data do not reflect it. Over 75% of the Blacks state that they never dream about their own death (J 80%, M 64%, A 62%); over 40% hardly ever or never think of their own death (J 69%, M 38%, A 47%); and only 19% acknowledge that they are afraid of death (J 32%, M 32%, A 22%). Fewer than half (48%) had ever felt close to dying themselves (J 31%, M 50%, A 37%), while 85% had never had "the unexplainable feeling that (they) were about to die" (J 88%, M 66%, A 85%).

Although some of the figures above do show Black Americans to be more engrossed in death than other ethnic groups, other findings are contradictory, and most certainly no such pattern can be demonstrated. Accepting our data at face value, we need to assume that Black Americans, especially the elderly men, have lower overt fear of death than other groups, and that the impact of their more frequent encounters with the death of others, especially the sudden and unexpected death of others, does not appear to differentiate them from other groups.

A pattern does, however, emerge in another quarter. We asked the respondents to evaluate the importance of seven losses that their own deaths would produce. These were (1) concern regarding their body after death, (2) inability to care for dependents, (3) uncertainty as to what would happen after death, (4) inability to continue having experiences, (5) grief caused survivors, (6) cessation of plans and projects, and (7) pain during the dying process. Each could be rated as Very Important, Important, or Not Important. On six of the seven, the Black Americans were more likely than any of the other three groups to claim the reason was Not Important; on the seventh, they were second most likely to make this claim. The mean percentage of Black Americans stating Not Important for the seven items was 62% (J 51%, M 50%, A 52%).

Several interpretations offer themselves. Perhaps the Blacks have the strongest need to present a "cool" front, both to the outside, i.e., the interviewer, and to themselves. Or, withdrawal of affect reduces chance for disappointment, and feeling that matters are not especially important means that their loss is not especially significant. A third possibility, of course, is that we inadvertently missed the reasons for not wanting to die that would receive the greatest responsiveness from the Black Americans, even though we did ask directly whether other reasons existed. Fourth, perhaps these respondents, due to the circumstances of their lives, are simply less engaged in the process of living, so that they perceive their own death as less important to themselves than do members of other ethnic groups. This would also explain their being less afraid of death. Nor is it unlikely that two or even all of these interpretations are contributory to the findings.

We could feel a little more satisfied with the last of the four interpretations above, were it not for responses to the question, "Would you tend to accept death peacefully or fight death actively?" Although slightly more Black Americans would fight death (B 38%, J 34%, M 34%, A 30%), differences are negligible. Also, Black Americans express a desire to live longer, as we discussed earlier. For these reasons, we reject the fourth interpretation, but feel it still requires airing.

SUPPORT SYSTEMS IN FACING DEATH AND LOSS

The way people handle the problems surrounding death tells us much about their style of life. There are very few new resources open to an individual who faces critical illness and death, either his own or that of a loved one. The process of making decisions is likely to be similar to decisions made under other circumstances. We have characterized Japanese American and Mexican American subcultures as familistic. Strong bonds of responsibility and reciprocal expectations within these families encourage the members to handle death-related crises with the family's own resources.

Generally speaking, Black Americans and Anglo Americans do not show this same pattern of exclusive dependence upon supportive family interrelationships. To be sure, family support is found, but its boundaries seem narrower, its scope more situationally determined. There are advantages to both types of systems. Those who depend less on their families may be more influential in initiating and utilizing other, non-kin sources of community and impersonal institutional support. A narrow familistic orientation may provide personal security at the risk of potentially losing one's entire support system by disaster or disaffection. It has been argued that the deprived socioeconomic conditions under which most Black Americans live continue to mitigate against the development of a strong, stable familistic system. Conversely, counter arguments emphasize that the survival of Black families in spite of immense stresses and disruptions is evidence for the existence of a strong underlying family structure. According to this position, adaptation to reality may have required substitute parents or dependency upon the Black community to replace a missing family member, but a basically strong family structure has been retained.

A number of responses from the Black American sample makes sense when viewed as projections of reduced options for intra-familial dependency, but a few others do not. Perhaps the most reasonable conceptualization in order that we may integrate these findings is that subcultural groups define for themselves areas and times in which family support can be expected and relied upon and those in which it cannot. These occasions reflect not only past history and tradition but also present reality. For example, with increasing age (particularly among women), there is an increasing tendency to turn to religious persons and symbols for comfort and to rely less upon relatives. Those active in churches have traditional sources of spiritual and social support. Generally speaking, these older Black Americans (like the older Japanese Americans and Anglo Americans) tend to rely less upon relatives and more upon other support figures.

Thus, we find that Black Americans are least likely to encourage family members to spend time with them during their terminal stages, if it be inconvenient (B 32%, J 36%, M 56%, A 44%). Similarly, they are least likely to be willing to carry out the last wishes of a dying spouse (B 65%, J 85%, M 78%, A 80%) even though the last wishes might seem senseless and provide inconvenience. When we asked to whom they would turn for comfort in time of grief, about half (B 53%, J 51%, M 54%, A 50%) of the Black Americans referred to some relative. For these respondents, family members still serve the vital need of emotional support in this sort of crisis.

But when we asked who would provide practical assistance during bereavement, the familistic-non-familistic dichotomy appeared again, with high proportions of Black Americans (42%) and Anglo Americans (45%) relying on friends, church members, neighbors, and other non-relatives (vs. 9% and 14% for Japanese Americans and Mexican Americans respectively). Those relying on relatives were again about half (B 50%, J 74%, M 65%, A 45%). On this question, too, we found a tendency to rely less on relatives as respondents increased in age and in devoutness. But with increasing education came *greater* expectations of help from relatives: this may actually be a function of age since the young are more highly educated. Black Americans were also least likely to select "the death of someone close" as being the greatest influence upon their attitudes toward death (B 26%, J 41%, M 39%, A 35%).

A similar pattern occurs in response to a series of questions regarding appropriate time periods following the death of a spouse during which various activities should be avoided. Mourning restrictions may be viewed as symbolic of the degree of disruption in the family when a member is lost, i.e., the more severe the restrictions, the greater the disruption and the stronger the interdependencies of the family members upon each other as opposed to other support figures. The activities included (a) remarriage, (b) wearing signs of mourning, (c) returning to work, and (d) resuming dating. Except for (c), the Black Americans were more likely than any of the other groups to feel that it was "unimportant to wait." By averaging the percentages of those who denied the importance of waiting for these four items, the Black respondents (followed by the Anglo respondents) were the highest (B 41%, J 24%, M 30%, A 38%). And when asked to compare their own restrictions with those of family members and of neighbors, a substantial percentage of Black Americans said that they did not know.

Although family members do not appear to provide as much of a support system for Black and Anglo Americans as for Mexican and Japanese Americans, the Black respondents were no less likely than either the Anglo or the Japanese American groups to express their grief overtly and publicly. Given a situation in which a spouse had just died, 42% of the Black Americans would feel sorry if they could not cry (although with increasing education level this worry declines), and 79% report that they would try very hard to control the way they express emotions in public. 64% say they would let themselves go and cry themselves out in private or in public or both. We shall have more to say about the public expression of grief among Los Angeles Black Americans in our discussion section below. Suffice it to say here that our professional respondents (chaplains, funeral directors, deputy coroners, ambulance drivers, physicians, nurses, etc.) show near unanimity in regarding Black Americans as freely expressive in time of grief. Thus, speaking broadly, one might characterize the four subcultures in this way: Mexican Americans are publicly expressive and incorporate this into their ideology; Japanese Americans are publicly inexpressive and find this consistent with their ideology; Black Americans and Anglo Americans, who respond to these questions about expression control almost identically, behave quite differently from one another, with the greatest discrepancy among the Black Americans whose expressive style allows for the acting out of feelings despite effort to exert self-restraint. This may be another case of adopting the dominant Anglo ideology.

Since the Black Americans in our study seemed to depend less on family members for support during the crisis of death and dying, where do they find support? Our data do not cover all contingencies, but there is evidence that religion and the church fill the gap, at least for some. More Blacks than Japanese or Anglos would call for a clergyman if they were facing their own imminent death (B 64%, J 51%, M 88%, A 53%), and many more cited their religious background as being most influential in their attitudes toward death (B 40%, J 13%, M 21%, A 25%). However, relatively few (7%) Black respondents would turn to a clergyman in the event that they knew of a friend's suicide attempt; most would contact either the police (44%) or a relative (26%).

In this regard, an interesting pattern emerged concerning belief in life after death. Although well over half of the Black Americans did "believe (they) would live on in some form after death," and virtually all who did also believed in a hell (B 96%, J 55%, M 88%, A 75%), relatively few of those believers also felt that "those in heaven watch over earth" (B 39%, J 100%, M 82%, A 83%). This is, we feel, a very important and unique element in our Black Americans' conceptualization of death. It is not simply a matter of denominational theology. Such a belief serves to cut off relationships abruptly at death, to make understandable existing misery, and to influence post-death behaviors such as grave visiting. When we consider that 100% of our Japanese American believers felt that those in heaven watch over earth, we begin to see the importance of ancestors in that culture and the importance of strong family ties as existing extensions of relationships that extend back several generations. Obviously, the Black family has less of this kind of ideological support.

The data suggest that the family provides less support through interactions in this life and less caring and guidance when they have gone on to their next life. The gap is filled by friends and by the church—and most probably by the resourcefulness of the individuals themselves. In spite of common belief to the contrary, we feel that the success of religion in playing such an important role is not its mysticism or other-worldliness but its ability to address itself to matters of the here and now.

Thus the Black spirituals were not simply representative of a deeply felt Christian fervor. They also expressed the desire for freedom from a life of slavery, a freedom that was possible through escape to the North but was more likely to occur through death. Considering these songs as containing a secret language of escape, freedom, home, and hope, many spirituals take on a new light, and death is very much involved in the message.

In this sense, the religiousness of Black Americans is this-worldly. "Familiarity with death emphasized in the spirituals expresses the secular norm of death with which the Blacks were so familiar . . . the Blacks were prepared to accept death" (Jackson, 1972). In our data and our other interviews, we sensed a theme of practical unsentimentality occurring among the Black respondents. This may be the product of the omnipresence of death in the Black community and in the hardships of living that nag and growl by the deathbed as by the crib, at the funeral home as at the market.

Even the most vocal institution for presenting an other-worldly perspective on this world seems to be pervaded with a down-to-earth orientation (and necessarily so, some would argue). In a study of Negro Protestant churches in the North and the Southeast, Johnston (1956) found that "the audience today is less responsive to the other-worldly appeal than it was in the past. Christians express and manifest less ardent belief and interest in the transcendental aspects of life" (p. 89). She found that urban sermons well reflected the fact that "clerical leaders are not especially anticipatory of a future life." In fact, in the sermons she analyzed, only one pastor in ten even referred to the attainment of Heaven or the avoidance of Hell as motivators for action.

Brown in "Black Religion — 1968" (in Nelson et al., eds., 1971) notes the function of ghetto store-front churches in organizing day care centers, collecting food and clothing for the needy, and serving the personal and social needs of the people. He writes, "Lots of times the smaller churches can reach them when the larger churches can't *because the smaller churches are more down-to-earth in a way the people understand*" (p. 22, emphasis ours).

Although some of the more extreme positions taken in the literature seem to be reactions to the inaccurate stereotyping of

Negroes as emotional, simple-minded and religious, there is certainly an element of practicality necessary for sheer survival under conditions of social and economic oppression (Blauner, 1970).

ARRANGEMENTS FOR DEATH

We make arrangements for our own death. We also make arrangements for the death of others, and we participate in arrangements made by others. Funerals, wills, life insurance, psychological readiness—these are the most practical arrangements that people make for death.

A significantly higher proportion of Black Americans had taken out life insurance than had other groups (B 84%, J 70%, M 52%, A 65%), although we do now know what proportion of those may be burial policies. Interviews with life insurance agents established that many Black Americans have these burial policies, i.e., insurance policies that will cover funeral and burial, but no more. Only following World War II did the major insurance companies begin to cover Blacks in more than token numbers, and then at higher premium rates, in keeping with life expectancy data. Partly because of this history of discrimination and partly because of personal contact and weekly collections, many Blacks, especially among the elderly, continue to purchase their policies from small companies with dubious records of payment. Although the premiums are extravagantly higher for the amount of pay-off and although stories of their not paying at all are common, a dollar a week paid to the friendly insurance agent who calls personally for the money seems easier, perhaps more natural, than sending a money order to a distant address each quarter.

Since so many Black Americans have life insurance, it might be assumed that they have also made other arrangements for death. Not so. They are no more likely than the other ethnic groups (1) to have a will (B 22%), (2) to have made funeral arrangements (B 13%), (3) to have begun payment for a cemetery plot (B 22%), or (4) to have arranged for someone else to handle their affairs (B 24%). and barely one in four has discussed death seriously with anyone (B 26%, J 16%, M 33%, W 37%). As might be expected, older persons more commonly have made death arrangements than middle-aged or younger adults.

FUNERALS

When a society treats a people as objects, accords them only minimal respect, and simultaneously blocks the channels by which respect can be achieved, the result is, predictably, a people who desperately seek ways to confirm some sense of self-worth and positive self-identify. Success must be achieved within the group but only with the limits set by the dominant culture, so that, for example, economic success can be achieved only to a point before it becomes threatening to some member(s) of the larger society and is curbed. In the ghetto, sexual prowess, aggressiveness, and styles of dress are avenues unpatrolled by "the Man" and hence become means by which esteem and honor can be constructed. Death is another. A dead person isn't particularly threatening to anyone (unless he is a symbol of martyrdom or a carrier of disease). A man can retrieve posthumously some of the esteem he was not permitted to garner in life. Whether it is the tribute of fellow Panthers or the eulogies of a local congregation or lodge, the message sounds clear, "a SOMEBODY has died."

The importance of the local church affiliation as a permissible support for self-esteem has its roots in the slave days of the Black American. Wade (1971) writes:

> "Indeed, in death the religious connection took on special meaning. Without it the slave should have been interred without ceremony and with little care in some out-of-the-way cemetery for colored people. The master or the city might provide the plot, and perhaps a wooden slab would mark the spot. But as a member of the congregation the passing was attended with due solemnity. The minister—sometimes white—presided, prayers were offered, and a procession of friends carried out the body to be placed in the church burial grounds among other parishioners. Thus the church, for a moment at least, became a surrogate family for the bondsmen. It was little wonder that a leading guidebook for white ministers could observe simply: 'Funeral services are much esteemed by the Negroes.'" (p. 69)

Lewis (1971), describes the funeral customs of a small Southern town:

> "An essential feature of religion and church membership is the expectation of a church funeral. Among the first questions asked after death are 'To which church did the deceased belong?' and 'Whom do you want to preach the funeral?' In many cases persons indicate long before their deaths the minister they want to preach the funeral. As in the case of other practices, there tends to be a basic pattern within which variations occur. The basic pattern combines these essential steps: return of corpse to the home the evening before the funeral; on the day of the funeral, body and funeral party are driven to the church . . . The corpse is borne into the church while the church bell tolls and the choir sings or the minister utters an incantation; a song is sung by the choir and audience; a scripture reading and/or prayer is delivered; a eulogy is rendered by the paster; a final view of the remains is taken by the audience; interment follows, with male volunteers filling the grave after final rites" (pp. 108-109).

Lewis notes that variations occur according to the community reputation of the deceased, his family's wishes, and local church practice. The viewing of the body may provide an opportunity to take a collection either in support of the family or of the church and its pastor.

The personal importance of the funeral ceremony isn't limited to the days of slavery or to the small town in the rural South. In Harlem also the ceremonial aspect of the funeral offers final elegance to a bare life.

> "Death, for example, plays a peculiar role in the life of this Negro ghetto. One first realizes this fact by walking the streets and gradually noticing the enormous number of funeral parlors. Undertakers are among some of the most respected members of the Negro middle class; Harlem is at least allowed to bury its own. For the Negro poor, death is often the only time when there is real luxury. Many of the Negro lodges and fraternal orders have death-benefit plans. Dying is a moment of style and status, at least in the impoverished world of the racial ghetto" (Harrington, 1963, pp. 69-70).

As is common among Protestants, most Black American Protestant churches have no formally prescribed funeral ritual dictated by a church hierarchy. Local church custom is followed. According to denominational procedures outlined in Habenstein and Lamers (1960), about the only generalizations that can be made are (1) that family members can select the equipment, music, participants, and place of service without dogmatic restriction, and (2) that the minister leads the procession from church to coach and from coach to gravesite, positioning himself at the head of the grave. This leaves room for considerable variation.

The following description of a funeral, taken from the notes of a non-Black observer, is not necessarily typical of funerals in the Los Angeles Black community. However, it does represent funerals held under the auspices of the fraternal order involved, and many of the events described were found in other funeral settings.

BLACK FUNERAL
January, 1972

A _____ funeral home is a very imposing structure. Patterned on a Near Eastern motif it looks both formidable and formal with its dome roof and gold-trimmed white stucco exterior.

Upon entering the large and thickly-carpeted lobby, overseen by two Black receptionists, one male and one female, I could sense that the programmed atmosphere was official, serious, and dignified. When I came to the entrance of the chapel, several middle-aged Black men were waiting to sign the register. Jabbing each other and joking, they smiled and laughed as they stood in line. This informality contrasted sharply with the decor and the general mood.

The chapel itself seemed like a combination of auditorium, theater, and church sanctuary. There was the carpeted floor, the long wooden pews, the stage with curtains, and in what I felt was a highly (perhaps overdone) dramatic tone, a huge dome ceiling with subtle blue-black lighting that was interspersed with small gold lights to give the effect of a night sky with stars.

About 200 people, all Black, mostly middle-aged but also young mothers carrying their babies, and groups of children and teenagers, were sitting silently. Most were conservatively dressed in browns and blacks, but there were some notable exceptions: some of the young adults were dressed in mod styles and some of the women, especially young adult and middle-age, wore straight-hair wigs (red and light brown), which contrasted vividly with the Afro styles of most of the teenage girls.

The stage itself was divided into two sections. On the left side was the podium and two Black ministers. On the right side, sitting on both sides of the coffin, were two men in formal black wear. One wore a high top hat and the other held a sword across his chest. Both were solemn. Sitting directly in front of them were other members of the lodge to which the deceased belonged. As the service progressed it was apparent that they played a meaningful role in terms of adding formality to the service, organizing and focusing the corporate feelings of grief, as well as acting as pall bearers . . . I was somewhat surprised, however, to see two young adults in the group, which primarily had older men. The "exalted leader" also was relatively young.

The service began with a prayer, followed by the reading of Scripture. Then a young woman (20's), probably a niece, came from behind the curtains to read the obituary. The obituary was mostly factual, noting where the dead man had attended school, that he had served in World War II and Korea, and that he was survived by several brothers and sisters, nieces and nephews, and many friends. The young woman then read a few telegrams that had been sent. She next read a resolution by the Lodge members, which expressed their grief, but also their belief that he was now in good hands. The young woman was not highly emotional or affected, but very serious and straightforward.

Another woman then began to sing. The song was intense and moving, not only because it was powerfully done but also because the woman was hidden behind the curtains and we thus had to listen without visual distractions. Soft crying could be heard here and there among the listeners.

The sermon was based upon a compilation of writings: Ecclesiastes 3 ("for everything there is a season . . . a time to be born, and a time to die . . ."), Paul Tillich, and the *Bridge Over the*

River Kwai. The main emphasis was that life should be lived to the fullest, that every day is precious, for death comes when and where it will. The minister was very articulate and spoke intelligently. The sermon was definitely a message to the congregation about the status of their own lives rather than a eulogy of the deceased (unlike some funerals where the words are centered almost completely around the dead person's life, accomplishments, beliefs, and example).

After another prayer by the minister, lines were formed by the ushers to pay last respects. As we filed by the open casket many women, even little girls, began to cry. One elderly woman in particular screamed and wailed, calling for her son and shouting that she would never see him any more. A funeral home attendant (a middle-aged Anglo woman) tried to restrain her physically from remaining at the casket, saying that "we know you love him" but that it would be best if she did not stay with him anymore. But the elderly woman kept saying "Please let me see my son one more time." Several women finally escorted her to her seat. By this time many people were crying openly, even one of the large middle-aged lodge members, and myself. Handkerchiefs were out everywhere, although most of the crying was still by women of all ages and older men.

After the lines ended and everyone was seated, the curtains in front of the casket were lowered, apparently to close from our view the taking of the casket to the hearse. However, the effect was somewhat like that of the final curtain coming down after the last scene of a tragic play in which we were somehow participants. For, as the curtains were lowered, the bright lights in the chapel were turned on and the subtle blue lighting of the dome ceiling disappeared. It was a signal that we were now re-entering everyday reality—the drama of the funeral service had ended.

Outside in the lobby people began to greet each other. The sound was almost irritating because the lobby was very crowded. People began to smile and laugh and talk. There were people, however, who avoided the lobby scene and immediately went outside to await the casket. Apparently these people were mostly relatives. They stood rather quietly. Many others were still in the lobby as the casket was loaded into the hearse. Only when the actual procession began to form did these people begin to go to their cars. A few of the middle-aged men were still laughing and talking vigorously in a good-natured, everyday fashion as they walked across the parking lot.

The procession to E _____ Cemetery was a hectic, disturbing experience. The route was along a busy boulevard, onto an equally busy freeway and then to another freeway. It was difficult and dangerous to try to remain in the procession, especially traveling the freeway at 60 miles an hour while cars were trying to switch lanes to reach an offramp and other cars were trying to get on the freeway. The motorcycle escort tried to keep the lines together but, just as the lady in front of me constantly looked in her rear view mirror to see if I was going to smash into her, I was looking in my rear view mirror to see if the person behind me wasn't following too closely. The whole thing damaged the credibility that we were actually in a funeral procession. There is something ironic about the feeling that you might get killed while attending a service for a dead person.

Arriving at the cemetery, we parked our cars. Most of the people walking to the gravesite engaged in quiet conversation. Lodge members wheeled the casket on a cart and placed it in position in front of the chairs where the brothers and sisters were seated. After a short prayer by the minister, lodge members took over the service. Their leader gave an eloquent message that emphasized the fleeting quality of this life and the need to put our trust not in material things that crumble away but in spiritual things. The words were carefully chosen and firmly recited at a moderately fast pace. This rather long oration was probably a standardized lodge ritual that the leader had memorized. At one point he mentioned the "widow and children" of the deceased, although Mr. J_____was a bachelor. During this recital an elderly lodge member removed the green leaves from the lapels of the other members. The leader then explained that the leaves were symbolic of life. The leaves were then placed upon the casket underneath the American flag that was draped over it. The elderly man then brought out a white apron and placed it also on the casket. The leader explained that the apron was symbolic of humility. After this the members of the lodge gave an oath in unison. The service was highly ritualistic. It is somewhat difficult to assess the reaction of the people to such a service (which is typical only for members of this fraternal order)—they were quiet and serious, and no one seemed to be crying. The atmosphere could best be described as somber.

As the service ended, people began to walk away although some stayed to talk with the members of the family, and the lodge members gathered in their own group. Only a few feet away a Chicano service had begun. Most of the Blacks continued to converse openly and walked in full view of the Chicanos. Some of the Chicanos stared at the Blacks, but no one bothered to say anything.

After the service, relatives and close friends gathered together at someone's home for dinner. Not being part of the group, I walked slowly back to my car and departed. (From the research notes of B. Ogawa.)

One striking feature of the service (and the setting in which it was conducted) was its impressiveness. Impressiveness communicates importance. Mr. J. was important. He and all those who participated in the service were worth something.

At this point, we find another of the contradictions that make research fascinating and frustrating. Although our informants, our own observations, and our reading all indicated that funerals were important in the Black American community, the respondents, in discussing their own future funerals, showed a much higher rate of indifference than the other groups (recall, also, that they felt reasons for not dying were relatively unimportant too).

While less than 10% wanted a big, elaborate funeral, and only 20% wanted many friends and acquaintances at their funeral, 14% and 24%, respectively, were indifferent or did not know—and this trend increased with age. Large proportions of Black respondents were also indifferent or undecided as to whether the family should select the clergyman (25%, with more men than women), whether the clergyman should be Black (52%), whether or not the casket should be open (40%), whether the funeral director should be Black (54%), whether children ought to be permitted to attend (30%), whether there ought to be a wake (22%, primarily men and persons who did not consider themselves devout), and where the funeral should be held (13%).

In each of these instances, more Black Americans than any other group state indifference or uncertainty. That this is not a response set is shown by the relatively low proportion of such responses to items concerning autopsies, using life insurance for funeral costs, being embalmed, and being buried rather than cremated.

The great majority of Black American respondents who were not indifferent expressed opposition to elaborate funerals, did not expect friends to participate in covering funeral costs, preferred a funeral with only relatives and close friends, desired Black clergymen (especially the older and younger men and the most and least devout—speculation regarding motivation occurred quickly) and Black funeral directors (especially middle-aged women and young men—the motivation here is more uncertain), did not want a wake, wanted the funeral in the church, did not oppose an autopsy, and wanted to be buried. For the most part, these responses were fairly similar to those of other ethnic groups, extreme differences occurring in only a handful of instances.

In reconciling the two opposing threads that we find—i.e., the attitude of practical unsentimentality versus the depth of feeling—we are drawn to an explanation based upon differing methodologies. In response to interview questionnaires, the preferred self-image is that of being "cool," of not caring, of not being susceptible to emotional pain. In the actual encounter, this self-image is overwhelmed by depth of feelings, and emotions are displayed. Often the emotional display is virtually required to avoid being viewed as unfeeling. In addition, our respondents were, for the most part, long-time urban dwellers, more sophisticated and farther removed from the rural South than many other groups of informants.

Such inconsistencies do not imply an attempt at posing or posturing or attempting to deceive, although this may have occurred. Rather, an apparent contradiction often exists between what people (in this instance, Black people) say they wish to do and what they actually do. In this situation, the differences were greater than usual. We might speculate that the conflict for survival has been sufficiently intense that overt admission of vulnerability must be denied. The reaction is reminiscent of the elderly who say, "Don't worry about me—I don't want to be burden to anyone." In part they mean it—they do not wish to be a burden. But they still want to be loved, remembered, supported. We feel that the Black Americans are saying much the same thing—"I don't want to be a burden, to increase the already difficult life of my family, to add to their expenses and their cares." This does not mean they wish to be forgotten or ignored, nor does it mean that they are unwilling to accept the burden and expenses of others.

Visiting the grave is not common, with fewer Black Americans having made such a visit during the two previous years than the other (No visit—B 71%, J 36%, M 55%, A 59%). Black Americans are as likely as not to touch the body at the funeral service (48% vs. 47%), but are strongly opposed to kissing the body (12% vs. 82%).

When we presented our information about infrequent visiting of graves at a conference of Black Americans and asked for assistance in interpreting the results, there was an immediate and strongly felt argument that the results were understandable in very simple economic and geographic terms. In Los Angeles, public transportation is relatively inefficient and expensive. Thus, it is difficult for the Black Americans to get to the gravesites. This was the rationale put forward to explain the low frequency of grave visiting.

It seems reasonable to us that when given alternative explanations of behavior—for example, one based on values and another on economics or geography—that the simpler, more immediate be preferred, provided it fits the data. In this case, it is contrary to the principle of "Occam's razor" to hypothesize some avoidance of contact with death, weak and short-term family ties, or practical survival orientation (with all the initial learning and environmental reinforcement involved), when the simple, readily verifiable facts of poverty, geographic distance, and poor transportation might account for our results.

The choice of explanation in this instance, however, is artificial in two senses. In a major sense the "facts" explanation conceals implicit values. For what one spends money on (however, little it be) reflects one's value priorities. If visiting my family's grave is important enough to me, I will do it despite geographic distance, poor transportation, and limited means. In a second sense, the choice of explanations is artificial in that *for our data* transportation and income are relative constants for all our groups and the indirect evidence we have for geographic distance to gravesites (birthplace, years in U.S., number of persons known who died in past two years, and presence of integrated cemeteries in sampled areas) indicates that if anything, gravesites are more accessible to Black Americans than, for example, the most frequently grave-visiting group, the Japanese Americans. Moreover, Black American respondents felt they need not visit as often or over such a long period of time as did the other groups.

Perhaps the most significant conclusion that can be reached is that, even though individuals who attend funerals more frequently are also likely to visit gravesites more frequently (r = 0.32), the same cannot be said for groups. Had the Black Americans not been included in this study, we might have assumed such a correlation, since the extent of funeral attendance and grave visiting was highly consistent among the other three ethnicities. Not so among the Blacks, who rarely visit graves but frequently attend funerals.

To close this section, we present a quotation that makes several points. In it, we see not only the response to death in a Black ghetto but also we find reflections of behavior existing in all four of our cultural groups. The gathering of the family, the record of last respects, comments on the body, and the funeral procession are common features to be found in each of these Los Angeles communities.

> "Natural death in the ghetto is usually an occasion when relatives are around. In my family when the word is spread that someone is dying (especially an older person) everyone who is able to get to the side of the deathbed proceeds to the designated place with 'all deliberate speed.' At least one member of the family is constantly at the bedside until the dying person has become the legally deceased. It is not at all rare for the bereaved to be present at death . . .

> "After death, it is the common practice for all families to then turn the body over to a mortician to prepare it for the funeral. The body, after preparation, is put on display for several days at the funeral parlor so that relatives and friends can pay their last respects. The body lies in state in a casket without a lid.

> "There is a myriad of reactions from people viewing the body of the deceased. Some gaze upon it with a rather wry smile upon their lips. Some come close to the body, touch it, and perhaps place a kiss upon the cold lips. Some of the closer relatives lose all control and cannot bring themselves to look at the body.

> "There is some public indication that there has been a death in the family. A wreath is placed on the front door of the home and of the place of business if there is such. It is standard procedure that if you cannot attend the funeral, you send flowers.

"The burial itself is a highly emotional ceremony for the participants. There has often been some very extreme behavior. Women have fainted upon seeing the body lowered into the ground. Children have tried to throw themselves into the graves to be with their parents and have had to be restrained physically. After the funeral and burial services there is usually a meeting of all the mourners with food and drink provided by the relatives of the deceased. This is quite often a big social gathering and the closest thing to a family reunion that may ever take place." (Carter, 1971, pp. 269-270.)

7

Japanese Americans

Few ethnic groups in the United States have experienced the wide swings of fortune that have taken place with Americans of Japanese ancestry. From the later part of the nineteenth century, when their immigration into this country began, the Japanese were admired for their industriousness and resourcefulness; work was available on the railroads, in the canneries, in lumbering, mining, and industry of the west coast. Yet, at the same time, with the widespread unemployment of Chinese laborers following the completion of the railroad, the Japanese were also resented. The same work habits that brought them favor with their employers created antagonism among those with whom they were competing for jobs (Kitano, 1969).

Nonetheless, they moved slowly into agricultural work, and although unable to own land in California, did work the land and eventually, through their children who were automatically citizens (the first generation were forbidden this privilege by virtue of being Oriental), came to control some of it. After rising gradually in status, income, and education, the advent of World War II and the relocation centers set back the Japanese American's progress immensely. Just as the young men were moving into higher education, an entire people was shipped into the wilderness, to live in substandard housing, guarded by armed Anglos and surrounded by hostile people and a hostile environment.

Simultaneously, the first generation Japanese Americans, the Issei, many of whom never fully gave up their initial intent of returning to their homeland, were effectively deposed as rulers of their families. In traditional Japan, the father dominated the home

120

until his son, usually his first son, was required to take over from him, but the son was expected to display proper deference. In the United States, not only was the old man not permitted to own land, but he was pulled up from his home and shipped off to camp, where his limits in understanding American society, his possible limitations in the use of English, and his lack of United States citizenship robbed him of his traditional dominant role.

The Japanese Americans did an amazing job of rebuilding after the war. Education was prized and encouraged, and the young responded with alacrity. Over the years, several areas of Los Angeles became home for large numbers of Japanese Americans, in spite of some attempts at housing restrictions. Although many were gardeners and small shopkeepers, increasing numbers moved into teaching, business, and the professions. At present, the Japanese American population of Los Angeles is 104,078 (1970 Census), second only to the 217,307 Japanese American residents of Hawaii.

Although the non-Japanese communities viewed the Japanese Americans as people who had "made it," and although overt discrimination was much reduced, the Japanese themselves often retained the ambivalence held by many minority groups that are not fully accepted by the general community. And the third generation Sansei, today's college-age youth, are eagerly and overtly seeking to carve out for themselves a sense of ethnic identity that will enable them to live effectively in a multi-ethnic community.

The Japanese Americans can be differentiated with reasonable consistency into age/generation categories. The Issei are steeped in the Japanese culture, often speak English poorly if at all, and have led much or all their lives in a Japanese enclave; they had a fairly high education in Japan (about eight years, which is equal to the White American group of the same age) and were not from families of poverty (Kitano, 1969). The Nisei (second generation) have achieved considerable success by general American standards, in spite of the hardships faced during World War II; they are well into middle age now and tend to be pleased with their rising economic fortunes and the educational success of their children, although the Relocation Camp experiences undoubtedly are cause for some bitterness, albeit usually unspoken. The Sansei (third generation) are more like their non-Japanese age peers, even in the way they insist upon their ethnic needs. The rate of out-marriage, especially for the women, is high. Some, like their Nisei parents, are still not fully aware of what they partake from their Japanese antecedents and what from their Anglo peers; others resent the double bind in which they have been socialized to a nonaggressive norm of behavior by their parents but rewarded for more aggressive behavior by their peers. Yonsei (fourth generation) are still for the most part too young to have made much impact upon the community.

Our data indicate that the characterizations of generation/age categories are well founded. Japanese Americans show marked differences between age groups in attitudes and behaviors related to death. It is also our impression (based on brief observations and interviews) that the geographic distinctions made by Japanese Americans are also important variables, so that our findings should be generalized beyond the Los Angeles area only with caution. On the other hand, the social class variable seems not so important in this group as in, say, the Black American group, so that we would suspect no major differences between our respondents' attitudes and behaviors and those of Japanese Americans in Los Angeles who are of professional or managerial status.

BACKGROUND

Of the four ethnic groups in our study the Japanese Americans had the highest median level of education (B 11.6, J 12.0, M 6.0, A 11.8). This 12.0 years of education is slightly lower than the 12.4 figure provided by the United States Bureau of the Census for male and female Japanese American (14 years old and older) median school years completed in the Los Angeles-Long Beach area in 1960. (Recall that our sampling method would systematically reduce respondents with higher education.) Japanese Americans in California are the best educated of all categorized groups, including Whites (Kitano, 1969). Occupationally, the Japanese American respondents differed significantly from Black Americans and Mexican Americans in having a lower percentage of unskilled workers (B 38%, J 14%, M 25%, A 15%) and a higher percentage of skilled workers (B 34%, J 46%, M 34%, A 41%).

Nearly one-half (45%) of these Japanese Americans were born outside of the United States (recall our sampling procedures over-sampled the elderly), and all but two of these foreign-born were born in Japan. The mean number of years that these first generation immigrants had lived in the United States was 35.6 years (compared with 21.5 years and 26.9 years for foreign-born Mexican Americans and Anglo Americans, respectively). The mean number of years lived in California was also high (B 20, J 30, M 25, A 25) indicating a relatively stable population in terms of geographic mobility. Such residence patterns may also indirectly index the relative propensities of local ethnic communities to attract and hold members. Shortly, we shall indicate some of the causes and results of the Japanese American community strength.

We feel that with some understanding of a few social structural elements and some of their related value orientations, many of the attitudes and behaviors related to death in the Japanese American community become understandable. The three social structural features we shall focus on here are (1) the family organization, (2) generational characteristics, and (3) community ties. The values and orientations that infuse social relationships with meaning and predictability include social sensitivity, controlled communications (notably controlled expression of emotion), shame, a work ethic, some formal religious concerns, contact with death, and funerary and mourning customs. These foci will be dealt with under individual headings. However, since the value of *social-sensitivity* permeates and clarifies all of the remaining topics, we shall begin with a discussion of its influence and, simultaneously, provide the reader with an overview of the discussion to follow.

The present analysis and the emphasis we have placed upon social-sensitivity are speculative. We are drawing on the experiences of both authors in living in Japan and in their personal and professional relationships with Japanese Americans, as well as on their academic work. Others have attended to the concept of social-sensitivity (e.g., Benedict, 1946; Caudill and Devos, 1956; Kitano, 1969; Lyman, 1971), but our speculations and our attempts to integrate these with data go beyond our predecessors in both kind and degree. (We, of course, acknowledge exceptions to our hypothesis and intra-group variability in these, as in all other, speculations in this volume. See also Reynolds, 1969 and 1976, for applicability to Japanese national character.)

SOCIAL-SENSITIVITY

By social-sensitivity we mean extreme concern with the evaluations and feelings of others. This concern leads Japanese Americans to be quick in picking up subtle social cues, to spend much time and thought considering others' evaluations of them-selves, and to avoid direct interactions that would upset others. The term "sensitive" is appropriate in two senses. It means both "alert" or "receptive" to signals that intimate others' thought and feelings, and it also means "easily hurt," "susceptible," and "tender," that is, to take personally or to be readily influenced by others' thoughts and feelings. To be sure, some measure of these characteristics may be found in all people but it is their degree, consistency, and extent of influence that typifies the Japanese Americans.

The relationships between this variable and the other values that we shall be exploring are readily drawn. The careful internal censoring of communications and the limits placed on emotional expressiveness among the bereaved are employed so as to avoid disturbing others and to preserve a non-threatening, non-burden-some image in their eyes. Shame, shyness, polite hesitation, and other aspects of the *"enryo* syndrome" (Kitano, 1969, pp. 103-105) are products of the extreme concern with others' evaluations of one's self. Even the achievement-oriented work ethic and the formal Buddhist and Christian practices and beliefs are strongly flavored by this social-sensitivity. Work and morality are defined primarily in social-situational rather than absolute terms and the degree to which *one is recognized socially* as industrious or morally proper may take precedence over industriousness and religiousness *per se.*

One can imagine the extent of the community pressure that can be mobilized and its effects on the socially sensitive community members. Group norms are effectively maintained as long as members remain within the broad geographic and interactional sphere of the Japanese American community. Yet there is no doubt that the Los Angeles Japanese American community maintains strong cohesiveness *despite* the diffusion of Japanese Americans throughout the Los Angeles area. Except for the relatively dense population of elderly Japanese Americans in the Little Tokyo area, we found the Japanese American population to be much more likely to be living in ethnically mixed neighborhoods than the other three groups. For example, only 11% of our Japanese American sample (B 87%, M 64%, A 61%) estimated their block contained ¾ or more members of their own ethnic group and fully 60% of our Japanese Americans (B 2%, M 9%, A 23%) said that less than ¼ of the people on their block were of their own ethnic group. These differences are highly significant.

There are a number of attitudes and behaviors related to this extreme social-sensitivity that we would like to mention here. Social-sensitivity is intimately tied to a strong commitment to in-group custom, rules, and propriety. Offending someone is less likely to occur, and less likely to be interpreted as a personal affront, if one has been behaving according to custom.

The funeral is a prime example of a situation in which people are emotionally "keyed up" so that great care must be taken not to upset them further. Under these circumstances the family is safer conducting the funeral service in the "proper" way. Fortunately the Japanese American funeral director is arbiter and repository of appropriate funerary conduct. He is consulted regarding such matters as the proper order of service, seating arrangements, the order in which the bereaved family enters and is seated, the order of incense burning before the casket, and when the family stands with the congregation and when it remains seated. It is his responsibility to arrange floral displays so that their position relative to the coffin corresponds to the closeness of kin ties to the deceased, relative prestige of the sender, and other complex variables. He must arrange the wreaths sent by relatives, friends, and organizations so that all are visible, while carefully preventing the flowers sent by corporations from appearing too conspicuous (thus avoiding accusations of advertising). He also defines the boundaries of responsibility for those who participate in the service. For example, he makes it quite clear to the pallbearers and the surviving family members that placing the armbands and gloves atop the casket as it is replaced in the hearse at the end of the service symbolizes the termination of the pallbearers' responsibility and the absence of any obligation to attend the next day's cremation or graveside service. Thus, the structured situation, in this case a ceremony governed by custom, assures the participants that no one is slighted or ignored on a personal basis.

Special difficulties are encountered when evolving custom provides no clear guidelines for appropriate behavior. For example, Christian Sanseis may be in conflict over whether or not to place an incense stick in the publicly-placed brazier when attending a Buddhist funeral, fearing it will symbolize a belief they do not hold. Similarly, Isseis and Niseis at a Christian Memorial Day service placed carnations on a Bible, in lieu of incense sticks in a brazier, but they seemed in doubt whether or not to make a formal bow, as is customary in the Buddhist Memorial Day ceremonies. The result was usually a shortened semi-bow accompanied by apparent self-consciousness. When the situation is emotionally charged and one's thought and feelings might be misinterpreted should behavior be individualized, Japanese Americans tend to feel most comfortable within the framework of prescribed ritual. The extreme individualism permitted in Mexican American funeral offers a sharp contrast.

Another device for handling sensibilities in situations with anxiety potential is the time-honored custom of the go-between. In Japan go-betweens may participate in negotiations prior to marriage, renting a house, gaining entrance to a university, getting a job, or any situation in which one wishes to monitor and control one's self presentation to avoid embarrassment, misunderstanding or direct conflict. Among Japanese Americans we have noted the presence of go-betweens representing the surviving family in interaction with the funeral director. When a Japanese businessman dies, the company president may make all funeral arrangements for the widow. Interviews in Fresno, California, indicated that a representative from the prefectural organization (the *kenjinkai*) will frequently handle funeral matters for the family. In Los Angeles we have observed nurses and physicians offering to make initial contacts with a funeral director for the bereaved. These are all examples of concerned but (relatively) emotionally-uninvolved intermediaries making sensitive arrangements under conditions in which there is potential for interpersonal difficulty. For the most part, in the other ethnic groups, such tasks are often perceived as the province primarily of those with extensive emotional involvement with the dead person, sometimes even the next-of-kin. Among the Japanese Americans, the "face," the feelings, and the communications of both the family and the funeral director are being protected by the good offices of the go-between.

In face-to-face communication such tactics as indirection, vagueness, politeness, and deflection are commonly used by Japanese and Japanese Americans. These tactics prevent immediate direct disagreement and confrontation. The listener is expected to interpret the speaker's vagueness in a positive, non-threatening light so that neither feels offended or attacked. One young minister spoke directly of the suicide of a Sansei youth while conducting his funeral service. Afterward, there was discussion among a number of participants concerning the propriety of such straightforwardness and its possible effect on the family's feelings and reputation. The consensus of at least some of those attending the service was that in these times, perhaps, such directness is acceptable, but the young minister who speaks publicly in this insensitive manner "lacks polish."

Putting this overview and discussion of social-sensitivity aside for the moment, we shall return to the more detailed description of three structural features of the Japanese American subculture: family organization, generational characteristics, and community ties.

FAMILY ORGANIZATION

The Japanese American family is characterized by an emphasis on reciprocal obligations. The result has been, until recently, a tightly-knit family unit in which one could expect and receive support over a wide range of life circumstances and problems. The cohesiveness of the Japanese American family structure is reflected in the absence of any divorced or separated person in our sample, compared to an average of 13% for the other ethnicities. Of the Japanese Americans, 71% were married, 16% never married, and 13% were widow(er)s. Although the mean age of the oldest person in the household (57 years old) is significantly higher than that of the Mexican (52 years old) or the Caucasian (49 years old), and is close to that for the Black (53 years old), differences in the mean ages of the respondents themselves fall far short of significance (B 46, J 49, M 47, A 48). The Japanese Americans are more likely to live with elderly individuals than the other groups, suggesting that they have more day-to-day involvement with the concerns of what it means to grow old and, perhaps, to die from illness in old age.

The price for this cohesiveness and security seem to be a lack of intimacy within the family and only guarded communication of feelings, especially of affection. Except with very small children, a display of physical affection—particularly any public display—is very difficult for Issei and Nisei. We would hypothesize that the emphasis upon what one *ought* to do for family members has stifled, or at least masked, communication to others that one *wanted* to be supportive, not only because of ritualized obligations but because of feelings of affection, personal concern, and personal desire. Early socialization and subsequent reinforcement may have been so strong that many individuals are not fully aware of the feelings of compassion that they do have. (Perhaps such a statement might be made about many ethnic groups in the United States.)

Given this perspective of family relations, it is apparent that Japanese Americans would develop feelings of self-worth which are more strongly attached to their family role than to any personal qualities they might have. The result is, again, a fair degree of security in knowing that others will behave appropriately to satisfy their needs because of the ascribed role *as family member*. The cost is the corresponding recognition that it is the individual *as family member* that others are responding to and not the individual *as a person*. Lack of self-confidence and low feelings of self-worth when interacting with persons outside of the family are penalties that are paid for this sort of intra-familial security. And, of course, any activity that would bring disgrace upon the family would signify that the Japanese American is no longer behaving within the reciprocal obligation system. The result might be that family members would retaliate in kind, thus threatening the very basis of feelings of self-esteem. Such a threat is effective in maintaining conformity to family-accepted social norms.

Several examples of this family obligation theme were found in the Japanese American interview responses. Japanese Americans showed the highest frequency of "Yes" responses to the query: "Would you carry out your husband's/wife's last wishes even if they seemed to be senseless to you and caused some inconvenience?" (B 65%, J 85%, M 78%, W 80%). Strongest among the Issei generation is the related expectation that the wife should be at her husband's deathbed to give the last cup of water, the last damp cloth on his brow, and to hear his last wishes. Japanese Americans were also most likely to count on their relatives to help with practical problems if their spouse should die (B 50%, J 74%, M 65%, W 45%). Although nearly two-thirds or more of the respondents from all four subcultures would permit children under ten years of age to visit them on their deathbed, it was the familistically-oriented Japanese Americans and Mexican Americans who most often specified that if the children were *their own relatives* it would be all right (B 11%, J 24%, M 18%, W 7%).

Strong family ties are developed early and extend even beyond the grave. They are reflected, for example, in the family's participation in funerals. A child may be taken to funerals and carried up to view the body as his family files by the coffin and bows to the deceased and to the survivors. And, although large numbers of Japanese American community representatives attend funerals (see below), it is primarily only the family (and not all those who attended the funeral service as in Black American and Mexican American subcultures) that attends the next day's cremation or graveside service, often at a *family* plot. It is within the family household that the dead person's spirit as *hotokesama* continues to participate in family life, receiving food and water, incense and conversation at the family shrine (called *butsudan* by Buddhists and *kamidana* by Shintoists).

But the reciprocal obligations aspect of family existence prevents the Japanese American respondent from encouraging family members to spend time with him on his deathbed if it causes some inconvenience for the family members. Only 36% of this family-focused subculture (B 32%, M 56%, A 44%) felt they could make this demand of their family. In one of our depth interviews a Sansei remarked "I wouldn't want my family to know (if I were about to die). They would worry too much. They would be super nice. I would feel guilty putting a burden on them."

A puzzling response pattern was the relatively low Japanese American concern with the thought that their death would cause grief to friends and relatives. Fewer felt this to be an important or very important reason for wishing not to die than the other groups (B 74%, J 62%, M 78%, A 79%). Perhaps to respond otherwise would be considered insufficiently self-effacing, i.e., suggesting that one is so important that his or her death would cause suffering to others.

In Japanese culture the structural details of family composition have been traditionally important. Special obligations and privileges came with being *eldest* son or *eldest* daughter. Surviving siblings in order of their birth had some say in the disposition of their deceased sibling's remains even though the dead person had several adult offspring. Japanese Americans pay less attention to birth order in determining responsibility for elderly parents, and primogeniture (inheritance by the eldest son) is no longer customary. (In Japan, the post-war Civil Code allots equal inheritance to all offspring but, in practice, the custom still exists; see Beardsley, et al. 1959.)

Decisions concerning the funeral service and burial of an Issei may still be dominated by his brothers and sisters over the wishes of adult Nisei offspring if the deceased did not make his wishes known before his death. It is interesting to compare the English language and Japanese language versions of the same obituaries in the Japanese American press. The Japanese language version contains much more detailed information about surviving consanguineal kin including names and their specific birth-order relationship to the deceased. Such information is helpful in determining whether or not one is obligated to attend the funeral service. During the service there is a prescribed order in which the immediate survivors enter the funeral hall: wife, eldest son, other sons according to age, married daughter's husbands and married daughters by age, then unmarried daughters by age, followed by parents and siblings of the deceased.

That blood ties remain important is reflected in the necessity, upon occasion, of returning half of the cremated remains of a Japanese American to Japan to reside with already buried parents, while retaining half for the spouse and offspring in the United States. One funeral director reports "pre-need" payments arriving from several places outside California and even from Japan because parents have been buried in Los Angeles.

Intergenerational Factors

Despite the protective familistic solidarity with which Japanese Americans confront the larger society and which they share with Mexican Americans, the Japanese Americans uniquely showed in their interview responses a considerable intragroup variation by *age*. There are major differences in the orientations of the Japanese American age/generation categories. In the following paragraphs we shall describe some of these differences and their influence on death-related attitudes and behaviors.

One of the barriers to intergenerational communication and understanding is that of language. Forty percent of the interviews were conducted primarily or completely in Japanese. Although many Niseis are bilingual to some degree, the language barrier is great between Issei and Sansei generations. The dual language structure of the community requires dual language newspapers (including obituaries), dual language thank-you cards for funeral gifts, and frequently, funeral and Memorial Day Services conducted by two sets of participants in two languages (demanding no little patience from the single language Japanese Americans in attendance). Buddhist services tend to emphasize the Japanese language, and Christian services emphasize English.

Psychological studies of Japanese Americans (DeVos, 1955, Caudill, 1952) characterized the Isseis as relatively rigid in thought processes and in the controlling of impulses, and conformist in the sense of tending to submerge the self in aligning with the group. They were careful in interpersonal relations and were likely to suffer more from in-family problems than from larger-group difficulties because the latter were strongly ritualized.

These characterizations, drawn primarily from responses to psychological projective measures, are well reflected in Isseis' reactions to death. The controlled acceptance with which Isseis undertake grieving, whether for the increasing number of friends who die or in preparation for their own death, is truly impressive. The attitude of acceptance of phenomenological reality (including death and suffering) has its philosophical roots in Buddhist teaching. It contrasts markedly with the attitude of Sanseis, who seek to understand and control the external world according to a more Western mode. This acceptance among the Isseis is not limited to death-related aspects of living. For example, it is reflected (rightly or wrongly) in the lack of resistance to Wartime Relocation and other forms of racial oppression endured over the past seventy years or more. Such an orientation is not passive but is active in aiming at adjusting oneself to what is perceived as inevitable reality rather than trying to adjust external reality to meet one's own needs. Buddhist teachings emphasize functioning according to one's condition, behaving "naturally."

The vaguely Buddhist faith of many Isseis has fostered some of the "in-family problems" mentioned above. Since funeral services are either Buddhist or Christian and never both, disputes sometimes occur over which is appropriate. Difficulties also have reportedly occurred between Isseis and Niseis regarding the purchase of a special Buddhist name. Every person who receives a Buddhist funeral is given a posthumous name which is buried with the body and also inscribed on the back of his tombstone. In the past, persons who had performed special service over the years at a temple would receive a special name from the main temple of that sect. Recently, however, it has become possible to buy a special name. This is perceived to be a wonderful opportunity by some Isseis and a now meaningless temple money-making scheme by their adult children.

Funerals, memorial services, Memorial Day Ceremonies, and other death related ceremonial practices in the Japanese American community require representatives of groups to make public bestowals or speeches or, at least, appearances. In our observations the Isseis seem most comfortable in these ritual representations while many Niseis and most Sanseis appear uncomfortable and self-conscious in these public roles.

Perhaps the Issei are the most superstitious of the three generations. They observe the general taboo on discussion of death, but, in addition, they are likely to know and practice numberless avoidances and positive acts to keep harm and death away from their family. For example, one way of reading the Japanese character for "four" is *shi*. But *shi* is a homophone for (i.e., pronounced exactly like) the Japanese word for "death," so this reading of the character is often avoided, as is the serving of four of anything, e.g., cookies or rice balls, or the selling of four of anything, e.g., tableware or chairs.

In our ethnographic forays we have occasionally encountered lonely, isolated Issei who stated they wanted to die, even some who asked us to help them die. "Isn't it better to kill someone who wants to die?" one old lady at a nursing home asked. But far more common than active suicide attempts, we encountered passive suicidal behavior such as refusing medication and/or food. We have mentioned already the sense of being a burden which comes with increasing age in a reciprocal-obligation oriented family. In our interview schedule there was a significant difference by age in response to the question concerning caring for one's dependents as a reason some people don't want to die. Compared with Niseis and Sanseis, Isseis (like the aged in our other subcultures) tended to consider this an unimportant reason for not wishing to die. One way that many peoples of the world have handled the diminishing exchange potential of old age is by investing themselves in their children so that later the children would "balance out the debt" when the parents have grown old. The difficulties accompanying the Isseis' unfulfilled expectations regarding their children, who grew up in a culture that devalues the aged, are outlined in a paper by Reynolds (1971).

But in many Issei there remains the independent pioneer spirit that prodded them to emigrate to a strange land. And most common of all among the Issei seemed to be the attitude expressed by one fine old lady, "I won't hurry my death, but if it comes I don't mind too much . . . life is like a breath of wind . . . rivers will flow on after I'm gone . . ." The same philosophy underlies the Japanese poem translated by Hearn (1899, p. 159):

In A Cemetery at Night

This light of the moon that plays on the water I pour for the dead,
Differs nothing at all from the moonlight of other years.

Although we consider all generations of Japanese Americans to be extremely concerned with presenting a positive social image of "face," the Nisei generation has particular difficulty in this area. Isseis, like old style Japanese, handle the artificiality that accompanies image presenting by aiming at "sincerity" (see Kiefer, 1974), at actually trying to *become* the self or selves they present, and by ignoring, denying, and avoiding inconsistent presentations. Sanseis either rebel against presenting a "front" or accept artificiality as part of modern life. But Niseis, in the middle, sufficiently marginal to be uncomfortable with phoniness, yet unable to deny or erase it, find themselves increasingly under attack by the critical members in the third generation.

Thus some young Sansei have been appalled by the lack of consistency and straightforwardness of their parents when the latter were observed removing the flags from Japanese American veterans' graves following Memorial Day Services (to be used the next year), or laughing and engaging in social banter immediately before and after solemn funeral services, or participating in lively parties following graveside ceremonies, or—in another area of life—refusing to seek professional counseling while beset by many family-related problems.

The Issei attitude of acceptance is often difficult for Sanseis to understand. The third generation of Japanese Americans has grown up in a culture with much more technological control over the external world than existed in the Meiji culture of the Issei. Sanseis have been taught to have a questioning, probing nature, to aim at *changing* the external world when it causes them discomfort. They learned not to accept but to understand. However, the essence of death is not easily understood, perhaps not understandable at all, and so the Sansei fears and avoids thoughts of death, a topic that doesn't yield to his rational strategy of dealing with his world.

Like other young people Sanseis tend to avoid funerals. Not only is this a function of their general avoidance of death-related activities but it is also a result of the unintelligibility of much of the funeral service itself, particularly the Buddhist service with its ancient chants and Japanese language emphasis. Sanseis generally have little religious contact, and even that is often superficial. The thrust in most churches is the social function rather than the existential confrontation. Thus Sanseis can be fairly successful at avoiding thoughts about death that are stimulated in a formal religious context. To be sure, following marriage some thought is likely to be given to death as life insurance is taken out. And, on occasion the sudden death of an acquaintance or loved one or the more remote and expected death of a grandparent provokes thinking on the subject but, generally, death remains an unpleasant, distant enigma best avoided in word and thought. As one Sansei put it, "I've never really thought of it . . . I think about it but not much . . . I don't like sermons on death. I think sermons should give you an uplift but (in the case of sermons dealing with death) you leave the church depressed . . . If someone wanted to know, then he should go see the minister." Another remarked, "I don't think I'll think of death for a long time; for me I think it's unimportant."

COMMUNITY TIES

The Japanese American funeral is a community event attended by representatives of groups, in broad contrast to Anglo funerals, which are attended by individuals, and Mexican Americans' funerals which are attended by relatives and intimates. A Japanese American who dies leaves behind a relatively large pool of potential funeral participants, because any group with which he was affiliated (even by knowing well one member of the group) or any group that was affiliated with a group (e.g., the deceased's family) of which the deceased was a member, would feel some obligation to send at least one representative to the funeral; the closer the relationship, the greater the number of representatives that should be sent.

Japanese American funeral directors estimate the number who are likely to attend the service by counting the number and size of the groups, including the family group, in which the deceased was a member and by evaluating his prominence in them. Floral displays include banners with the name of the group that sent them. The service itself includes tributes by representatives of various groups, sticks of incense in Buddhist funeral ceremonies, and stalks of flowers in Christian funeral ceremonies.

Similarly the various Memorial Day Services in the Los Angeles area for Japanese Americans invariably include opportunities for representatives of appropriate groups, whether they are representing

Buddhist churches, Veterans of Foreign War posts, or business organizations, to pay public homage to the deceased.

That persons participate in these services as representatives and not as individuals is illustrated neatly in an observation made at one of the Memorial Day Services:

> "During the floral presentations in the Buddhist Service, as the next to the last person was being called forward by the conductor, a Nisei woman who was not called as representing an organization but who apparently thought that the organization had been accidently bypassed came to the front with flower in hand to await her turn. The conductor, noticing her and obviously disturbed, hurriedly tried to find out who she was since she was not on the list. He conferred with the Nisei man who had just placed a flower in front of the monument and seemed relieved to find out that he hadn't made a mistake. He then informed the woman that her organization was already represented. *With this the woman turned around and quietly walked back to her seat still holding her flower.* As an individual she could not go ahead and present the flower" (Noted by B. Ogawa.)

It is perhaps in this light that one can most profitably view the Japanese American interview responses that they desire their funeral minister (B 62%, J 79%, M 74%, A 68%) and funeral director (B 39%, J 65%, M 47%, A 40%) to be Japanese American, i.e., to be representatives of their community. This tendency was especially strong with increasing age.

Obon is the Japanese American equivalent of the Mexican American celebration of the All Souls Day and All Saints Day. On the festival days of Obon the souls of the dead return to spend a joyful period with their survivors, dancing, banqueting, and socializing. Obon has become a time of folk dancing and carnivals for the Japanese American community with the major overt reminder of the death element being only in the public reading of a list of the sponsoring Buddhist church's members who died during the preceding years.

Death in any community involves a rearrangement in relationships and a shifting of responsibilities. It becomes important to communicate to community members that someone has died and to identify the deceased so that community members can respond appropriately. In Hawaii Japanese American deaths are announced publicly via the daily (mailed) newspapers. During the funeral services Japanese Americans file past the coffin bowing to the deceased and then to the survivors, symbolically communicating recognition of these relationships as well as feelings of sympathy. This long file of community peers who, for various reasons and in various roles, have made the effort to attend (with koden, i.e., a gift of money in an envelope) is an impressive and moving display of group solidarity.

During the period from 1920-1940 Japanese Associations in California established and maintained graveyards. Today vaguely defined Japanese American sections in a number of public cemeteries in Los Angeles are common. These sections reflect not only earlier social policies to segregate races but also Japanese American desires to be buried near others of their community, particularly family members. Group monuments to Nisei veterans and members of prefectural organizations are to be found in some of these cemeteries.

Another facet of the group orientation of Japanese Americans is expressed in the custom of gift giving. A typically Japanese way of expressing appreciation as well as influencing the other party to "think well of one" is to give gifts. Gift giving occurs in death-related situations just as it occurs in any social situation. Gifts are given to hospital staff by patients and their families. Gifts are given to the survivors of the deceased in the form of *koden*, and gifts of various sorts are returned to those who contributed to the funeral. Gifts are given by mortuaries to church and hospital Christmas funds and temple building programs. Thus there is a complex flow of carefully selected presents of appreciation in exchange for hoped for esteem and good wishes which serves to bind the community together.

It is interesting, and often mentioned by those we interviewed, that the Sansei actively participate in this gift giving (especially in the *koden* tribute), even though in many other attitudes and behaviors relating to death they seem alienated and far removed from Issei and Nisei.

CONTROLLED COMMUNICATION

Nearly every death-related professional in our study who came in contact with members of several ethnic groups and thus had comparative perspectives characterized the Japanese Americans as quite controlled in their expression of grief. We consider this to be a special case of the general Japanese American emphasis on controlling expressions of all kinds, including verbal expressions, that might upset others.

In our interview we asked three questions that are directly related to this topic. Less than half the Japanese Americans (B 52%, M 59%, A 42%) said they would worry if they couldn't cry after the death of their spouse. Over 80% said they would try very hard to control their expression of emotions in public (B 79%, M 64%, A 74%). Finally, 71% said they would let themselves go and cry themselves out in public or in private or both (B 64%, M 88%, A 70%). In the last question there were significant differences within the group by sex and age: women and younger persons of both sexes were more likely to say they would cry themselves out.

Of course, each group has its own frame of reference for what constitutes "emotional control" and "letting go." A further complication is the Japanese American's tendency to utilize subtle and indirect communications of affect. Payne (1970) has written a thoughtful account of Japanese American responses to pain and death based on her experiences and interviews. She reports that Japanese American doctors and nurses learn to watch for indirect evidences of pain such as squinting, grimacing, and paleness in patients who are not likely to communicate intense agony verbally, even, in some cases, right up to death. Similarly, body tension is one of the cues which Japanese American funeral conductors observe to signal the need for a supporting hand when a family member is taking a last look at the deceased. We have observed a sort of "eloquent restraint" among aged Issei widows during funeral services for their husbands. Such behavior reflects the Japanese values *enryo* ("restraint") and *gaman* ("forbearance"), much written about in psychocultural descriptions of Japanese culture. These values involve holding back one's own desires and expressions of distress so as not to upset others. However, this "holding back" can be done in such a way as to make it noticeable, thus communicating both "I am in need of something" or "I am upset by something" and "I am suppressing this fact out of deference to you" or "I am suppressing this fact in order to let you know of my good breeding." But younger Japanese Americans seem to be adopting more Western affective reactions. Our observations at funerals suggest that Sansei women are the most likely to cry and that Sansei men show even more controlled restraint than Nisei men, indicating a shift toward the strong normative dichotomy between men and women in the permissibility of tearfulness in dominant middle-class American culture.

The *otsuya* (or wake) and *makuragyo* (a form of Buddhist last rites) traditionally provided the immediate family with non-public opportunities to express grief. However, these pre-funeral services are not as common as in the past. The Buddhist emphasis on acceptance of inevitable reality and self-control is reflected even in the pacing and sequence of the funeral service. The ceremony in a Christian funeral comes to a climax with the processional viewing of the body, but after those attending a Buddhist service have viewed the body, a good deal of the ceremony remains to be carried out. The expectation in the Buddhist form is, of course, that after viewing the body the survivors will still be sufficiently self-possessed to continue participating in the ritual. Recently, some Buddhist families who prefer the format of the Christian ceremony have rearranged the order of the Buddhist ceremonial elements so that the viewing of the deceased comes at the end of the service.

We have asserted that many Japanese Americans have difficulty in communicating unpleasant or disheartening information, whether by emotional outburst or otherwise. Thus, the broadly human problem of telling another person that he or some loved one will probably soon die becomes especially difficult for the Japanese American. In fact, there appears to be a great deal of ambivalence about whether to tell at all. We have recorded a number of cases in which families have turned to doctors, nurses, social workers, ministers, and priests seeking their advice on whether or not to tell an aging Issei of impending death. The advice they received was usually noncommital (these professionals did not want the responsibility of deciding either), so it was fortunate in a number of cases that the dilemma was solved by the dying patient himself broaching the subject.

Almost half the Japanese Americans (B 60%, J 48%, M 37%, A 71%) thought a dying person should be told that he is dying. The special problem involved here, of course, is who should do the telling. Of those who stated that a dying person should be made aware of his condition, 29% believed a family member to be the appropriate informant. Of those who preferred that the dying individual not be told, significantly more Japanese Americans mentioned that it would cause greater pain for the dying and that it could precipitate an earlier death. Again, the assumption is that the individual lacks ego strength and should be protected from an upsetting communication.

Like the other ethnicities, Japanese Americans generally felt that a person dying of cancer senses his imminent death without being told (B 81%, J 80%, M 78%, A 89%). Also like the others, most Japanese Americans would themselves wish to be told if they were dying (B 71%, J 77%, M 60%, A 77%). Again, the implication appears to be that "others can't handle the information, but *I* can." Middle-aged (especially middle-aged men) and more highly educated Japanese Americans were significantly more likely to want to be told. Like Black and Anglo Americans, about half this group felt they could tell someone that he is about to die (B 51%, J 47%, M 19%, A 52%). Middle-aged women reported significantly more difficulty with this task than did the other Japanese American women.

Telling patients of the death of a fellow patient is another problem in which the extreme sensitivity to the feelings of others plays an important part. As in many other convalescent care facilities, the local Japanese American practice appears to be to isolate a dying patient, either in a separate room or in a room with confused patients, who, it is hoped, will not be aware of what is happening. When the death occurs, patients are hustled into their rooms so they won't observe the body being wheeled away. Most of the nurses avoid questions about their "missing" fellow patients. When pressed, they may respond that a patient has moved or has been transferred. In one case, the inquiring patient's reply to such an evasion was, "Or perhaps she died" "I wouldn't know about that," was the nurse's untruthful but protective reply.

One nurse at a local Japanese American facility tells inquisitive patients the truth about fellow patient's deaths. She is a socially recognized exception, and even in her case there are limits put on her by the sensitivity of the relatives of the deceased. For example, in one case, a patient was moved out of her room when she became critically ill. Her roommate cried all day. The critical patient weakened and eventually died but the family asked that her former roommate not be told. At our last contact the nurse not only felt unable to tell the former roommate, who would be sad and angry at not having been told before, but she could not tell any other patient either for fear they might tell the dead patient's friend.

This incident exemplifies some of the common problems engendered by this sensitive, controlled, protective, indirect communication style. Interpersonal complications, misunderstandings, lack of needed information, and suspended credence become the cultural price one pays for the value, "Do not burden others with your sorrow" (Habenstein and Lamers, 1960, p. 55).

The strategies one uses in dealing with others are often the strategies adopted for dealing with oneself. Here we would like to extend the idea of controlled communication, essentially a social action, to intrapersonal psychological processes. The psychological analogues of this pattern of interaction are denial, suppression, and repression. In other words, upsetting information is withheld from self-awareness or the ego in much the same way it is withheld from others.

Only a handful of Japanese Americans report that they think of their own death at least weekly (B 34%, J 10%, M 37%, A 25%), and one-third claim they *never* think of their own death (B 14%, J 33%, M 10%, A 22%). Comparing these significantly different responses with the equally significantly higher incidence of funeral attendance and grave visiting of the Japanese Americans, we must at least consider the possibility that denial or suppression is operative in some responses here. We are reminded of the comment of a young Nisei visitor at the Japanese American nursing care facility when asked about his mother's absent roommate. He replied that he had noticed she was not doing well but that he did not dare ask what happened to her, i.e., he had correctly assumed that she had died, but he preferred not to know for certain.

Compared to the others, slightly fewer Japanese Americans admitted ever dreaming about their own death or dying, but differences were not significant (B 22%, J 20%, M 36%, A 38%). Older Japanese Americans were significantly less likely to report such dreams than younger persons. The constriction of fantasy and the suppression and denial of upsetting thoughts and recollections have been reported elsewhere for Isseis (DeVos, 1955). Our data also show it as being most evident in the older generation.

SHAME

Personal embarrassment and the associated embarrassment to one's family underlies, in a negative way, much of what is basic to Japanese American culture just as a genuine warm concern for others underlies it in a positive way. For example, grave decorations and offerings of cigarettes, gum, fruit, nuts, beer, and incense represent both a continuing sensitivity and concern for the feelings of the deceased and also a need to keep up family graves to satisfy the eyes of the community. The beautification of Issei and veterans' graves just prior to Memorial Day and the relative haste with which some individual graves are tended and then left reflect the emphasis on obligation and shame avoidance that is found in such public display among some Japanese Americans.

Gossip provides a fairly effective sanctioning force in the well-knit Japanese American community. Families try to prevent any hints of narcotics, unwanted pregnancies, family feuds, mental illness, or suicide from filtering out to the community. We have encountered cases of persons hastily tidying up the yard when a death in the family portended visits by community members. Suicides are often concealed (sometimes with the cooperation of the physician), often with no obituary and only a private funeral.

Our interviews indicate that Japanese Americans were no more likely than other respondents to have ever known someone who killed himself (B 25%, J 22%, M 31%, A 29%). However, they were significantly more likely to have known a suicide that had been subsequently concealed and reported as a natural or accidental death (B 5%, J 20%, M 7%, A 5%). Our interviews with professionals turned up numerous cases of this sort. Kitano (1969) also reports an instance of a suicide that had been publicly declared an accident.

In an earlier interview study of close relatives of successful suicides, two points were made with extreme consistency by Japanese Americans: first, suicide did not run in their families, and, second, *they* would never consider killing themselves (Reynolds and Kitano, unpublished data). Our experience suggests that such reactions may be universal rather than limited to one ethnic group.

This Japanese American concern with social reputation, with what others are thinking, extends not only to the family reputation, but also to the reputation of one's occupation and one's employer. For example, one reason given why nursing home staff suppress information about deaths is that it would hurt the facility's reputation among the Isseis, some of whom already consider it a "last stop." Similarly, as noted above, families who bring an elderly Issei to such a facility may feel defensive and uncomfortable lest others misinterpret their action as signifying rejection or abandonment of the elderly parent.

WORK ETHIC

Norbeck (1965) writes of the moral import of thrift and industry in Japan: "The lazy person in Japan is more than merely lazy; he is regarded as untrustworthy and morally unsound" (p. 20). Similarly, Caudill and DeVos (1956) have argued that diligence and long-range goal striving were values that contributed to the success of Japanese Americans in a culture dominated by very similar values.

That dying would mean the end of all their plans and projects was unimportant to nearly half the Japanese American sample (B 66%, J 44%, M 51%, A 64%). and only 8% (B 6%, M 13%, A 6%) said they would first attempt to complete projects and tie up loose ends, given six months to live. Nor would Japanese Americans return to work any sooner than other ethnicities following the death of a spouse.

In general, our data support the presence of some special valuing of work or, perhaps, of competence in general but, in perspective, it lies within a value hierarchy below the social and reputation-preserving values discussed above. Nevertheless, dying is particularly distressing to a person who is bothered not only by pain and the knowledge of his approaching end but by the additional anguish of not being able to function independently. "I can't do anything for myself," indicated an extremely sorrowful state-of-being for one elderly patient. Part of the Isseis' willingness to die (discussed above) comes from the failing eyesight and mental capacities, the inability to use hands and legs in fruitful production, the dread of being a burden. One outspoken Nisei remarked that facilities now devoted to the care of older people might be better utilized to help hungry children "who will be productive."

The Japanese American work orientation is also reflected in the unique scheduling of funerals. A major reason why Japanese American funerals are held in the evenings is so that people need not miss work to attend.

RELIGION

It is difficult to assess the influence of religion on Japanese American attitudes toward death. What influence there is tends to be philosophical rather than centered about a God figure, and is expressed through ritual rather than personal commitment.

About half (51%) of our Japanese Americans gave Buddhism as their religious affiliation; 15% considered themselves Methodists, and 12% (B 6%, M 0%, A 12%) had no religious preference. The slight difference among the ethnic groups, with relatively few Japanese Americans considering themselves more devout than others (B 20%, J 12%, M 18%, A 18%), did not reach significance.

In Japan one is generally given Buddhist rites at birth and death. But the sense of affiliation or identification with the congregation, there as here, in Buddhism as in Catholicism and Protestantism, is often only nominal. When we asked whether or not the respondent would call for a priest or minister on his deathbed, over half the Japanese Americans (B 64%, J 51%, M 88%, A 53%) replied that they would. At the time of their spouse's death, only 22% (B 32%, M 33%, A 28%) would first turn to God or a priest or minister (those who would are significantly more often older persons), and no Japanese American would first turn to church members for practical help in time of grief. On the other hand, 20% of the Japanese Americans would first contact a priest or minister if they knew someone who was seriously contemplating suicide (B 7%, J 20%, M 25%, A 20%).

Buddhism, like Christianity, comes in many forms so we must be careful in explicating what "traditional Buddhism" is like. In many ways, Japanese Americans do not appear particularly religious in terms of traditional Christian or traditional Buddhist practices. Their limited acceptance of life after death (only 47% believed in life after death, with 11% believing in heaven, 20% mentioning some spirit form, and 16% referring to other forms) is consistent with some forms of Buddhism, but inconsistent with Jodoshinshu Buddhism to which many of these respondents claimed adherence. Some Japanese American Christian clergymen have told us that young ministers tend to deemphasize the concept of an afterlife (just as we found among Blacks), and there is a general avoidance of the topic of death in Sunday morning sermons from Japanese American pulpits.

Yet a theistic ideology is present in some responses, especially among the older Japanese American respondents. Compared with other women, elderly women were significantly over-represented among the 63% of Japanese Americans who agreed that accidental deaths show God's hand working among men. And non-theistic moralism is far from absent in the Japanese Americans' responses. Older people (especially older women) and the least well educated were more likely than chance to be among the 43% of Japanese Americans who felt that most people who live to be at least 90 years old must have been morally good.

One theme does run through both Buddhist and Christian folk theology, however: *acceptance.* One Japanese American Methodist minister wrote the following in response to several items on a special questionnaire we had constructed: "(There is) a need *to accept* accidents as part of life . . . Expressions of appreciation on the part of the bereaved help to further the reality of death *to be accepted.*" "The need *to accept* all of life (tragedies, good, etc.) must be stressed" (emphasis ours). The same words could have been written equally by a Buddhist priest.

Under half (41%) of our Japanese Americans felt that people should be allowed to die if they want to. Neither this percentage nor the reasons they gave for their responses were unique. However, when we asked for the reasons of the 51% who replied that people should *not* be allowed to die, we received a preponderance of moralistic rationales that were non-theistic in essence, a marked difference from the other subcultural groups who organized moralistic arguments within a theistic-religious framework.

Observations in the predominently Japanese American convalescent care center indicated that, at one time or another, nearly every patient had expressed a wish to die, although these were rarely if ever turned into actual self-destructive behavior. We suspect that such reactions are common to all ethnic groups. Patients appeared to accept their status, that of the traditional sick role, without particular resistance, and placed themselves in the hands of the physician, not indefinitely but until clearly perceived evidence of neglect or inadequacy soured the trust. Such patience seems to be related to the Buddhist value placed upon allowing situations (in this case, the *healing* situation) to "ripen" naturally without forcing them to conclusion as the stereotypic Westerner is wont to do. As long as social relationships are harmonious almost any situation is endurable. But the burden of unfulfilled reciprocity bears heavily in the Issei's mind.

Belief in Life After Death

In almost all religions, the existence of the individual prior to birth and subsequent to bodily death has been important. Although our Protestant (Black, some Japanese, and Anglo), Catholic (Mexican American and some Anglo), and Buddhist (Japanese American) respondents all have their origins in religious groups whose theologies are quite specific about the form of life after earthly death, we anticipated finding considerable variation both between and within groups.

In response to a direct question, nearly half the Japanese Americans believe they would live on in some form after death (B 59%, J 47%, M 40%, A 66%). Consistent with their respective theologies the more devout were significantly more likely to believe in an afterlife than were the less devout. What was characteristically Japanese American was that 43% of those who believe in an afterlife conceptualized it as returning in *spirit* form rather than living on in heaven or paradise (24%). and *all* of the 12 persons (B 39%, J 100%, M 82%, A 83%) who believed in heaven felt that those in heaven watch over earth. Such beliefs underlie the communication between survivors and deceased that takes place at the butsudan and gravesite, permitting family ties to extend even beyond death. Interestingly, in both of our familistically-oriented subcultures (i.e., in both Japanese

American and Mexican American subcultures) there are even special provisions for the afterlife of children. In the Mexican American folk subculture the souls of dead children become little saints or angels. According to the folk-Buddhism of at least some Los Angeles Japanese Americans, dead children become little Buddhas. Since children are "good" and "good" people have passage into "the world mind," the possibility of death leading to nirvana and Buddhahood is not alien to the Japanese Americans.

There are two senses in which the dead can be considered yet with us. Hearn (1899), writing at the turn of the century, described them both. In one sense, the dead have bequeathed to us life and ways of knowing our world. Through countless generations they passed on love and hope and information which converge in each person's life only to fan out again to his offspring. In this sense, the unseen presence (the spirit, if you will) of our ancestors is continuously among us. But there is another sense in which many Japanese and Japanese Americans believe that the spirits of recently deceased family members take a special interest in family affairs. In this sense the spirit is more personalized. For some Japanese Americans the spirit can be talked to and, for many more, it can be "felt to," i.e., one can express the same loving feelings toward and sense the benevolent protective concern from someone even *after* his death that were felt during his life. An aftertaste is a somewhat similar phenomenon—it remains very real even after its source has disappeared, and both experiences seem to fade with time.

Six of those Japanese Americans who believed in a heaven also believed in a hell; five did not. Thirty-four Japanese Americans thought death is simply nothingness or the end of life, four thought of it in terms of sleep, nine simply didn't know how to conceptualize death, and the remainder offered such descriptions as "full of ashes," "a beautiful thing," "it's up to Buddha," "body stops functioning," etc. The final item in this section asked the respondent his *wish* about life after death. Only half (B 80%, J 51%, M 69%, A 83%) of our Japanese Americans wished there were life after death; 19% (B 6%, M 14%, A 8%) wished there were none.

Why should it be that comparatively few Japanese Americans wish there were life after death? Is life lived so fully in this sphere that Japanese Americans feel it is unnecessary to live beyond their allotted time? Or can it be that the pressures of social-sensitivity in this life makes blackness, the end, nothingness preferable to an afterlife that might demand the same sort of carefulness and image-protection which are demanded in this life? "World weariness" is the translation of a common motivation expressed in suicide notes in Japan. A major component of "world weariness" seems to be heavy responsibility with no relief in sight. The degree of world weariness may vary considerably and the satisfactions one exchanges for responsibility and preservation of "face" may be much greater among our Japanese Americans than among those Japanese who killed themselves. Nevertheless, similar thoughts and feelings may underlie our Japanese Americans' indifference toward an afterlife that might perpetuate the same burdens borne here.

Again we need to look at Eastern concepts of time. These tend to be that time is cyclical and continuous, while Western views are that time is linear and discontinuous. Life and death, similarly, are seen as parts of a cycle in Eastern thought, rather than as a dichotomous being-non-being. Buddhism does not limit its alternatives to ordinary life versus nothingness, since nirvana is often defined as a state of pure bliss, very unlike "life." (We are indebted to Dr. Christie Kiefer for offering this interpretation.)

So it may be that Japanese Americans do not desire life after death, but, rather, nirvana which they would not properly classify as *life* after death, but rather as withdrawal from the repetition of reincarnations.

CONTACT WITH DEATH

Japanese Americans most certainly did not escape existential contact with the death of others, since 83% had known someone personally who had died during the previous two years. In general, the elderly (especially older men) had known more persons who died and more persons who had died of natural causes than the young. As was typical of all groups, relatively few deaths were by other than natural causes. Although 75% of all Japanese Americans knew people who had died naturally, a much smaller number were acquainted with people who had died in accidents (19%), in war (5%), by suicide (3%), or by homicide (0%).

The actual rates for Japanese American suicides and homicides in Los Angeles County were indeed fairly low (based upon 1970 Census data and 1970 data from the Los Angeles County Coroner's Office). The suicide rate for Japanese Americans was 12 per 100,000 population (B 12, M 5, A 20), while the homicide rate was a remarkable 1 per 100,000 (B 40, M 7, A 6).

Fewer Japanese Americans knew someone who was dying under circumstances in which a decision had to be made whether or not to inform him of his coming death (B 40%, J 29%, M 45%, A 42%). We would suspect that, far from there being fewer such cases in the Japanese American community, it is rather that personal and family desires for privacy and controlled communications are responsible for these findings. Nonetheless, in instances that were known, the Japanese Americans did not differ from other ethnicities in the proportion of cases that were actually told (B 63%, J 60%, M 44%, A 69%) or for which information was provided by the physician (B 74%, J 67%, M 64%, A 80%).

Selecting two contrasting cases from our field notes, we can illustrate some fairly typical responses of Japanese Americans to this issue:

> Mr. K was dying of cancer. His wife came to the nursing home every morning and remained the entire day. Soon she would be alone, he told her, so talk with the children about his approaching death. It was *unmei* (fate)—*shikataganai* (it could not be helped). She had thought at first it was his being in the convalescent facility and not at home that was causing him to weaken—or perhaps it was the doctor. But she came to realize that he would lose ground under any condition. Nothing could be done to save him. She did not appear to utilize denial or any other such mechanism—she related effectively to reality without losing feelings of warmth for her dying husband.

> An old man told his eldest son that he suspected he was dying of stomach cancer (his wife had died of the same disease). He hinted that he would not be around much longer. The son, not wishing to take the responsibility of telling his father that the self-diagnosis was accurate, first approached the physician for support. The doctor told him there was no need to tell his father. "He is an old man—let him die in peace." The son then called a family meeting to inform the other children, in part to enable him to share the responsibility for informing their father or maintaining secrecy.

Relatively few Japanese Americans had ever felt they were close to dying themselves (B 55%, J 29%, M 54%, A 38%), and fewer reported contacts with persons already dead (B 55%, J 29%, M 54%, A 38%). Of those who had experienced such an encounter, one-third stated that they psychologically felt the presence of the deceased rather than seeing, hearing, or touching the dead person directly. However, several psychic experiences were related. One respondent discovered a camera, lost previously on a trip, on a fence across from his father's grave, although he insisted the loss occurred far from the cemetery. Another saw a ball of fire approach the door of his home. Such an apparition is a culturally-shared symbol of death in Japanese folk knowledge. Personal accounts of having seen fireballs portending death are not uncommon among Issei or older Nisei in Los Angeles.

The ancestral shrine (or butsudan) in Buddhist homes is a focal point for interest in and communication with deceased family members just as the gravesite or deposited cremains seem to be for other Buddhist and Christian Japanese American families. Yamamoto and Imahara (1970) report on a sample of Buddhist and Christian Japanese American widows, 65% of whom sensed the presence of their dead husbands (see also Kalish and Reynolds, 1972).

About 12% of this ethnic group had had the unexplainable feeling that they were about to die (B 15%, M 34%, A 15%), and only 17% had had this feeling about someone else (B 37%, M 38%,

A 30%). There were no major differences between the groups in the frequency with which these feelings about others actually seemed to predict their deaths. About half (47%) of those Japanese Americans who had these feelings said they were always correct, while about a third said the person(s) did not die subsequently.

Facing One's Own Death

About two-thirds of all groups said they would accept death peacefully rather than fight it actively. Interestingly, within our Japanese American sample there was a tendency for the least devout to be more accepting of death. Given the Buddhist emphasis on accepting one's natural state and adjusting constructively within it, we expected the opposite trend. It may be that the combination of a culturally-standardized norm of public self-depreciation and a nebulous quality to the Buddhist religious affiliation has confounded the self ratings of degree of religiousness in this group. Middle-aged women showed a significant tendency to accept death and to endure pain in silence. Such responses conform to recognized and named values within the Japanese American community (e.g., *gaman*), which were described above in the background section on communication and expression control.

Of the Japanese Americans 31% said they were afraid to die (B 19%, M 33%, A 22%). Fewer respondents made this response in each increasing age category. Japanese Americans were most influenced in their attitudes toward death by the death of somone close (41%), being close to death themselves (18%), and their religious background (13%). These same reasons were the top three selections of the other three groups but with varying rankings. There was a significant difference only between Japanese Americans and Black Americans who rated religious background very high. Given the sensitive interpersonal orientation of Japanese Americans and their relative lack of concern with formal religion as the ultimate source of personal values, it is not surprising to find deaths of others as more influential in determining the respondents' attitudes toward death than religious training.

Japanese American expectations and wishes about when they would die or how they would die were not unique in any way. Typically, elderly persons both expected and wished to die sooner than younger persons. Japanese Americans, like Anglos, greatly preferred to die at home (B 44%, J 72%, M 54%, A 61%) rather than in a hospital. However, nearly a third of the middle-aged Japanese Americans preferred to die in a hospital, a significantly high percentage compared to older and younger Japanese Americans. Here, perhaps we have competing desires to handle death within the family (as other serious issues are handled there) and to protect family members from the distress of death and the burden of caring for a dying person.

THE TRAGEDY OF DEATH:
ATTITUDES, CUSTOMS, RITUALS

The sorrow brought about by the loss of others derives from many factors. One aspect concerns the kind of death suffered by the dead individual; another aspect is a function of the roles performed by that person most recently, i.e., the tasks that now fall upon others. Other determinants include the closeness of the relationship with the deceased and the ability to resolve guilt. In response to these feelings, numerous customs have developed in which the living pay homage to the dead, whether to propitiate desires for revenge, to utilize the spirit for protection and good fortune, or to provide an opportunity for catharsis and an expression of family and community solidarity.

Many, perhaps most, people have contemplated what a "good death" means for them. Half of the Japanese Americans considered slow death to be more tragic than sudden death (B 58%, J 50%, M 50%, A 68%). Although all groups tended to see the deaths of youths as most tragic, the Japanese Americans were significantly more likely than the others to believe that middle-age deaths were most tragic (B 8%, J 22%, M 6%, A 5%).

Considerably more Japanese Americans than other respondents considered the death of a man to be more tragic than the death of a woman (B 10%, J 34%, M 9%, A 16%); all other ethnicities having a greater percentage believing a woman's death the more tragic of the two (B 38%, J 29%, M 36%, A 25%). There were no significant differences related to the sex of the respondent on this item. In fact, a somewhat higher percentage of Japanese American women than men considered a male's death to be more tragic. Of course, men have traditionally occupied the seats of power and esteem in the Japanese culture, and women have remained humbly (but not altogether impotently) in the background. Perhaps a man's death would be likely to have more impact on the Japanese American community than upon other communities, since the man generally represents his family unit in community affairs. Without his presence the status and visibility of his wife and children would be greatly diminished. This could tip the balance toward perception of greater tragedy in the death of men than women. It is very likely that those who chose women's deaths as more tragic were interpreting the influence of females in the family as greater than that of males, especially in terms of their influence upon children.

Japanese Americans did not differ significantly from any other ethnic group in selecting as the most tragic ways to die, accidents (32%), homicides (32%), suicides (10%), and natural death (1%). However, in judging which of the above were least tragic, many fewer Japanese Americans chose natural causes (B 76%, J 64%, M 83%, A 87%) and many more picked suicide (B 14%, J 26%, M 14%,

A 7%). Why should suicide be considered least tragic by over one-fourth of the Japanese Americans? Previous research indicates that is it not because of traditional Japanese admiration of certain kinds of suicide (admiration no longer as strong in Japan as it once appears to have been).

Mourning and Funeral Customs

Several interview items dealt with norms surrounding the period of mourning following loss of a spouse. Of the four subcultural groups, Japanese Americans and Mexican Americans responded in terms of the most conservative and restrictive norms. Although the differences were not always significant, the trend was consistent across these six items, whether it was the time period prudent to wait before going out, remarrying, ceasing to wear black, returning to employment, or the frequency with which one ought to visit a spouse's grave. These items could be considered an indirect index of the strength of family ties or they might be perceived as the strength of community norms and the need to retain *face* by adherence to these norms. In the case of the former, when relatively strong ties are disrupted, as by death, symbolic behaviors reflecting the disruptions are likely to be more intense and prolonged. If the latter, the presentational self would require the longer evidence of mourning. It is likely that both pressures work in concert.

Few Japanese Americans (B 30%, J 17%, M 17%, A 25%) felt it was acceptable to start going out with other men/women any time after a spouse's death; 34% (B 11%, M 40%, A 21%) felt the minimum wait should be two years or longer. Attitudes toward remarriage were along even more conservative lines. Fourteen percent of the Japanese Americans (B 34%, M 22%, A 26%) felt it unimportant to wait any minimum time, 26% (B 11%, M 20%, A 11%) set at least a two year minimum wait and 21% said that one in their age category should never remarry (B 5%, M 13%, A 1%). On this item, a relatively low level of education and increasing age for each sex and for both sexes combined were significantly associated with conservative views.

One type of response to the normative restrictions on widows and widowers in the Japanese American community has been the growth of church-related organizations that bring such people together. The *fujinkai*, or Issei women's organizations, have increasingly become *widows* organizations as wives who had come to the United States to marry much older husbands understandably outlive their spouses. One organization, called the "We-Are-One" Club, was begun for *Nisei* widows and now has grown to include both sexes and divorced persons, as well. This organization began in 1969 in response to the frustrations of Nisei widows who were receiving pressure from their deceased husbands' families to remain in the family's sphere and not remarry. In addition, going out with other males provoked community gossip or immediate conclusions that they were about to be married. Existing organizations, such as Parents Without Partners, were Anglo-oriented, and the Nisei widows did not feel at home in them. The group now numbers 40-50 and meets monthly with programs including special speakers (from among such professions as lawyers, financial counselors, psychiatrists, child psychologists, and education experts) and parties.

Wearing black as a sign of mourning is a gradually disappearing custom in American society. Almost half the Japanese Americans (B 62%, J 42%, M 52%, A 53%) felt it was unimportant to wear black, 26% felt it appropriate to wear black for up to a month, and only 14% (B 5%, M 28%, A 1%) saw the need to wear black for a year or more. Our observations at funerals and Memorial Day Services confirm that these attitudes are well-reflected in the clothing that is actually worn. Even the Japanese American funeral directors no longer exclusively wear black suits while conducting funerals. Black arm bands for close relatives and officiants in the more traditional funeral services are surviving tokens of this color symbolism.

Over half the Japanese Americans (B 78%, J 53%, M 64%, A 82%) felt that a week or even less away from work following the death of a spouse would be sufficient. Over one-third (B 17%, J 39%, M 27%, A 9%) considered a month or longer to be necessary minimum period to wait. It seems that here we have contrasting pressures from the work ethic and the desire for social propriety.

Visiting the grave of the dead spouse is an act that varies considerably in meaning from culture to culture. Japanese Americans and Mexican Americans answered quite similarly as to the fewest number of times one ought to visit a spouse's grave in the first year after the death. Fifty-eight percent of the Japanese Americans and 59% of the Mexican Americans (B 13%, A 35%) felt that a minimum number of visits was 6 or more. Eighteen percent of the Japanese Americans (vs. B 32%, M 19%, and A 11%) felt that once or twice was sufficient. Only 7% (B 39%, M 11%, A 35%) felt it unimportant to visit at all. In the *fifth* year following the death 30% of the Japanese Americans (B 10%, M 18%, A 6%) still felt it necessary to visit the grave six or more times and only 8% (B 52%, M 29%, A 43%) considered visiting unimportant. We previously discussed the meaning of grave visitation in terms of retaining intra-family obligations even after death, as well as maintaining one's community reputation. However, at this point we would insert that our observations confirm the reality that Japanese Americans *do*, in fact, visit graves more frequently than the other groups. Japanese American sections of Los Angeles cemeteries are conspicuously well-kept with numerous visible signs of recent visits. Families who visit their children's gravesites weekly and elderly persons who visit their spouses' gravesites each week are known and discussed within the community.

Part of the high frequency of grave visiting among Japanese Americans can be traced to the Buddhist requirements for post-funeral services on the first, seventh, 49th and 100th day following the burial and then on yearly anniversaries. However, the appropriate days vary considerably from community to community and family to family in Japan and in the United States so that what remains (even among non-Buddhist Japanese Americans) is the general sense that one is obligated to visit the gravesite at intervals (regular or irregular) following burial.

A series of related questions dealt with the respondent's wishes for his own funeral. Few respondents in any group desired a large, elaborate funeral. Japanese Americans significantly more often preferred a funeral with only relatives and close acquaintances (B 58%, J 83%, M 58%, A 63%) to one with lots of friends and acquaintances. But these unassuming attitudes do not conform to the actuality of funerals in the Japanese American community. In fact, funerals tend to be largest in this subculture because of the wide range of group representatives obliged to attend and because the *koden* gift offering brought by those attending makes larger funerals economically feasible. We were reminded of the obituary of a prominent Issei pioneer who died in 1970 at the age of 90: "His lifelong sense of duty and humble indebtedness to his community was strongly felt when recently he told some of his close friends, 'when I go I want a simple funeral'." (*Rafu Shimpo*, No. 20,089, Monday, June 22, 1970). The funeral actually required 13 receptionists, 12 ushers, and three floral registrars. There were 19 honorary pallbearers and an estimated 700-800 in attendance. This was somewhat large even by Japanese American standards and a far cry from "a simple funeral."

We included the next item specifically to get information about a custom existing in the Japanese American community. The respondent was asked whether or not he expected many friends and/or relatives to share in the expenses of his funeral. In the Japanese American subculture it is customary to bring to the funeral a gift of money in a small envelope with the giver's name written on it. This is called *koden*. The giver's name and the amount of the gift is recorded and retained by the bereaved so that they will know the appropriate amount to reciprocate should someone in the giver's family die. In addition the bereaved family usually had prepared individual packages of tea or coffee or *sembei* soy crackers for the guests at the funeral, though this has evolved in the past ten years or so to gifts of postage stamps, and most recently, to thank you cards announcing a donation to charity in the guest's name. Only the Japanese American ministers and non-Japanese are not expected to bring a *koden* offering. Large floral displays from individuals and organizations, with banners announcing the giver and, often, his relationship to the deceased surround the casket. The family may feel obligated here, too, to reciprocate a money gift of, say, $35 to those organizations that sent flowers. The system of record-keeping and reckoning of appropriate gifts and counter-gifts is fairly complex. And, although even Sansei youth who object to many Japanese American customs participate in the *koden* system, there have been efforts to simplify it further—for example, by recording the names of those who brought *koden* but not the amounts. As one insurance agent put it, the koden is a kind of Japanese group insurance as opposed to the individual policies of American society.

The sharing of funeral expenses is not restricted solely to the Japanese American group, however. Moore (1970) has written of the importance in the past of the *mutualista* burial societies for Mexican Americans as a formalized means of cooperative handling of funeral expenses. "In 1970, a young student at the University of California at Riverside told me of a *mutalista* that his wife belonged to until she married. The group at the time consisted of about 600 members, descendants of a colony of Mexican immigrants who had settled in San Gabriel, California. There were two classes of funeral; 60 cents and $1.60. Even in 1970, that was enough to amplify family funds and provide for a decent funeral. This student was surprised to find that '*mutalistas* are alive and well': he had not heard of any such groups in his own community in Los Angeles" (p. 7, footnote).

Clark (1959), too, found burial societies called *funerarias* with large Spanish-speaking membership in the San Jose poverty area cutting across Protestant-Catholic denomination lines. Clearly, however, formal burial cooperatives do not play such a prominent part in the lives of Los Angeles Mexican Americans, Blacks or Anglos.

Significantly more Japanese Americans replied that others would share in their funeral expenses (B 27%, J 43%, M 30%, A 27%), but we had expected the percentage to be much higher. In subsequent checking, we learned that our translation might have been somewhat misleading for this question—to our knowledge, the only item so affected. In our attempts to use identical wording for each of the ethnicities, we avoided the use of the term *koden* in both English and Japanese versions. Therefore, although the English-speaking respondents appeared to recognize the *koden* was included in the possible customs we were asking about, some Japanese-speaking respondents expecting, but not finding, the familiar term may have assumed that we were not including *koden*. Perhaps the biggest effect of *koden* and large community participation in funerals was manifested in the Japanese American's estimations of what an "adequate" funeral would cost—the mean estimate was $1,948 compared with $1,075, $1,209, and $1,179 means in the other subcultures. Sixty-one percent of Japanese Americans (B 17%, M 28%, A 29%) estimated that an adequate funeral would cost over $1,400 with no significant intragroup differences by age or education.

Most respondents in all groups considered the selection of a minister for their funeral to be a family responsibility. This was especially true of the Japanese Americans (B 62%, J 79%, M 74%, A 68%). Fifty-nine percent of the Japanese Americans preferred their casket be open provided there was no disfigurement (B 51%, J 59%, M 51%, A 39%).

Of all the groups Japanese Americans responded least often that they would touch the body of their dead spouse at a funeral service (B 51%, J 31%, M 76%, A 51%). Younger persons (especially younger men) would be significantly more likely to touch the body than their elders. Similarly, kissing the body, while unlikely in the Japanese American and Black American groups (B 13%, J 12%, M 59%, A 33%) is a practice significantly associated with our youngest age group, especially young men. Two funeral directors told us that the Japanese Americans virtually never touch nor kiss the bodies. One commented, "I don't know exactly why they don't, but we don't encourage it—we might have to touch up the make-up afterwards . . . At times they do kiss the body—love is strong, I guess." More probable, and in keeping with other sources, was the rationale provided by one funeral director that the corpse is cold, hard, and unresponsive. The shock of this non-responsiveness is upsetting to many Japanese Americans. It is almost as if the reciprocal obligations of family life are projected on and expected from the family member—even in death.

As noted earlier it is not uncommon to see small children at Japanese American funerals. Thirty-one percent of these Japanese Americans (B 15%, M 47%, A 27%) were opposed to having children under ten years of age in attendance at their funeral. Opposition came significantly more often from women and from the less devout.

The *otsuya*, or wake, is not held very often in Los Angeles any more. Nowadays the wake and funeral service are combined in a single evening funeral ceremony for the family and/or community followed by a private graveside or crematorium service the next day. The *otsuya* is still common in Hawaii and in other areas of California. It is still held in Los Angeles on occasion primarily to meet the special requests of Hawaiian-born Japanese Americans and Japanese Americans of Okinawan descent. Of our Japanese American respondents, 41% wanted a wake (B 25%, M 68%, A 22%) and 46% did not. There was significant inverse relationship between desiring a wake and level of education.

Where, then, ought the wake be held? Half of those desiring a wake wanted it held in a church (B 27%, M 21%, A 15%). Older people most often chose this location. About equal quarters chose a funeral home (B 49%, J 24%, M 68%, A 50%) and their own home (B 24%, J 26%, M 11%, A 30%). The last location was most often selected by the youngest age groups.

Few Japanese Americans (15%) thought there would be drinking of liquor at their wake or funeral (B 36%, M 39%, A 23%) or the taking of tranquilizers (B 38%, J 16%, M 50%, A 41%).

Seventy-three percent of this group would prefer to have their funeral service in a church, 18% in a funeral home and 3% at home. Church services are almost a necessity due to the large turnout at Japanese American funerals.

About equal percentages of Japanese Americans would object to an autopsy (33%) and embalming (29%) of their body. On the latter procedure there were a couple of significant intra-group differences with old persons and more devout persons tending to be indifferent whether or not these procedures were performed.

In Japan preference regarding burial or cremation varies from region to region. Burial is preferred in the Shinto religion. However, in large metropolitan areas, cremation is the nearly universal practice employed for disposal of the body. In our Japanese American sample, 53% of the respondents preferred cremation (B 4%, M 5%, A 18%), 33% preferred burial and 11% were indifferent. Middle-aged Japanese Americans were most likely of the three age groups to prefer burial. These percentages are in close conformity to the estimated percentages of type of disposal of the body (by generation) provided independently by Mr. Fukui, the director of a large Japanese American funeral establishment in Los Angeles. Again, it appears that Japanese American behavior is conforming closely to their verbalized preferences. Two practical advantages to cremation stressed by Mr. Fukui are (1) it allows more time for the family to select an appropriate spot to deposit the remains, and (2) it allows for easier transportation of remains, permitting more family geographic mobility. Thus, even if the family moves around in Los Angeles they can find a nearby place for depositing and visiting the deceased. In addition, cremated remains can be divided and part of them sent to Japan.

The majority of Japanese Americans preferred to have their remains deposited in Los Angeles (60%). A small percentage (11%) would prefer to have their remains sent back to Japan. The reasons for selecting the place for depositing their remains included the following: it was the respondent's birthplace (10%), there is a family plot located there (15%), consanguineal (blood-related) kin live there (27%), conjugal (marriage-related) kin live there (24%), and other reasons (23%, including the influence of salesmen and personal philosophical attachments to the sea). In no culture is one's final "resting place" solely a personal matter. Particularly among Japanese Americans, with grave-visiting an important element of family and community expression, the choice is likely to involve socially derived considerations.

So far we have discussed attitudes, beliefs, and expectations regarding funerals and mourning, i.e., "What is it that people *say* they do?" We have already noted that, with regard to funeral matters, there is no great discrepancy between attitudes and behavior in the Japanese American subculture. Attending funerals is a community responsibility, a necessary activity in maintaining family and group reputations, an informal funeral insurance guarantee through *koden* exchanges (see above), and a way to show respect and concern for the deceased and their survivors.

Eighty-four percent of the Japanese American sample had attended at least one funeral in the preceding two years (B 67%, M 60%, A 55%). More Japanese Americans had attended eight or more funerals during this period than had failed to attend any (17% vs 16%). There was a significant relationship between increasing age and increased number of funerals attended. Japanese Americans had also attended funerals more recently than the other groups (52% within the past six months—B 39%, M 34%, A 28%). Again, the significant trend was for the elderly to have attended most recently.

Of all the groups, fewest Japanese Americans had not attended a grave other than during a burial service (B 71%, J 36%, M 56%, A 59%) in the preceding two-year period, and 34% of them (vs. 3%, 14%, and 8%) had visited graves five or more times. Increased frequency of grave visiting was associated with increasing age. Grave visiting is often a family affair among Japanese Americans, and even when an individual comes to the cemetery (to clean off the marker, to place fresh flowers or fruit or gum or candy or a glass of some favorite beverage), he often does so conscious of himself as representative of his family or some other group.

However, Japanese Americans didn't visit or talk with significantly more dying persons in the preceding two years than did other groups (58% had visited none vs. B 62%, M 61%, A 68%). Nor were they more likely to have ever told someone he was going to die (6% had vs. B 7%, M 4%, A 4%). The upsetting nature of these interactions would tend to make them avoided whenever possible (i.e., whenever avoidance would not cause embarrassment to those involved).

With the generally high frequency of funeral and graveside activities, one might expect that Japanese Americans would have made numerous preparations for their own death. We suspect, rather, that the social focus of these death-related events enables Japanese Americans to avoid much consideration of the personal implications of human mortality. Planning for one's own demise, however, may evoke thoughts and feelings difficult to handle by avoidance, denial and suppression—so it is far easier to avoid the planning altogether. And talking with someone personally about experiencing death or handling one's affairs falls within the category of inflicting unpleasantness on others—a behavior of the sort the socially sensitive Janapese American tends to avoid.

Seventy percent of the Japanese American sample (B 84%, M 52%, A 65%) had taken out life insurance. Few Japanese Americans had made out a will (B 22%, J 21%, M 12%, A 36%). Fewer still had made funeral arrangements (B 13%, J 11%, M 8%, A 14%) or arrangements to donate their bodies to medicine (B 2%, J 3%, M 1%, A 8%). Those who had done any of this planning were generally elderly (especially elderly males).

SUMMARY

Clearly most of the specific death-related attitudes and behavior of Japanese Americans make sense within the framework of the related themes of social sensitivity and community cohesion. Protection of others, avoidance of disturbing communications, and mutually supportive pursuits are not unique to this ethnic group. But the consistency and intensity of these orientations thrust them to prominence in our interpretive scheme and alert us to the probability that these same orientations find unique expression in other groups, as well.

8

Mexican Americans

Mexican settlers in Southern California date back to the period when the entire area was part of the Mexican nation. Following annexation by the United States and the almost simultaneous discovery of gold, the northern California area received immense numbers of prospectors and settlers, while "in southern California the situation was completely different. There were very few important changes for nearly a generation after the Gold Rush. Mexican *rancheros* owned the land; the Indians/Mexicans did the work; the Anglo settlers were few and unimportant" (Moore, 1970b p. 18). However, when the railroad finally connected Los Angeles directly with the east (1876-1877), the influx of Anglos quickly turned the dominant Mexican group into a small minority of the population. "(This) ended most of what remained of Mexican ownership of the great ranches and transferred the land to the not-too-gentle management of financiers, railroad developers, town planners, cooperative colonizers, and irrigation companies" (Moore, 1970b, p. 19).

Today, a century later, the early Mexican impact upon the Los Angeles area is primarily manifest in street names and Spanish (often pseudo-Spanish) architecture.

The descendants of the original Californians are, for the most part, either well assimilated into the middle- and upper-class communities of Los Angeles—perhaps identifiable by retention of the surname—or else lost to basic ethnic identification altogether through out-marriage. Elsewhere in the country, this has not been the case. In sections of New Mexico and Texas and elsewhere, persons of Mexican ancestry have lived for generations with full awareness of their early origins and strong attachment to both Mexican and United States affiliation.

Mexicans began to move to Los Angeles in the late 1920's; 40 years later, this city had more Mexicans than any other North American community except for Mexico City itself. Although living primarily in the *barrios*, the Mexican Americans have slowly spread, not only enlarging the boundaries of the *barrios* but also beginning small enclaves in various sections of the area and to some extent moving into previously all-Anglo (and occasionally all-Black) neighborhoods.

Throughout this book, we comment casually about *the* Black or *the* Mexican or *the* Anglo or *the* Japanese American. We explicitly recognize differences according to age, sex, generation, religiousness, education, and social class. We say relatively little about differences according to the section of the country in which the individuals have lived or the length of his experience in this nation. Persons of Mexican background living in the sections of Los Angeles where we did our interviewing share values with those living in rural Texas, with those in Albuquerque, and with the migrant worker on the Illinois spinach farms, but they also differ from them in some respects.

Nor are the cogent differences only attributable to geography. One must not confound Mexican, Mexican American, recent Mexican immigrant, *barrio* dweller, and poverty-level Mexican, all living within a twenty-minute drive of each other. This problem, which exists for all ethnic groups, has an extra element of subtlety with the Mexican Americans. We have turned to contemporary Mexican writing as source material for the interpretation of Mexican American orientation toward death without clearly demonstrating the extent to which those living in the United States still represent their country of origin. In this chapter for example, we refer to such writers as Paz, who writes of Mexico, but realize we can only attempt to evaluate the relationship of his work to the Mexican Americans in Los Angeles.

Whether Mexican Americans in Los Angeles or those in the United States as a whole will eventually be sharply different from their Mexican relatives south of the border is presently unpredictable. Several circumstances suggest that they may retain closer ties with their country of origin than have other immigrant groups.

One compelling factor is the Spanish language. Grebler, et al., (1970) found that, of the lower-income Mexican Americans included in their Los Angeles investigation, half had some difficulty with English. Our interviewers partially confirmed this—one-half of these interviews were conducted in Spanish, and 65% were mostly in Spanish. One might infer that those preferring the interview to be conducted in Spanish had difficulty in speaking English; an alternative hypothesis is that people may prefer to discuss emotion-arousing concerns in their native language.

Inability to speak English provides a kind of barrier to the learning of some general (i.e., Anglo) cultural attitudes and behaviors regarding death. It is not that learning Anglo norms would or should lead to their adoption. Nor is the language barrier impermeable. There are ways of learning about Anglos in Spanish, and much learning does occur nonverbally, e.g., by observation. But so much of culture is learned verbally that when language barriers are combined with social distance and segregation in housing and in jobs, fewer death-related aspects of Anglo culture, especially values and attitudes, are likely to be known. Thus, the intrusion of Anglo norms is less likely to be a force leading to diversification of response, particularly since these Mexican American respondents averaged fewer years lived in the United States and more years lived in another country than did the other three ethnic groups we surveyed.

Regardless of the diversity of Mexican Americans in the nation, or even in Los Angeles, those participating in our study showed the greatest *intra-group consistency* in their ideology of death. They displayed relatively few internal differences in ideology when analyzed by age, sex, education, and degree of relative religiousness. They seemed more certain of their own preferences for funeral ritual and mourning restrictions, for example, and they had apparently considered these matters and were both familiar and comfortable with the boundaries of what they felt was acceptable behavior.

DEATH IN THE MEXICAN AND THE MEXICAN AMERICAN CULTURES

Mexico has seen many changes over time in attitudes and ritual devoted to death. From the human sacrifices of the Aztecs to enhance and protect the quality of life in the populace (Vaillant, 1941; Soustelle, 1955) to the business of disposal of remains according to modern Federal law and Department of Public Health order (Habenstein and Lamers, 1960), customs have changed considerably. And when one considers that life expectancy in Mexico has increased from 39 years in 1940 to 67 years in 1968 (World Almanac, 1971, p. 541), it is not surprising to find that expectations concerning death are in flux also. Variations in death-related attitudes and behavior extend geographically as well as temporally. Descriptions of the customs of the people of Oaxaca (Green, 1969), Morelos (Lewis, 1951), a Mexico City slum (Lewis, 1969), Yucatan (Redfield and Villa, 1934), and Sonora (Osuna, 1970) are scattered throughout the literature.

Yet according to one knowledgeable informant, the dead in many small towns today receive the same rituals that were performed a century and more ago. Furthermore, the geographical variability in attitudes and rituals is far from universal; it is not uncommon to find communities at considerable distance from each other using almost identical ceremonies. Many authors have written of the death symbols in traditional Mexican art and life. Paz does so particularly well, here with contrasting examples for effect:

> In a world of facts, death is merely one more fact. But since it is such a disagreeable fact . . . the philosophy of progress . . . pretends to make it disappear, like a magician palming a coin . . .

> Death also lacks meaning for the modern Mexican . . . The word death is not pronounced in New York, in Paris, in London, because it burns the lips. The Mexican, in contrast, is familiar with death, jokes about it, caresses it, sleeps with it, celebrates it; it is one of his favorite toys and his most steadfast love. True, there is perhaps as much fear in his attitude as in that of others, but at least death is not hidden away: he looks at it face to face, with impatience, disdain or irony. "If they are going to kill me tomorrow, let them kill me right away." (1961, pp. 57-58)

Some of the similar thematic sayings told us by Los Angeles Mexican Americans include "Que triste seria la vida si no existeria la muerte" (How sad life would be if there were no death); "Todo se puede evitar menos la muerte" (One can avoid everything but death); and "La muerte no tiene prejucios" (Death has no prejudices). Of course, sayings like these are in no sense restricted to Mexican Americans, but they do succinctly express some of the cultural themes we will discuss in this chapter.

The recognition that we brush elbows with death daily finds expression not only in Mexican art and folksayings, but death may exist alongside Mexican Americans in person. There is some cultural acceptance of the possibility of contact with persons after they have died.

Clark (1959) found that many stories of contact with apparitions or ghosts circulated in a San Jose Mexican American community: "Once my brother-in-law, Trine, was driving to Los Angeles to bring me and my mother back to San Jose. Trine's brother had died a few weeks before that. As he was driving along the road, all of a sudden he heard his brother talking to him from the seat right next to him. He said his brother rode quite a ways with him and talked to him, but he was too scared to turn around and look. He knew his voice, though—it was him all right" (p. 148).

A slight majority of our Mexican American respondents reported that they had "experienced or felt the presence of someone after he had died" (B 55%, J 29%, M 54%, A 38%). Although most having this experience indicated that it occurred in a dream, the event had a reality not normally associated with dreams. This may reflect a less rigid demarcation between living and no-longer-living. Although Trine was frightened, the experience was not necessarily unpleasant, and similarly, over half of the Mexican Americans we interviewed who reported such encounters described them as pleasant or positive. Nor was the experience unique: such encounters are much more common than usually assumed. (See Kalish and Reynolds, 1973, for fuller discussion of this topic and related data.)

Thus on the one hand we find a kind of acceptance of death and its symbols, as a motif in art and in ceremony. On the other hand, the Mexican American's acceptance does not let him escape strong emotions, considerable involvement, and frequent fantasies of personal death and the death of others. We will return to this theme in our later discussion of the data.

But we do not wish to imply that the attitudes of Mexican Americans are indistinguishable from those of Mexicans. Changes that might distress the relatives back in Sonora or Jalisco can often be observed. For example, we made extensive efforts to observe a Los Angeles celebration of the "Days of the Dead," which we naively expected would be a community celebration of All Saints' Day and All Souls' Day that would take place much as the Obon Festival or Memorial Day ceremonies do in the Japanese American community. Simply put, our search was fruitless.

The pomp and ceremony of the Catholic Church found a responsive audience among the Indians in Mexico, aiding the priests in their attempts at conversion. Moore (1970b) has written of Mexico: "Indian customs were incorporated into the Spanish Catholic rites—both on the Day of the Dead and at the normal funeral. Candles, water, flowers, food, and incense are provided for the dead in the villages on the Day of the Dead" (p. 278). We observed some Mexican American individuals and families among the many Catholic families who brought flowers to freshen their loved ones' graves and lit candles at Mass, but these rituals are also part of general American Catholicism.

We visited two Masses on All Souls' Day in the East Los Angeles Catholic cemeteries called Resurrection and New Calvary. The Masses, as were the holidays generally, were "catholic" in both senses of the word. When Mexican Americans participate in these services, it is *as Catholics*, i.e., mixed (as their graves are mixed) among Irish, Italians, and others. The services were in English, although other Catholic programs that involve large numbers of Mexican Americans are given in Spanish. The casual air in which the Mass was conducted comes through clearly in one observer's notes:

> Adults made up almost the entire congregation. The handful of children that were there were pre-school age and younger. They were given a lot of freedom. They were not forced to kneel whenever the adults did; they were allowed to roam at least an arm's length away from whoever brought them (one little boy about three or four years old played a bit by romping around on all fours near

his mother), and they were dressed colorfully. Reds, blues, polka dots, and so forth were worn, but I didn't see any child dressed in black.

The adults were also dressed colorfully. They wore anything from red pantsuits to yellow dresses. Some (not all) of the older people wore darker, more somber colors (blacks, navy blues), but these were always balanced by the more colorfully dressed. Not all of the women used the traditional headpiece. Some people who attended also wore their working uniforms.

The adults also had some freedom at the mass. The older people did not feel that they had to kneel or stand if it was difficult to do so. They were not invalids, for they had been able to walk up the mausoleum steps. Casualness was very much accepted. One woman brought a large paper bag into mass with her. Some carried flowers.

Some adults did not feel obliged to stay in one spot during the mass. Besides the people leaving and arriving during the mass, some roamed around the mausoleum. One woman walked around one particular area looking at the names on the crypts. Several women talked very quietly to each other.

Some people, who hadn't already left before the mass was over, started walking toward the exit at the same time the priests starting marching down the aisle to signify the mass's ending.

(Research notes of J. Masuko)

Following the cemetery service we drove through much of East Los Angeles searching for signs of candy skulls, toy skeletons, or *pan de los muertos* (bread of the dead), traditional symbols of this day in parts of Mexico. We found none. In fact, we were greeted with uncomprehending looks at Mexican American bakeries and candy stores. Only a few persons knew what we were looking for and they could not tell us where these symbols of the homeland could be found.

Whether this change in custom implies some form of acculturation or whether it foreshadows development of views and values neither Anglo American nor Mexican cannot now be predicted.

Some Sampling Biases

Before describing the persons we interviewed, we must reiterate some of our sampling biases. These become apparent when we note that 61% of our respondents were born in Mexico, compared to 13% in Los Angeles, 11% elsewhere in California, and 14% in other Western states. the 1960 census reports only 20% of Spanish-surname persons in California being born in Mexico, and the 1970 census report for Los Angeles County indicated 39% of Spanish-surname persons were born in Mexico.

In addition, almost as many young and middle-aged Mexican American respondents were born in Mexico as elderly respondents, although 1960 census figures showed the foreign-born to be much older than the native-born. What led to these apparent inconsistencies?

We purposely over-sampled the elderly and eliminated anyone under the age of 20. Equally important, we limited our interviewing to neighborhoods with high ethnic density level. Both factors would increase the proportion of respondents with traditional values and the proportion who speak Spanish. Recent immigrants tend to enter through the more ethnically established sections of the city, and Los Angeles has had a recent surge in immigration from Mexico. From the work of Moore (1968), who describes results from a much broader sampling in Los Angeles in 1965-66, it becomes apparent that those Mexican Americans living in the neighborhoods we visited were not a random sample of all Mexican Americans in the county. Our sampling approach guaranteed an over-representation of individuals with low formal education, recent immigrant status, and limited job skills. The same bias is present in our sampling of all ethnic groups and should cause little concern for cross-group comparisons, but does suggest caution in generalizing from these data, especially data reported in percentages, to other communities.

The census data can be explained by additional factors. First, since many immigrants are either not legally in the country or are eager to avoid any unnecessary encounters with government officials, they are likely to avoid any symbol of the federal apparatus, including census takers. A recent *Los Angeles Times* article estimated that 300,000 illegal immigrants were now living in Los Angeles. The Mexican American community registered strong complaints that their numbers had been underestimated by the 1970 census-taking methods. Second, the Spanish-surname persons are not identical with Mexican Americans. In Northern California, substantial proportions of Spanish-surname individuals have their origins in Panama, Guatemala, and other nations, although this is not so much the case for Los Angeles County.

Those foreign-born in our sample had lived in the United States for an average of 21.5 years with a range of from over one to 65 years. Most came from the west coast of Mexico, with fewer from the central states, and only a handful from areas scattered throughout north-central Mexico. Respondents in the total Mexican American sample had lived in California for an average of 25 years.

In addition, our data showed relatively little difference between generations as to whether the interview was administered in English or in Spanish. This, plus our own observations, suggests more comfortable communication between generations and greater ability to transmit tradition from first to third generation. When adequate control for social class and ethnic density is made, the Mexican American younger persons are more likely to be able to speak the language of their country of origin than are comparable Japanese Americans—or, for that matter, Americans of Jewish, Italian, Greek, or most other backgrounds. Undoubtedly also the easy accessibility to the Mexican border makes cross-national visits with relatives more common, aiding in the preserving of customs and language skills.

DEMOGRAPHY

Certainly the reality within which one lives has an effect on one's conception of death. Consider the world in which living and dying take on meaning for those in this Mexican American sample. The lower-middle and lower income Mexican Americans are most prominently concentrated in the East Los Angeles area. In the urban *barrios* there is a familiarity with life—and a familiarity with death.

This is a world of low formal education. Of our four Los Angeles groups in lower- and middle-income areas, the Mexican Americans had significantly less education, with an average of slightly better than six years of completed schooling. This is consistent with the relative lack of education found in Mexican American populations in the Southwest generally (see Grebler, et al., 1970, pp. 142-179), but represents a lower level of education than Moore (1968) reports for Mexican Americans in Los Angeles.

Forty percent of the respondents in our sample were housewives, 25% were working at unskilled jobs, and 34% at skilled jobs. Only two respondents could be called "professionals." Again, this seems to be much the same occupational ratio found among Mexican Americans in the Southwest (Grebler, et al., 1970, pp. 205-228), while being lower than that found among Mexican Americans in Los Angeles (Moore, 1968), as expected from our sampling procedures.

Nearly 90% of our sample considered themselves to be Roman Catholic. It is no wonder that the tombstones of Mexican Americans are, for the most part, engraved with religious symbols and set in Catholic cemeteries. As we shall see, there is a great amount of variation among those labelling themselves "Catholics" when we examine their beliefs about an afterlife, orientations toward priests, and attitudes related to a deity. But, however the Mexican American, even the Protestant Mexican American, has personally chosen to respond to his world, his choice has necessarily taken into account the Roman Catholic Church. The influence of the Church as a reference point in constructing an ideology of death cannot be ignored as we encounter the overall consistency and certainty of response that characterizes our Mexican American group. Moore (1970, p. 85) estimates the percentage of Mexican Americans who are Catholic to be "no less than 95 percent."

In comparing themselves to most members of their faith, 17% of the Mexican American sample felt they were more religious, 50% felt they were as religious, and 32% felt they were less religious than others.

Relatively low divorce rates and high valuing of strong family ties (Moore, 1970; Edmonson, et al., 1957) have been found among Mexican Americans specifically (see Grebler, et al., 1970, pp. 351-353). Our respondents were also from intact households: 73% were married, 10% had never been married, 8% were widowed, and some 10% were separated or divorced. To be sure, there are nonpracticing, nonbelieving, anti-Church Mexican Americans, and there are disorganized and broken homes in the *barrios*, but these are atypical. When death slices into these tightly-knit families there is a special depth to the loss, but, on the other hand, it is within the large, supportive family that the Mexican American is likely to find solace and practical aid in time of grief. We were somewhat surprised to find that the mean age for the oldest person living in the respondents' households was only 52 years, not significantly different from the means for the Black American and Anglo American groups. We were aware of the lack of community facilities designed for care of the aged (we knew of only one such facility at the time, Catholic-sponsored, in East Los Angeles) and of the expressed value and observed concomitant behavior of caring for the old within the family (Madsen, 1969; Clark, 1959). As a result, we expected a relatively high mean age for the oldest person in the household in both the Japanese American (where we did, in fact, find it) and the Mexican American samples. We are not certain whether these findings are due to the lower life expectancy of Mexican Americans, to the recent influx of non-elderly, or to other factors.

In sum, one might briefly describe this sample of low- and middle-income Mexican American adults (mean age of 47) in Los Angeles *barrios* to be family-centered, church-influenced, restricted in terms of education and occupation and strongly tied to both the United States and Mexico by emotional and interpersonal bonds. For a careful statistical description of Los Angeles Mexican Americans, we refer the reader to Grebler, et al., (1970) *The Mexican American People* or Moore's (1970) *Mexican Americans*. Steiner's (1969) *La Raza* provides a more impressionistic and journalistic description.

CONTACT WITH DEATH AND THE DYING

Now, what sorts of experiences with death are to be found in the Los Angeles *barrios?* What is the reality in which the Mexican American ideology of death develops? We can shed some light on this topic from several sources: the respondents' self-reporting of experiences, our interviews with professionals in appropriate fields, reported deaths in the local ethnic press, and statistics from the Los Angeles County Coroner's Office. We will discuss two related issues. First, we will describe the extent to which our respondents have experienced the loss of others through death, although we will discuss the impact of such loss later. Second, we will describe the kinds of communication with the dying that the Mexican Americans see as being appropriate.

According to their own reports, the Mexican American respondents were about average in not having known anyone who had died during the previous two years (B 10%, J 17%, M 19%, A 26%), and slightly less likely than average to have known 8 or more persons who had died (B 25%, J 15%, M 9%, A 8%). Thus, whatever contact with the dying and the dead they have had cannot be attributed simply to having known more such persons.

Nor did examination of other, related items reverse this interpretation. Mexican Americans are *not* more likely to have attended at least one funeral within the two previous years (B 67%, J 84%, M 60, A 55%), nor to have visited a dying person during that time interval (B 38%, J 42%, M 39%, A 32%), nor more likely to have told someone about his imminent death (B 7%, J 6%, M 4%, A 4%). Although these items, for the most part, are not statistically significant, we simply want to make the point that differences between Mexican Americans and other ethnicities in a variety of death-related interactions are negligible.

The deaths of acquaintances were primarily due to natural causes. Ninety-six percent of those who knew someone who had died during the two previous years had lost at least one acquaintance by natural causes as compared with 34% who lost acquaintances by accidents, 10% by war, 5% by suicide, and 4% by homicide. Again, these figures hover near our averages.

The rate of reported suicide is relatively low among Los Angeles Mexican Americans (about 5 per 100,000 persons compared to 12 for Black Americans and Japanese Americans and 20 for Anglo Americans) and the homicide rate of 7 per 100,000 is about the same as the Anglo American rate of 6 and much lower than the Black American rate of 40. When we compared these data from the Los Angeles County Coroner's Office with the above reports of our respondents, we found that all of the groups showed consistency between the rates of homicides and personal knowledge of homicide victims. However, Mexican Americans seemed to know of more suicide cases than their suicide rate would indicate. The reason for this discrepancy may lie in the Catholic Church's teaching that suicide is a mortal sin against the fifth commandment, "Thou shalt not kill." In our sample a few more Mexican Americans than Black Americans and Anglo Americans had known of concealed suicides, perhaps because the Catholic Church normally refused to bury suicides, but, perhaps more importantly, because the disastrous and everlasting consequences of suicides made for ready recollection during the interview. On the other hand, some members of the Mexican American community believe that certain prison deaths reported as suicides were actually homicides.

Our content analysis of *La Opinion*, the major Spanish-language newspaper in Los Angeles, indicates that *La Opinion* carried references to death by *accident* significantly more often than the three other ethnic newspapers. The newspaper also significantly more often reported deaths of young people (particularly in the ten-years-and-under range), of Catholics, of students, and of blue collar workers.

Contact and Communication

One of the recurring themes in this volume is the issue of whether to and how to communicate an awareness of his terminal condition to a dying person. The Mexican Americans are least likely to encourage such communication (B 60%, J 48%, M 37%, A 71%). Similarly, they are least likely to wish to be told themselves, given such circumstances (B 71%, J 77%, M 60%, A 77%). About as many Mexican Americans as others (except for Japanese Americans) actually knew someone who had been dying under conditions where awareness was a matter of concern (B 40%, J 29%, M 45%, A 42%), but fewer of these (i.e., those responding affirmatively) stated that the dying person was actually told (B 63%, J 60%, M 44%, A 69%), which appears consistent with the general feelings concerning awareness of dying.

Why do these Mexican Americans take this position? While it is true that nearly 90% state that the patient will already sense that he is dying, the other groups are in full agreement, so that cannot produce differential responses. Many Mexican Americans feel that knowing of his imminent death makes it harder upon the patient and harder upon others. Later we shall discuss these responses as efforts to protect themselves and others from the inevitable distress of having to confront such an unpleasant reality.

THE FAMILY

Much of the general outline of response concerning death can be understood within three important dimensions of traditional culture: family (especially women), religion, and feelings. It is the woman who holds the family together with bonds of service and affection. And, in a sense, she may be seen as interweaving ties between the family and the Church. These ties are felt on a deep emotional level, the public expression of which is relatively freely permitted.

THE FAMILY PROTECTIVE NETWORK

Within the family there is a protective network for helping the dying, and their survivors, handle the emotional problems associated with death. Of all the groups, Mexican Americans were most likely to state they would not want children under ten years of age to attend their funeral (B 15%, J 31%, M 47%, A 27%). A somewhat smaller number (B 34%, J 22%, M 34%, A 25%) would not want children under ten to visit them if they were dying. Our interviews with Mexican American funeral directors support the interpretation that the family tries to shield children from the tragedy of *personal* contact with emotion-filled death scenes. Young children are seen as not yet ready to handle the impact of tragic feelings and/or to discharge these feelings through appropriate emotional expression. At the same time, several informants have been mystified by these findings. Their experience has been that young children are frequently in attendance at funerals and are basically not kept back from the dying.

Perhaps we can distinguish here between the tactics for handling emotion used by Mexican and Black Americans on the one hand and Japanese and Anglo Americans on the other. The former seem to try to discharge feelings through their active expression, and the latter seem to attempt to dampen the feelings with composed control. Our interviews with coroners, funeral directors, and hospital chaplains confirm our own observations regarding expressions of grief in these communities. The social consequences of the latter tactic may be burdensome. Of course, individual members of these subcultures do not elect an either-or position regarding these tactics but exhibit each in degree.

This protective (perhaps *empathic* is a more appropriate term) motivation may underlie the relatively frequent response of these Mexican Americans that dying persons should not be told they are dying (B 29%, J 39%, M 58%, A 22%) because it's harder on them and on those telling them. Relatively few (B 51%, J 47%, M 19%, A 52%) felt they could tell someone he was about to die. Protectiveness may also underlie the relatively high proportion of Mexican American respondents who stated their desire to die in a hospital (B 21%, J 16%, M 34%, A 14%) in contrast to dying at home (B 44%, J 72%, M 54%, A 61%). Here again, some informants found these data difficult to accept at face value. Perhaps a more practical explanation will suffice. Since, of these four ethnic groups, the Mexican American has the lowest educational and job skills level, we assume he also has the lowest income level. He may, therefore, feel that he is better off in a public hospital, where he can receive medical (although not always personal) care, than at home, where his presence might make major demands upon his family and upon available space. In any event, only one-third of these Mexican

Americans did state a preference for dying in a hospital, while over half wished to be at home.

Of course, dying in a hospital need not mean dying in isolation away from one's family. Our informal observations and interviews with professionals indicate that Mexican American families commonly arrange for shifts of visitors to spend time with hospitalized family members and, when not actively opposed by the hospital staff, even "camp in" for long periods at the bedside of the seriously ill or dying person.

It may be true that "the elderly Mexican American (in Texas) accepts death as a valued experience, a thing of beauty, and an entrance into another world that is real. For him death is an inevitable event that takes place in the presence of his entire family" (Madsen, 1961, p. 233), but the older people in this study are no more likely to wish to die at home than are the young.

Of all groups, the Mexican Americans were most likely to respond that if they were dying they would encourage their families to spend time with them even if this caused some inconvenience for the family members (B 32%, J 36%, M 56%, A 44%). Yet more than the other ethnic groups, the Mexican Americans consider *very important* reasons for not wanting to die to include no longer being able to care for dependents (B 26%, J 42%, M 37%, A 44%), and causing grief to relatives and friends (B 19%, J 14%, M 38%, A 29%). More eager to spend their last hours with their close friends and relatives, the Mexican Americans also express more concern about the meaning their loss would have to others. They want the warmth and affection of others, but not at the price of becoming a burden.

The Family Supportive Network

Joan Moore (1971, p. 277) writes, "Uniformly, one meets the flat assertion that the funeral is the most significant family ceremony among Mexican Americans . . . Family members from remote points make a special effort to come together for a funeral, particularly that of an old person." This gathering of friends and, especially, relatives seemed to be what a significant number of these Mexican American respondents had in mind when they stated they would rather have a large funeral with many people attending than one with only relatives and close acquaintances (B 21%, J 9%, M 33%, A 8%). Although these statistics show relatively more Mexican Americans select the large funeral, on an absolute basis more persons of all ethnic groups prefer the more intimate funeral size. In this sense, perhaps, the primacy of the nuclear family is being asserted.

The Mexican Americans were most likely of the four subcultural groups to desire their remains to be disposed of in Los Angeles (B 54%, J 60%, M 67%, A 51%) or outside the United States (B 1%, J 11%, M 20%, A 3%). Here, too, decisions related to burial are made with the larger family in mind. Family members have responsibilities to one another that are not severed even by death. (See also Osuna and Reynolds, 1970, pp. 259-262).

Respect for the dead is expressed publicly in various ways. Along with the Japanese subcultural group, the Mexican Americans relatively frequently visited graves, and the wearing of mourning black extended over the longest period for this group. (Interesting to note, as the level of formal education increased there was a significant trend to shorten the period during which black was expected to be worn, and one Mexican American funeral director said that black armbands were rarely worn except for the days of the wake and funeral.) Fairly strict proscriptions surround the public mention of anything negative about the deceased. People have much to say about the positive, often ideal qualities of the dead person (particularly this is said of older women). Such opportunities to remark on valued traits may be utilized as an important socializing reinforcer for the culture. On the other hand, one social worker remarked that the custom prohibiting speaking ill of the deceased inhibits opportunities to express dissatisfaction and aggression with consequent emotional ill effects from such "bottling-up." The half humorous recounting of faults and foibles permitted at Japanese American funerals is not acceptable within the Mexican American emphasis on the tragedy of the loss. Humor is one resource that provides the Japanese Americans with some emotional distance from an event so that the all-important composure can be maintained. Such composure, for the Mexican American, would be interpreted as cold and unfeeling, hence devalued and to be avoided.

Although between 50% and 54% of each group would turn to a relative for comfort should their spouse die, it is particularly the Japanese Americans and Mexican Americans who turn to the family at such a time for assistance with practical problems such as preparing meals, babysitting, shopping, and cleaning house (B 50%, J 74%, M 65%, A 45%). Among Mexican Americans, next-of-kin and very close relatives of the deceased may be expected to devote themselves to the grieving. Practical activities, with their demands on the survivors' energy and intellect (and their value as distractions and anchors to the world of everyday reality) are likely to be handled by relatives outside of the immediate family. As might be expected, there is a significant difference between sexes, with Mexican American women more likely to turn to relatives for practical assistance in time of grief (F 75%, M 53%) and males more likely than females to depend upon no one (F 13%, M 29%). This difference is in keeping with our understanding of the familial consolidating function of the Mexican American woman. Based upon the 1965-66 probability sample, Moore (1971) points out that nearly half of the Mexican Americans interviewed would seek advice or help from a family member for a personal matter, but the percentage drops, especially for men, when the concern is political or involves city government.

The two subcultures we have described as most familistic, the Mexican Americans and the Japanese Americans, also appear to be the most conservative in terms of the duration for mourning. We asked how long after loss of spouse before "you personally consider it all right for a _____ to" remarry, stop wearing black, return to employment, and begin dating. The blank was filled with the age group, ethnic group, and sex of the respondent. Although specific answers varied, the Japanese Americans and Mexican Americans were consistently more likely to opt for the longer formal mourning period and least likely to feel that waiting was unimportant. The Mexican Americans were also likely to wait a longer period of time before worrying that crying and other forms of grieving had been going on for too long.

The question about remarriage indicated an interesting sidelight. About 10% of the entire sample, primarily but not completely elderly, felt that remarriage was *never* appropriate for someone like themselves (B 5%, J 21%, M 13%, A 1%). Perhaps this is not simply the reflection of cultural expectations. One wonders if the personal investment in a deceased spouse does not require a longer period of disengagement and redirection in familistic cultures than in individualistic ones.

There is also a general tendency to handle problems within the framework of available within-community resources, particularly the family. Writing about a rural poverty area in Texas, Madsen (1969) states, "The Chicano is raised in the belief that a family should be a self-sufficient unit in an unstable world. The family should provide for all its members and be the source of assistance in time of trouble. The individual's dependency on the family is instilled in the child from his earliest years," (p. 224).

Consistent with Madsen's assertions is the low utilization of available public health (including mental health) facilities by Mexican Americans. Perhaps this low utilization is produced by an unwillingness to seek help from strangers, as Madsen contends. More probable, however, is the lack of bilingual staff (physicians, nurses, aides, clerks), transportation problems, awkward scheduling requirements, and history of dealing with health care givers who understand little or nothing of their cultures and needs. In at least one instance, a mental health clinic staffed by bilingual personnel had a very high rate of community utilization, with a large proportion of the cases being self-referrals. This is simply another reminder that we need to consider both psychosocial factors and practical/economic factors in judging matters such as the utilization of health services.

Kiefer in a paper presented at Southwest Anthropological Association Meetings (1972) notes that Mexican Americans in California have had geographic accessibility to extended kin residing in Mexico so that immigration to the United States does not involve the isolation from relatives that forced Japanese Americans to form non-kin cooperatives based on prefectural origin or occupation. Not only Japanese Americans, but fairly large percentages of Anglo and Black Americans have migrated away from the locations of large kin networks, so our Southern California Mexican Americans may have kin resources unavailable to the other groups. We suspect, however, that at least as important as geographic propinquity, is the *value* placed on kin ties as resources. Our depth interviews with Mexican Americans indicate instances of relatives flying, bussing, and driving in from all over the United States for a funeral—it is not only those nearby who attend.

Throughout our work with the Mexican Americans, we have been impressed by the importance of the family—not in the sense that the family is important among Japanese and Japanese Americans, i.e., as the locus of control, of shame and pride, and of self-identity, but rather as the locus of emotional support, of control through warmth, and of shared activity. Since the family is important, the death of a family member is important, requiring attendance at the funeral, due respect through mourning, and fulfillment of reciprocal family obligations via helping the survivors. Mexican Americans appear to have maintained the kinds of family relationships that permit calling upon others for emotional and personal support, while at the same time having the sensitivity to protect people from openly acknowledging the personal encounter with their own death or with that of close relatives.

Whether this is psychological denial occurring in a culture marked by social and ritualistic acceptance is an intriguing point. We shall discuss this at greater length later.

RELIGION

It is difficult to overestimate the effect of the Catholic Church on the ideological constructs of most Mexican Americans, whether male or female, young or old, members of Protestant or Catholic congregations. The precepts of the Church have filtered down (with some distortion in the process) to influence markedly the taken-for-granted understandings of daily life.

The symbols of the Church inevitably are likely to be in evidence at the time of death. Mexican American respondents reported significantly more often than others that they would call for a priest or minister on their death bed (B 65%, J 51%, M 88%, A 53%), and, as one might expect, this was increasingly the case with increasing religiousness.

Last rites, now called "the annointing of the sick" or "sacrament for the sick" to broader the meaning of the term, are a special kind of institutionalized comfort ritual. They may be dreaded as the symbol to the dying patient that all hope is gone. They may be delayed as long as possible by the family so that they will not appear to have given up hope too soon. Notes are usually entered in a patient's hospital records whenever the priest visits so that the bereaved family can draw some comfort in the knowledge that their loved one was ritually prepared for death. These rites can be administered any number of times. It may be difficult, in fact, for the dying person of Mexican descent to *avoid* this ritual if his family is devout. We refer the reader to an insightful novel by Fuentes (1964) for the description of the struggles of Artemio Cruz to die free of the Church. Although the author and the setting are Mexican, we feel that implications for Mexican Americans are still abundant.

Religion is tightly interwoven with the other threads that we are considering within the tapestry of the Mexican American subculture: family, feelings, and women. The close connection between religion and family is readily available in the literature, e.g., "The family is sanctioned by religious symbols and by the injunctions of the priest" (Vogt and Albert, 1966, p. 261; see also Madsen, 1964, p. 17). The tie between faith and family is reflected in the interview responses of our Mexican Americans, as well. We found that with increased religiousness came the increasing importance of avoiding death so as not to cause grief to family and friends. And, although they would first turn to their family for comfort if their spouse died, the Mexican Americans' second resource is God and the priesthood (first two choices combined: B 49%, J 29%, M 58%, A 44%). Our finding that more religious persons in our sample desired larger funerals may be related to the desire for more elaborate ritual but, more likely, it represents the desire to have the extended family and friends (perhaps parish-related acquaintances) participate in the event.

Given the generally accepted close relationship between women and the Church in Mexican and Mexican American cultures, we expected more clearcut differentiation between the sexes on items such as self ratings of religiousness or beliefs in an afterlife. But, aside from the extremely high tendency of women to report they would call for a priest when dying (F 95%, M 80%), there were no such significant differences. There was a significant positive relationship between degree of religiousness and considering the death of a woman more tragic than that of a man, again underscoring the close relationship between religion, the family, and women.

Bellah (in Vogt and Albert, 1966, p. 239) writes: "The religious world of the Spanish-Americans is highly dramatic . . . it provides rich opportunities for the expression of feelings." In no way does the faith of the Mexican American Catholic serve to suppress the outpouring of feelings at time of grief. Rather, it validates the assembling of loved ones so that emotions can be publicly and freely expressed and it thus permits the social support system of the extended family to be fully operative.

To be sure, religious belief provides comfort and prescriptions for thought and action during the unsettled period following a loss. But it places no special pressures to take a non-grieving public posture serene in the knowledge that one's loved one is in a better place and all will be reunited again one day. Among fundamentalist Protestants, including Mexican American Protestants, it is clear that too much expression of grief reflects a lack of one's faith and is therefore to be avoided (provided the deceased was a "believer").

The contrasts between Mexican American Catholics and Protestants are, we feel, useful ones to elaborate, despite the relatively small numbers of the latter. The contrasts point up some of the taken-for-granted conceptualizations of most Mexican Americans. One Protestant minister puts his feelings this way:

> Death is a door opening to God's home . . . We really believe this, so death for us is easier to take . . . Of course, we grieve, we're only human but we grieve according to whether that person who died was a believer of God . . . If you have hope that you'll see that person again someplace, sometime, you won't feel as bad . . . We don't despair like others . . .

Awareness of the need for grieving is fairly consistently accompanied by a skepticism of the genuineness of extreme expressions of grief. But when extreme expression is the norm within one's subcultural group, the fundamentalist believer is in something of a double bind.

The minister continues:

> People often cry all night because they've been drinking all night! Their sorrow is not sincere. The expression of grief depends on how emotional people are . . . That is something very hard to judge . . . Someone who doesn't show any emotions appears or is judged as someone who doesn't care . . . I personally don't need to show others how I feel about my mother's death . . .

When our Catholic Research Assistant attended a Protestant velorio (wake) service, four differences between this one and those Catholic wakes she had attended immediately stood out. The first was the lack of publicly displayed crucifixes and religious figures. The second was the silence:

> I didn't hear anyone crying at all, not even softly. The mortuary was quiet in spite of all the people.

Third was the large number of floral wreaths. And the fourth was the substantial number of men in attendance. Our impressions of Mexican American Protestants are based upon a limited sample, but we did find considerable consistency within this sample.

Another aspect of faith involves the extent of fatalism. Madsen (1964), for one, considers its roots to lie in the religious orientation of Mexican Americans. "Do what one will, everything is as God wishes" (p. 16). More recent social philosophers may see its perpetuation caused by the social, political, and economic powerlessness of the Mexican American people, although recent sociopolitical movements suggest that younger Mexican Americans are increasingly seeing the way out of poverty as being through their own actions.

It is no longer considered appropriate to speak of "fatalism" in Mexican American culture, for the term has been used to justify, perpetuate, and mask inequalities of opportunity in education, housing, and employment. Yet in some areas acceptance of the inevitable is the most realistic and healthy of attitudes. When all efforts have failed to save a young child's life or when a father of four dies in an auto accident, then all the sophisticated technological control over our world is of no use in erasing death's message of man's ultimate helplessness and mortality. It is in such circumstances that his world view provides the Mexican American with appropriate expression and meaning to his grief. And it is by experiencing and bearing grief that one becomes a mature man or woman.

To deny the appearance of a type of fatalism in our data would be to misrepresent what exists—or, at the very least, what the authors see as existing—whatever the political implications of such a position may be. However, we would like to suggest an alternate approach to this phenomenon. Consider the statement: "The secret of happiness is not expecting too much out of life and being content with what comes your way" (Grebler, et al., 1970, p. 436). Usually this is interpreted as denoting passivity on a passive-active dimension. We would offer another dimension: changing the self versus changing the environment. In that sense, the previous statement connotes that the speaker is making the change within himself. The low-income Mexican American often has no apparent alternative to doing this. His control of the external environment is minimal, so adaptation or adjustment of self is a realistic option, perhaps the only viable road to survival.

In the area that concerns us most, that of one's own death or the death of a loved one, adjustment within oneself may be optimum. Ross (1969) refers to acceptance as being the final state of a successful sequence of understandings that precede death. Denial, avoidance, random or frantic activity, anger, these are all common responses to death, but are usually felt to be necessary preludes to the eventual culmination in acceptance. Perhaps the Mexican American's ability to accept the locus of control being outside of his own hands may serve him well as a mourner. He can express his sense of loss honestly without being burdened by feeling that he has left some task undone that might have altered the course of events.

Consistent with this speculation is the fact that a sizeable proportion of Mexican Americans felt that people cannot hasten or slow their own death through a will-to-live or will-to-die (B 12%, J 15%, M 38%, A 15%). Similarly more Mexican Americans opposed the notion that people should be allowed to die if they wish (B 47%, J 51%, M 69%, A 39%), and more believe that "Accidental deaths show the hand of God working among men" (B 63%, J 63%, M 71%, A 56%). Such responses make sense when we see the broader ideological context according to which life is held in God's hands. Life remains something mysteriously given and mysteriously withdrawn. How can man presume to take upon himself what is a divine prerogative? Interestingly, a number of Mexican Americans remarked that a suicidal person is one who does not fear God. It is a *sin* to kill oneself, not only according to official Church dogma, but in the folkview of these respondents, as well.

FEELINGS

Everyone undoubtedly has feelings about death, his own death and dying, the loss of others through death, and the general and abstract concept of death. No one would realistically claim that the Mexican Americans, or any other group, have *more* feelings or *more intense* feelings. However, we can describe what those interviewed *say* about their expression of feelings and what we have observed of this expression of feelings. In these regards, our community survey data are confirmed by our more subjective observations, i.e., that the expression of feelings by Mexican Americans about their own death and dying are more intense and that their expression of feelings of loss through the death of others is more intense.

Before discussing relevant findings, we wish to pursue the previous issue a little further. The James-Lange theory of emotions postulated essentially that behavior preceded feelings, i.e., the individual ran away from a menacing opponent and this action (or, perhaps, the entire setting) elicited feelings of fear. More recently, Festinger's cognitive dissonance model has suggested that feelings and attitudes often become consistent with each other so that persons behaving contrary to their "true" attitudes frequently end up altering their attitudes. Thus people who feel socially obligated to express grief might well come to feel that such grief was actually felt. We previously stated that our data can be considered only descriptive of expressed emotion—we do not wish to exclude the possibility that differences in expressed emotion do underlie differences in felt emotion.

Taking our data at face value, however, Mexican Americans are slightly more willing to admit fear of dying than the other groups (B 19%, J 31%, M 33%, A 22%). However, they are *not* conversely less likely to claim to be unafraid, as logic might dictate. Rather, the differences occur in the neutral category, with fewer Mexican Americans responding with this neither/nor position.

Some other differences are not substantial, but a pattern does seem to appear. Thus, Mexican Americans also dwell more than most others upon their own dying, doing so at least weekly (B 34%, J 10%, M 37%, A 25%) and claiming less often that they never think of their own death (B 14%, J 33%, M 10%, A 22%). Earlier we noted their greater willingness to accept the inevitable in a variety of situations. This does not occur in regard to their peaceful acceptance of their own death (B 59%, J 66%, M 65%, A 63%), where they responded very much as do the other groups.

We find feelings concerning death more pervasive in other ways, as well. On five questions involving actual death encounters, dreams about death, and unexplainable feelings about dying, the Mexican Americans were most likely to have experienced three of them and came within one or two percent of the others. Thus, Mexican Americans tend to report (a) more frequent unexplainable feelings that they were about to die (B 15%, J 12%, M 34%, A 15%); (b) more such feelings about others (B 37%, J 17%, M 38%, A 30%); (c) second highest frequency of dreams about their own death (B 22%, J 20%, M 36%, A 38%); (d) second highest frequency of mystical encounters with the already-dead (B 55%, J 29%, M 54%, A 38%); and (e) more experiences in which they felt close to dying themselves (B 48%, J 31%, M 49%, A 37%). Although differences between Mexican and Black Americans are virtually nil, a pattern does emerge.

These responses appear to verify the common assumptions that Mexican Americans find death and dying more pervasive and more likely to enter into their day-to-day living. This occurs even though their actual behavior does not bring them into contact with the dead or the dying more often than the other groups (except for the Anglos). As stated earlier, these Mexican Americans are no more likely than Black Americans and Japanese Americans to have known someone who had died recently, to have attended a funeral, or to have visited a dying person. We are not asserting that Mexican Americans avoid participation in these acts, but that their greater preoccupation with death and dying does not arise from more frequent contact with the dead or dying.

Preoccupation with death can be interpreted as counter-phobic (indeed, the recent emphasis on the study of death may itself be counter-phobic), and we do not exclude the possibility that this view has validity. Another alternative strikes us as making at least as much—probably more—sense. Many people believe that, in order to live fully, death must be faced effectively, that becoming involved with death and bringing it into your life actually is liberating of the self. Prior to an honest facing of one's own death, we tend to have feelings of omniscience and to plan as though the results of our planning would be permanent. Facing death drives home the truly finite role of man: nothing is forever, this too shall pass. Having recognized that life shall not stretch into an infinite future, people can more effectively deal with the concerns of the day. To do so requires some acceptance of the inevitable and acceptance of one's finite being.

Thus, the striving, middle-class Anglo and his European counterparts (and counterparts everywhere) who seek to accumulate and increase their possessions and their virtues, finds that the annihilation of the self that attends their death becomes overwhelmingly painful. Put simply, you can't take it with you. The Mexican and the Mexican American surround themselves with reminders of death, which is everyone's fate, and are therefore much less pressed to seek and strive, but prefer to live their day. Becker (1974) insists that the terror of death is inevitable, and that customs and rituals attempt to diminish this terror. The Anglo population, according to Becker, has lost its myths and heroes and makes self-conscious attempts to reduce death anxieties, all of which are bound to fail.

Perhaps the tendencies we found among Mexican Americans are merely an accommodation to poverty and to feelings that the poverty is insurmountable, but we prefer the suggestion by Dr. Margaret Clark (personal communication) that these views represent not only an adjustment to the present poverty, but also to the permanent reality of ever-present and inevitable death. She explains the acceptance of death by the Mexican Americans as also being encouraged by their feelings that the interrelationship between the supernatural and nature is very close; the individual spirit lives on after the death of the body, so that more continuity between life and death can be found. This resembles the other familistic group in our study, the Japanese Americans.

Not only are strong feelings concerning death and dying more pervasive among Mexican Americans, but emotional responses to the death of others are also of greater moment. We previously mentioned that the two familistic cultures studied, the Japanese Americans and the Mexican Americans, were most likely to adhere to longer mourning periods. If these two groups resemble each other in this regard, they are miles apart on the kinds of emotional expression considered appropriate for mourning.

To speculate again, we believe that a familistic orientation is also a kind of effort to achieve immortality by investing oneself in family members (and by procreating others) who will live on and replenish the inroads that death makes in the family organism, extending far into the future. Thus the very existence of the familistic orientation means that the family is likely to offer immortality, over and above whatever formal religious structure offers. Whether this should enhance or diminish acceptance of earthly death cannot be readily foretold, however. The Mexican Americans are not only most capable of expressing their grief overtly, but they are less anxious about physical contact with the dead body.

Our data show the following: more Mexican Americans report that they would worry if they could not cry at the death of a spouse (B 42%, M 59%, J 42%, A 42%), would try to control their grief in public (B 21%, J 17%, M 36%, A 26%), would be more likely to cry themselves out (B 64%, J 71%, M 88%, A 70%), and would be substantially more likely to touch (B 51%, J 31%, M 76%, A 51%) or to kiss (B 13%, J 12%, M 59%, A 33%) the body at the funeral service.

Two factors run counter to this general trend in our data, however. We found that with increasing education came an increasing tendency to respond "yes" to the question "Would you try very hard to control the way you showed your emotions in public?" We would interpret this trend as a response to dominant cultural norms. Moreover, 94% of the middle-aged males (40-59 years old) in our sample responded they would try to control the public expression of their feelings under these circumstances. Although those Mexican Americans we asked uniformly agreed that one does not lose his reputation for being masculine by crying over the loss of a loved one, nevertheless these middle-aged males felt some curbs on the freedom with which they could show their inner state.

On balance, the Mexican American respondents indicate the same amount of objective encounters with death and dying but more pervasive subjective encounters; they admit to more fear and greater overt expression of grief. All of these factors are exhibited in their funerals.

FUNERALS

Funerals bring family members together in a religious and personal ritual deeply involved with feelings. Except for (a) being more likely to desire a funeral with many friends and acquaintances, (b) wanting a wake, and (c) preferring the wake and (d) the funeral service to be held at the funeral home rather than the church or family home, the responses of Mexican Americans on questions concerning funerals were not conspicuously different from the other ethnic groups. This only points up the limitations of community surveys, because the authors and their informants would agree that funerals in the Mexican American community differ substantially from those in the Black, Japanese, or Anglo American communities.

Perhaps we can best illustrate this by describing two occurrences in which the Mexican American and Anglo American cultures produced near clashes due to lack of mutual understanding regarding the meaning of funerals.

The first of these was at the gravesite of Reuben Salazar, the Mexican American journalist who was killed by police action while sitting at a bar. At the conclusion of the highly emotional and well attended burial service, an official of the cemetery asked the crowd to leave. No one moved. He became indignant and threatened to call the police. After another long pause, the mourners began slowly to disperse.

The second event was the funeral of a Mexican American who was well known and highly esteemed in the San Diego area for his work in helping farm workers' children enter college. He was killed in an automobile accident. At the churchyard, the mourners who had followed the procession from the church remained after the priest said prayers at the graveside and left. The cemetery caretaker, not himself Mexican American, forbade them from staying while the coffin was lowered into the ground, a rule at the cemetery. A few left, but the majority remained. Then a mourner brought out his guitar and began to play a piece that the dead man had particularly liked; others also played the guitar and sang, with the mourners at times joining in as a group, many of them through streams of tears. Finally, the Anglo caretaker returned and said, "You people have to leave—if you don't, I'll call the police!!" The mourners became angry and refused to leave until *they* felt ready.

Both cemetery officials were behaving as they normally did, adhering to rules and regulations with which they were familiar. Their experience had undoubtedly shown them that mourning behavior was fairly controllable and that funeral and cemetery services could end at the time the formal ritual was over, although in both instances the cemeteries were frequently used by Mexican Americans, and the officials should have been sensitive to their cultural traditions. They were responding to behavior boundaries of time and space, and the authors are in accord with the general principle that, for society to function, certain mutually acceptable limits need to be placed upon emotional expression. However, the importance of funerals in general for Mexican Americans, and of these two in particular, led to different kinds of behavior than the cemetery directors had encountered, and the authors feel that much greater leeway in permissible funeral behavior must be accepted.

During such periods, the stifling of the natural outpouring of feeling seems unduly cold and cruel to the Mexican American. It takes time to properly appreciate and express one's feelings of respect and loss. One should not be hurried in the emotions being expressed during these moments. It would seem that the services provided by a cemetery should be in accord with the traditions and values of those receiving the services, not those providing them. And one ought not feel required to isolate himself from others when grieving. The sharing of grief is a force which can bind loved ones close together. (This, of course, is in contrast to the Japanese American orientation which tends to emphasize the disruptive negative aspects of such feelings with the result that they are to be controlled and expressed privately or only with one's closest kin and friends.)

Lest our comments be taken as an unfair attack upon rules and regulations established at cemeteries, we feel obligated to provide some explanation. Most funeral directors have to cope with mourners who have climbed into the coffin or jumped or fainted into the grave opening. The moment of lowering the casket into the grave is often especially upsetting.

Reynolds (1970) in his analysis of a Mexican funeral held in rural Mexico wrote:

> Interactions within any group are structured by their shared expectations and limitations on behavior. The Mexican people have been described as a communal, group-oriented people with relative congruence and conformity in attitudes and behavior within the family group (Romano, 1968). Although it does seem to be the case that this funeral ceremony drew participation and cooperation from a large social group, it also provided for a great deal of independent, individualistic activity that ought not be overlooked. A group pays the price of a certain amount of disorganization and unpredictability when it permits individualistic variation. It is to the valued independence in human interaction and its consequences for these Mexican people that we turn briefly now.
>
> One of the striking features of this funeral complex was its informality. There were few rules that were formalized and rigid. When decisions regarding the funeral details were to be made, there was neither a formalized set of persons to make them nor a regular means for arriving at them (with the exception of the binding wishes of the deceased). Instead, general discussion by those present, those interested, and those affected was necessary to arrive at some group consensus. Similarly, the timing of the beginning and ending of the ceremonies was generally unformalized. That is, the rosary was not set for a specific time but rather began when it seemed that enough people had congregated. In the same way, the graveside ceremony had neither formal beginning nor formal ending—the priest having arrived and gone before most of the procession reached the cemetery and people arriving and leaving at various times (though many waited to leave until some members of the immediate family had gone). The point I wish to emphasize is that the ceremonial events were not time-scheduled nor were there, in general, specific events that formally marked the beginning and end of the ceremonies so that a participant could say at a point in time, "Now the ceremony has begun; now it has ended." Nor could all the people turn away simultaneously with the sense that a particular ceremonial element was finished. Rather, arriving and leaving was timed within broad limits according to the convenience of the individuals and subgroups of participants.
>
> In this light it is interesting to note that there was no fixed procession route from the cathedral to the cemetery. And, in fact,

cars were scattered along several routes, some taking short cuts and arriving before the family.

One of our most helpful informants was Mrs. R., the funeral director of the first Mexican American mortuary in Los Angeles, founded in East Los Angeles over 50 years ago and still operating. Mrs. R. made five major points regarding the funeral behavior of Mexican Americans, and we have integrated these with our community survey findings.

First, the Mexican Americans, especially the women, are very emotional, so that sometimes it is necessary to call a physician and to use tranquilizers. More Mexican Americans expected tranquilizers to be used at their wake or funeral than any other group (B 38%, J 16%, M 50%, A 41%).

Second, Mrs. R. stated that "when death comes, all come," even if they had only met the deceased once or twice. This is particularly true of low-income persons. Family and friends are likely to help pay for funeral and other expenses (compare this custom with the difficulties of meeting basic funeral expenses under conditions of extreme poverty in Mexico City, described by Lewis, 1969). Just 30% of the Mexican Americans expected friends and relatives to make such contributions, indicating that they do not differ particularly in this regard from the other groups (B 27%, J 43%, M 30%, A 27%).

Third, people show sympathy by attending the evening wakes. More Mexican Americans wished to have a wake than members of other groups (B 25%, J 41%, M 68%, A 22%), and of these, more wanted the wake at the funeral home than at the church or family home. Generally, funeral services (i.e., funeral masses) *per se* are held in the mornings, so most people with jobs cannot attend. The Japanese Americans made adjustment for working persons by scheduling public funerals the evening before the private graveside service.

Fourth, Mrs. R. mentioned that about 10% of her clients were elderly persons with "pre-need" trust accounts. Although our own data are not actually comparable, we did find that few Mexican Americans made funeral arrangements in advance (B 13%, J 11%, M 8%, A 14%). This appeared to be part of a pattern, however, since the Mexican Americans were also less likely to have taken out life insurance (B 84%, J 70%, M 52%, A 65%), less likely to have a will (B 22%, J 21%, M 12%, A 36%), and less likely to be paying for a cemetery plot (B 22%, J 26%, M 12%, A 25%).

We assume that all these figures can be explained by economic and educational differences among the groups studied. That they were no less likely than some of the other subcultures to have discussed their eventual death (B 27%, J 16%, M 33%, A 37%) or to arrange for someone to handle their affairs (B 24%, J 17%, M 25%,

A 42%) suggest that death-related money matters did not receive prior planning, although death-related social considerations did receive such planning.

Fifth, whether Protestant or Catholic, Mexican Americans rarely desire cremation. Our findings agreed. Of the four ethnic groups, the Mexican Americans were most likely to desire burial (B 84%, J 33%, M 89%, A 66%), shared with the Black Americans the lowest acceptance of cremation, and shared with the Black and Japanese Americans the lowest acceptance of donating their bodies.

Burial often occurs in the cemetery where other family members are interred although use of a family plot is not usual. From various sources, we received unusually consistent views of funerals and wakes in the Los Angeles Mexican American community. Coroner's office investigators, hospital chaplains, priests, and funeral directors see the grieving process at different stages in time, but all report the coming together of large numbers of supportive people, family and friends, and the outpouring of emotions with little constraint.

If descriptions of behavior are consistent, interpretations of the same behavior are not. Thus, one funeral director states, "Latins are more emotional. Their family ties are stronger—at least than Anglos. Anglos are more reserved. Our people stay here at the mortuary sometimes until late at night, after the rosary. Anglos don't—they usually go home right away, after the rosary. Also, Mexican people like to see the body one last time, so the morning of the funeral they come to the mortuary first before going to church. Anglos don't do this."

And a Catholic priest, of Spanish descent, says, "Latins feel more deeply with more sincerity than Anglos. They manifest their feelings openly." Both the funeral director and the priest mention that the Mexican Americans visit the body, while Anglo Americans do not. They also both refer to the custom of throwing a handful of dirt on the casket after it has been lowered into the grave. "Protestants place a flower on the casket, but Latins—they don't mind getting their hands dirty—they just grab some dirt."

A Protestant working in a funeral home, however, makes the same point in a different fashion. "Catholics leave the mortuary messy—cigarettes, ashes, and they stand around telling jokes. Sometimes they drink. With Protestants, we don't have these problems. Another difference—the priest usually charges $20 or $30 or even $35 for the service, but the Protestant minister does it for nothing."

And another Protestant: "Latin people never talk about details. They just say they want Papa removed. They're usually too upset to talk anyway. Anglos go into detail on what they want done. They talk of embalming, like they would say 'I don't want so-and-so embalmed.' They're more restrained. We don't have much weeping when we remove the body, but the rosary is when all hell breaks loose. You should hear them in the chapel. I would say that was the peak of emotions. The other night a guy threw himself into the casket and threatened to kill me. Yes, the rosary is the worst time. The people are really hard to manage and you don't want to provoke an argument. The morning after the rosary, I dump the casket into the limo and go pick up the family and drive them to the church. If they are Latins, they only weep, but Anglos talk a lot more. You never know if you're going to pick up a bunch of drunks or jokers or if they're going to be haggling over who's going to get the insurance. Latins do weep more, I guess. They feel everything deeper. They're not pretentious. Anglos are more cynical."

Another mortician describes the drinking at funerals as mostly by the young, who—he felt—had a guilty conscience and did not want to face their own deaths. "The best thing for people like that is to go up to the coffin and touch the body. To reach out and touch it. Then they'll know that it doesn't move and can't hurt them."

These comments are representative of others we heard, but we wish to repeat the caution that these are impressionistic comments by individuals who have had most of their experience as a death-related professional in the same limited geographical area. The image we came away with is that Mexican Americans tackle death and dying head on, while Anglo Americans try delicately to keep it at arm's length. The graphic representation of our image is the Mexican American grabbing a handful of dirt, while the Anglo is handed a flower. Whether the respondent is Catholic or Protestant, Mexican American or Anglo American, favorably disposed toward Mexican American habits or critical, he will acknowledge the greater depth of expressed feeling exhibited by the Mexican Americans and he may assume this to represent a greater degree of actual feeling and sincerity.

FINAL COMMENTS

Death is very much a family event for the Mexican American. A death may pull together geographically separated family members both physically and psychologically as no other event can. Notice how clearly this social dimension is reflected in the responses of the Mexican Americans. Significantly more often than the others, Mexican Americans said that: (1) if they had six months to live they would focus their concern on others and be with loved ones, (2) they would encourage their family to visit even if it was somewhat inconvenient for family members, (3) they would want funerals with lots of friends and acquaintances, (4) they would like to be buried in Los Angeles or Mexico (where loved ones are buried), and (5) they would like to have a wake preceding their funeral service.

Within the security of a tightly supportive family, the Mexican American feels free to express his feelings of loss and hurt in individualistic and socially-prescribed activity. Significantly more often than the other groups, Mexican Americans responded (1) that at the death of their spouse they would let themselves go and cry themselves out, (2) that they would worry if they *could not* cry, (3) that they would be likely to touch the body of the deceased, and (4) that one ought to wear black for a year or more.

At the same time they are protective of family members' feelings. Again, significantly more often than the other groups the Mexican Americans felt (1) that a dying person should not be told of his impending death because it is harder on him and on others, (2) that they could not tell someone he was about to die, and (3) that they did not want children under ten years of age visiting them on their deathbed (there was no significant difference here between Black Americans and Mexican Americans) or attending their funeral.

Of course, the Roman Catholic Church may mean something different to the (Mexican American) old and the (Chicano) young, the man and the woman. Nevertheless, its tenets provide some framework for organizing thoughts about death. And it is with this in mind that some of the interview responses make the most sense. Ninety percent of the Mexican American sample considered themselves Roman Catholics. Significantly more often than the other groups, Mexican Americans responded (1) that they would call for a priest or minister on their deathbed, (2) that people cannot slow or hasten their death by a will-to-live or a will-to-die (that's in God's hands), and (3) that people should not be allowed to die if they want to (God gives life and only He has the right to take it away).

And the Mexican American respondents significantly more often than the other groups considered the interview to be a *positive* experience (B 33%, J 34%, M 73%, A 35%).

So we return to our earlier differentiation between death as a concept and a symbol and death as something that happens to people I know—and to me. Based on our data the Mexican Americans in this study seem to accept death readily as an abstract concept and they seem to recognize and accept the reality of death at the existential level as well, even while admitting their fear of death and their wish to put thoughts of personal death aside, both for themselves and for their loved ones. We need to select our words carefully: the Mexican American appears to wish to avoid thoughts of the death of his loved ones and of himself, but death seems highly pervasive in his thoughts and dreams nonetheless, and we would hypothesize that he copes with these distressing thoughts by mastering death through ritualistic acts, through dwelling on it until the anxiety is worked through, and through integrating it meaningfully into life.

To the extent that they retain their rootedness in La Raza (Mexican People and Culture), death is integrated with life. It is recalled in the songs and poetry, in holidays and celebrations, in the paintings and religion. Death is embraced in the funeral ceremonies and provides the stage and setting for dramatic expression of grief and anguish. Death is something to be thought about and talked about. Although our Mexican American respondents have not uniformly done so, there is consensus that one should acquaint oneself with death and grow from the acquaintanceship. The Yaqui Indian man of vision called "don Juan" taught Castaneda (1971, *A Separate Reality*, Simon and Schuster, New York): "Every bit of knowledge that becomes power has death as its central force. Death lends the ultimate touch, and whatever is touched by death indeed becomes power" (p. 183).

9

Final Statements

Senior Author's Summary Statements

We have now analyzed hundreds of pieces of data, have spent hundreds of person-hours of time and effort, have used hundreds of dollars of computer time, and have written innumerable hundreds of words. Where has it led us?

First, and perhaps most important, we have found immense diversity, not only across groups, but within groups and subgroups. Thus, although most people state they would want to be told if they were dying, a sizable minority indicate they do not wish to be told; although a majority would prefer to be home when they are dying, another sizable minority would rather be in a hospital. The lesson in this is that no program for the dying or ideology about the dying will fit all cases, except for programs or ideologies that are flexible enough to account for a wide range of individual differences.

Now that the media and the health and mental health professionals have "discovered" death, the dying are less likely to be ignored or isolated (although the changes in rhetoric have far outdistanced the changes in action). However, there is the constant danger of replacing outdated rigidities with modish rigidities, so that the assumption that everyone should die in hospitals (which replaced the earlier ideology that no one should) is becoming replaced again by the new ideology that no one should die in hospitals. The assumption that the dying did not wish to talk about their own imminent death is becoming replaced by the assumption that the dying all wish to talk about their own imminent death.

We believe that our data show "the dying" as a stereotype does not exist. We certainly find modal responses or common responses, but not universal responses. To know what the modal or common responses are can help in developing appropriate policy, in improving clinical skills, and in encouraging subsequent research, but it cannot appropriately be applied to all cases.

Second, we have certainly established that differences between groups exist in terms of death-related attitudes, values, expectations, experiences, and social and religious customs. These differences are substantial for age and ethnicity; they are less clear for sex. In some instances, the sociocultural forces shared by the Japanese Americans and Mexican Americans caused these two groups to appear most similar, while the Black and Anglo groups also seemed alike. On other issues, the low income and limited formal education of Blacks and Mexican Americans placed them on one side of the fence with the Japanese and Anglo Americans on the other side. And there were occasions when three ethnic groups clustered around one norm while the fourth appeared to be quite different.

Third, we have also shown that individual differences exist within groups and subgroups. Not that this knowledge comes as a surprise to anyone—we all recognize the existence of such differences, but we sometimes function as though everyone, or everyone having certain characteristics, thought and wished and behaved alike. In essence, we hope that we have helped readers improve their abilities to understand what—for example—the elderly Mexican American man might expect when he is dying, but we also hope that this will not lead to new stereotypes replacing the old.

Fourth, we have—as project directors—gained a great deal of respect for the views put forth by those we interviewed. Obviously this is a somewhat selected group, since those who find death and dying too stressful to discuss refused to be interviewed. But our turn-down rate was not unduly high, very little higher than surveys with much less affectively demanding topics. We felt that people responded with care, consideration, and honesty.

And finally we have accumulated a substantial amount of information, much of it presented in this volume and the various articles and talks that emerged from the project. We believe these data can serve several purposes. They can provide a comparison for studies done in other kinds of communities (other ethnic or religious groups, other regions of the country, other nations, rural or small town communities); they can be used to evaluate health and social policies; they can give guidance to health and mental health clinicians; they can be used to develop related programs.

Our respondents had contact with the dying and with death—through knowing people who had died, through attending funerals, through gravesite visits, through visiting the critically and terminally ill. The elderly are more likely to have had these experiences; the Anglo respondents were less likely. Most respondents would agree with the "experts" that the dying know they are dying, that people by and large should be given a reasonable indication of their prognosis, even when terminal and that they consider themselves capable of handling a terminal prognosis.

Future research can use this monograph as a jumping off place, moving in either of two directions. The first is to administer comparable materials to other communities; the second is to select certain of the questions we included and to probe the answers in greater depth. We would particularly encourage the latter. We feel a great need to understand more of the richness and depth that surrounds what we have presented as a checkmark on a piece of paper.

Thus we talk a great deal about "fear of death" but we have little if any research data to tell us what people mean when they use that phrase. We see changes in mourning customs, but we lack a good natural history of the mourning process, based on what people actually do. We know that many people confront their own deaths, but do not die at that time, yet we know almost nothing as to what the effects of such an experience are. We have all sorts of theories about the impact of touching or kissing a body at the funeral, but we have little understanding of what this action signifies to the person doing it and what later effect it (or its absence) will have. We have learned that Anglos are more likely than others to consider the death of an infant or child as most tragic, but we have little information on which to develop the implications of that finding into greater understanding of the nature of the family in various ethnic groups.

We could easily continue this discussion. The point is already clear. Our study focussed on breadth; we now hope that there can be many studies focusing on depth.

Junior Author's Summary Statement

Death is an inescapable aspect of each person's reality. Across time and culture, men have devised a variety of ways of handling the psychological, social, economic, and political consequences of death and the processes of dying and of grieving. In the decade since this project was initially conceptualized, the awareness of the general public and of the individuals immediately concerned with death has burgeoned. While still in part taboo, the topic of death has received considerable coverage in the media, has been the basis for countless workshops, has been formalized in hundreds of college and a number of high school courses, and—most significant—can be discussed in informal gatherings without arousing anxiety and overt or implicit avoidance among the participants. Programs to aid the dying have been established—Ars Moriendi in Philadelphia, the Shanti Project in the San Francisco area, the hospice movement initiated in New Haven are just a few among many.

We feel that this publication has appeared at just the right time. The danger of ritualizing new procedures—albeit improved new procedures—to replace inadequate previous procedures is growing. While Elisabeth Kubler-Ross is moving into new ground, many of her followers (and we feel that the term "followers" is appropriate) are setting her five stages in concrete. Now that hospitals, social services, and schools are opening up for examination of old myths and stereotypes, we need to be cautious that they not be replaced with new myths and stereotypes.

Dying and death occur in a social context. People do not live alike and they do not wish to die alike. Individual differences can too readily be obscured by clinical and research findings that certain attitudes and values suggest new procedures in enabling people to cope with their own dying and the dying of others.

We have attempted to focus on the diversity of feelings and beliefs and expectations regarding death, dying and grieving. We have tried to show how these feelings, beliefs, and expectations are embedded in the sociocultural settings of the individuals involved. The psychosocial sequelae of death have been relatively little explored in the light of their obvious theoretical and practical import in developmental psychology, personality, social structure, and cross-cultural studies—not to mention their immense implications for meaningful, humanistic behavior.

For the theoretician and the scholar, our study has aimed at presenting some hypothesized relationships between demographic variables, culture, and orientations toward death. We have presented enough information about our data bases so that the social scientist can decide for himself the relative probabilities of the links we proposed.

For the "practicalist," the person who—for professional or personal reasons—must encounter death and dying, we have presented some alternatives for living. We have attempted to set these alternatives for living into a meaningful historico-cultural context. We described what appear to us to be some of the consequences of various alternatives of meaning and behavior related to death.

What do people think about death? *How* do they think about death? How do they organize their understanding of an event, an experience, a phenomenon that is uniquely unknowable in the rational sense in which we generally speak of "knowing" something? Since those who could best inform us of the realities of phenomenological death are no longer capable of communicating about their experience on any systematic, verifiable way, it is impossible for us to accumulate a rationally-derived data base for testing out the "truth" of various ideologies of death. Yet individuals do have conceptions of death and dying that permit them to deal with their own dying and the deaths of others (and, incidentally, to respond to questions on the subject with a great deal of internal consistency within the universe of possible responses.) And they share elements of their ideologies of death with their neighbors, the members of their religious group, their age mates and so forth.

In the chapters above we described the understandings of death in four Los Angeles ethnic groups (Black Americans, Japanese Americans, Mexican Americans and Anglo Americans). We described the world of reality in which these ideologies are embedded. And we examined the behavior and feelings that flow in natural and expected response from these ideologies.

Death is the condition *par excellence* in which to find operating the social construction of reality. It is no wonder, then, that in our samples we found the greatest differences in ideologies of death to be associated with differences in culture and not differences in sex or age or level of education (though, of course, differences were found in these other dimensions as well since they, too, reflect human differences within and across cultures).

In order to explore the subject of death and bereavement in these four ethnic groups we gathered information of several sorts. A community interview survey, interviews with persons in death-related occupations, participant observation in death settings (terminal wards, funeral services, coroner's facilities, etc.), content analyses of local ethnic newspapers and ethnic literature, depth interviews with selected respondents, and statistical information on rates of death by various causes provided the data base for our analyses set against the culture-historical background of our ethnic groups, age and sex cohorts, and so forth.

The community survey interview schedule covered four general topical areas:

1. The respondent's own death—thoughts, dreams, plans, expectations, wishes, fears, worries, and his own funeral;
2. The death of others—telling another of impending death, frequency of death of acquaintances, mystical experiences;
3. Survivors—acceptable and unacceptable grief reactions, expectations in mourning behavior;
4. Death in the abstract—tragedy of different types of death, mass death, life after death, suicide.

There are essentially four sorts of descriptive comparisons that were used in the analysis of our interview results:

1) One was the comparison within each subcultural group itself. Thus, we characterized the Black Americans in our sample as perceiving themselves to be about as devout as others of their religious faith—64% responded they are about the same, 20% that they are more devout, and 16% that they are less devout. The question to be answered by this comparison was "how did each group respond?"

2) A second comparison was that among the groups. From this perspective the Black Americans in our sample were seen to consider themselves more religious than did our respondents in other groups. For example, 84% of the Black Americans considered themselves to be equally or more religious than others of their faith as compared with 64% of the Japanese Americans, 68% of the Mexican Americans, and 64% of the Anglo Americans. The question to be answered here was "how do the groups compare with one another?"
3) The third sort of comparison involved a breakdown within a particular ethnic group by age, sex, education level and so forth. Thus, we showed that Mexican American women more frequently responded that they would call for a priest if they were dying than did Mexican American men. The question here was "What are the variations within each group by age, sex, etc.?"
4) Finally, we pooled our data from the ethnic groups to see if the dimensions of age, sex, education level, and so forth would show significant differences regardless of ethnicity. We found, for example, that, whatever their ethnic background might be, as people grew older they attended more funerals, thought *more* about and thought *more positively* about their own death. The question to be answered here was "What human dimensions cut across the subcultural groups?"

We feel strongly that it is important to avoid the pitfalls of over-generalizing either from data or from personal experiences. Our findings have established to our satisfaction that ethnicity, age, sex, and social status all influence views of death—but this is virtually a truism and did not require this lengthy study. We have pointed out what some of these differences are, hoping to enable future researchers and future practitioners to avoid an inevitable tendency to ignore such differences. We hope that the middle-class, middle-aged Anglo researcher or practitioner will remain aware that the non-middle-class, the non-middle-aged, and the non-Anglo are likely to have views that differ from what appears to be the "norm."

Nor do we wish to leave readers with the impression that the views within ethnic, age, social status, or sex groups is uniform. We found major differences within such groupings as well as major differences between such groupings. And even regional differences, which our study barely touched on, cannot be ignored. Thus, we found that Blacks and Anglos shared certain world views that influenced their responses to dying, but that they also differed in significant ways. Japanese Americans and Mexican Americans seem to share a familistic approach to death and dying, but they differed considerably in how they expressed this familistic attitude. Moreover, individual differences within each group are substantial, and we tried to make note of these also.

As must happen with much research, we wish that we could consider the entire study as a pilot study for a subsequent investigation. It required this major effort to learn what we needed to learn more about, to develop procedures that would permit us to know what procedures would improve the study. We sincerely hope that others will extend what we have done to other ethnic groups, to the same ethnic groups in other settings, with other questions and issues, with foci on personality variables or family roles or health status or. . . . We have provided a broad background that needs supplementation by more intensive and specific investigations. And, of course, time is also a variable, so it would be appropriate to do a follow-up study, with improved methods and instruments, to see what has remained the same and what has changed in a setting that is similar to ours.

The data were rich, complex, and, occasionally, contradictory. We shall not attempt to summarize them here. In each chapter we have described the currents and themes that we see underlying the interview responses and observed behaviors and content analyses.

In the text and appendix we have provided the reader with enough of the data so that he can make his own interpretations.

We close with a quote from the field notes of Brian Ogawa, a Japanese American research assistant on the project. The vignette is a scenario of the orientation and import of our study.

"Between the Christian and Buddhist Memorial Day Services I was standing by the graves across from the Japanese monument. A Caucasian woman was placing flowers on a nearby grave. A Japanese American woman was standing close to her apparently waiting for the Buddhist service to begin. She was looking intently at the gravesite where the Caucasian woman was kneeling. As the woman stood up, the Nisei lady softly said to her, 'It looks like a new grave.' Obviously appreciating the concern shown her, the Caucasian put her arm around the Japanese and said with tears in her eyes, 'Yes, my husband died three weeks ago.' They stood there for a few minutes, together, looking at the grave."

Bibliography

Abrahams, Roger D. *Deep Down in the Jungle.* Chicago: Aldine Publishing Company, 1963.

Alexander, I.E., Colley, R.S., and Adlerstein, A.M. Is death a matter of indifference? *Journal of Psychology,* 1957, *43,* 277-283.

Back, K. Cited in R. Kastenbaum, Meaning of time in later life. *Journal of Genetic Psychology,* 1966, *109,* 9-25.

Baldwin, James. Man Thousands Gone. *Notes of a Native Son.* Boston: Beacon Press, 1955.

Beardsley, Richard K., Hall, John W., and Ward, Robert E. *Village Japan.* University of Chicago Press, 1959.

Bellah, Robert N. Religious systems. In Evon Z. Vogt and Ethel M. Albert (eds.), *People of Rimrock.* Harvard University Press, 1966.

Benedict, Ruth. *The Chrysanthemum and the Sword,* New York: Houghton Mifflin, 1946.

Bengtson, V.L., Cuellar, J.A., and Ragan, P.K. Group contrasts in attitudes toward death: Variation by race, age, occupational status, and sex. Submitted for publication, 1976.

Blauner, Robert. Death and social structure. *Psychiatry,* 1966, *29,* 378-94. (Reprinted in B. Neugarten (ed.), *Middle Age and Aging.* Chicago: University of Chicago Press, 1968, pp. 531-540.)

Blauner, Robert. Black Culture: Myth or Reality. In Norman E. Whitten and John F. Szwed (eds.), *Afro-American Anthropology,* New York: The Free Press, 1970.

Bullins, Ed., (ed.), *New Plays from the Black Theatre.* New York: Bantam Books, 1969.

Bureau of Census. Current Population Series P-20, No. 79 2-2-58.

Carter, W.B. Suicide, death, and ghetto life. *Life-Threatening Behavior,* 1971, *1,* 264-271.

Casteneda, Carlos. *A Separate Reality*, New York: Simon and Schuster, 1971.

Caudill, William. Japanese American personality and acculturation. *Genetic Psychology Monographs* 1952, *45*, 3-102.

Caudill, William and George DeVos. Achievement, culture and personality: The case of the Japanese Americans. *American Anthropologist, 58:* 1102-1126, 1956.

Chapman, Abraham, ed., *Black Voices—An Anthology of Afro-American Literature.* New York: The New American Library, 1968.

Chenard, M. Unpublished doctoral dissertation, 1972.

Christ, Adolph E. Attitudes toward death among a group of acute geriatric patients. *Journal of Gerontology, 16,* 1961, 56-59.

Clark, Margaret. *A Community Study — Health in the Mexican American Culture.* Berkeley and Los Angeles: University of California Press, 1959.

DeVos, George. A quantitative Rorschach assessment of maladjustment and rigidity in acculturating Japanese Americans. *Genetic Psychology Monographs* 1955, *52,* 51-87.

Dickstein, L.S. Death concern: Measurement and correlates. *Psychological Reports,* 1972, *30,* 563-571.

Diggory, James C., and Rothman, Doreen Z. Values destroyed by death. *Journal of Abnormal and Social Psycology,* 1961, *63,* 205-210.

Donaldson, Peter J. Denying death: A note regarding some ambiguities in the current discussion. *Omega,* 1972, *3,* 285-293.

Dore, R.P. *City Life in Japan.* Berkeley and Los Angeles: University of California Press, 1958.

Dorson, Richard M., (ed.) *American Negro Folktale.* Greenwich, Connecticut: Fawcett Publications, Inc., 1970.

Edmonson, Munro S., Madsen, Claudia, Collier, Jane Fishburne. *Contemporary Latin American Culture.* New Orleans: Middle American Research Institute, Tulane University, 1957.

Erikson, E.H. *Childhood and Society* (2nd edition), New York: Norton, 1963.

Evans-Pritchard, Edward E. *Witchcraft, Oracles, and Magic among the Azande.* New York: Oxford University Press, 1937.

Exton-Smith, A.N. Terminal illness in the aged. *Lancet,* August 5, 1961, *2,* 305-8.

Feifel, Herman. Older persons look at death. *Geriatrics,* 1956, *11,* 127-30.

Feifel, Herman. The taboo on death. *The American Behavioral Scientist,* 1963, *6,* 66-67.

Feifel, Herman, and Jones, R. Perception of death as related to nearness to death. *Proceedings of the 76th Annual Convention of the American Psychological Association,* 1968, *3,* 545-546.

Feifel, Herman, et al. Physicians consider death. Proceedings of the *75th Annual Convention of the American Psychological Association*, 1967, 2, 201-2.

Frazier, E. Franklin. *The Negro in the United States.* New York: Macmillan, 1949.

Fuentes, Carlos. *The Death of Artemio Cruz.* New York: Farrar, Straus and Giroux, 1964.

Fukuyama, Y. The major dimensions of church membership. *Review of Religious Research*, 1961, 2, 154-161.

Fulton, R. The sacred and the secular: Attitudes of the American public toward death, funerals, and funeral directors. In R. Fulton (ed.), *Death and Identity.* New York: Wiley, 1965, pp. 89-105.

Glaser, Barney G., and Strauss, Anselm L. *Awareness of Dying.* Chicago: Aldine, 1965.

Glock, C.Y., and Stark R. *Religion and Society in Tension.* Chicago: Rand McNally, 1965.

Gorer, Geoffrey. The pornography of death. In W. Phillips and P. Rahv (eds.), *Modern Writing.* New York: McGraw-Hill, 1959, 157-188.

Gorer, Geoffrey. *Death, Grief, and Mourning.* New York: Doubleday, 1965.

Grebler, Leo, Moore, Joan W., and Guzman, Ralph C. *The Mexican-American People. The Nation's Second Largest Minority.* New York: The Free Press, 1970.

Green, Judith Strupp, *Laughing Souls: The Days of the Dead in Oaxaca, Mexico.* San Diego Museum of Man, Balboa Park: Popular Series, No. 1, May 1969.

Grier, William H., and Price, M. Cobbs. *Black Rage.* New York: Basic Books, 1968.

Habenstein, Robert W., and Lamers, William M., *Funeral Customs the World Over.* Milwaukee: Bulfin Printers, 1960.

Hall, G. Stanley. A study of fears. *American Journal of Psychology*, 1897, 8 147-149.

Hall, G. Stanley. Thanatophobia and immortality. *American Journal of Psychology*, 1915, 26, 550-613.

Handal, P.J. The relationship between subjective life expectancy, death anxiety, and general anxiety. *Journal of Clinical Psychology*, 1969, 25, 39-42.

Hannerz, Ulf. What ghetto males are like: Another look. In Norman E. Whitten and John F. Szwed, (eds.), *Afro-American Anthropology*, New York: The Free Press, 1970.

Harmer, Ruth M. *The High Cost of Dying.* New York: Crowell-Collier, 1963.

Harmer, Ruth M. Funerals, fantasy, and flight. *Omega*, 1971, 2, 127-135.

Harrington, M. *The Other America: Poverty in the United States.* Baltimore: Penguin, 1963.

Hearn, Lafcadio. *In Ghostly Japan.* Boston: Little, Brown, and Company, 1899.

Hendin, Herbert. *Black Suicide.* New York: Basic Books, 1969.

Hinton, John M. The physical and mental distress of the dying. *Quarterly Journal of Medicine,* 1963, *32,* 1-21.

Huston, Zora Neale. *Mules and Men —Negro Folktales and Voodoo Practices in the South.* Philadelphia: J.B. Lippincott Company, 1935.

Ivey, M.E., and Bardwick, J.M. Patterns of affective fluctuation in the menstrual cycle. *Psychosomatic Medicine,* 1968, *30,* 336-345.

Jackson, Maurice. The Black experience with death: A brief analysis through black writings. *Omega,* 1972, *3,* 203-209.

Jeffers, Frances C., Nichols, C.R., and Eisdorfer, C. Attitudes of older persons toward death: A preliminary study. *Journal of Gerontology,* 1961, *16,* 53-56.

Johnston, Ruby F. *The Religion of Negro Protestants.* New York: Philosophical Library, 1956.

Joseph, Stephen M. *The Me Nobody Knows — Children's Voices from the Ghetto.* New York: Avon, 1969.

Kahana, Boaz, and Kahana, E. Attitudes of young men and women toward awareness of death. *Omega,* 1972, *3,* 37-44.

Kalish, Richard A. An approach to the study of death attitudes. *American Behavioral Scientist,* 1963a, *6,* 68-70.

Kalish, Richard A. Some variables in death attitudes. *Journal of Social Psychology,* 1963b, *59,* 137-145.

Kalish, Richard A. The aged and the dying process: The inevitable decisions. *Journal of Social Issues,* 1965, *21,* 87-96.

Kalish, Richard A. Non-medical interventions in life and death. *Social Science and Medicine,* 170, *4,* 655-665.

Kalish, Richard A. Sex and marital role differences in anticipation of age-produced dependency. *Journal of Genetic Psychology,* 1971, *119,* 53-62.

Kalish R.A., and Johnson, A.I. Value similarities and differences in three generations of women. *Journal of Marriage and the Family,* 1972, *34,* 49-54.

Kalish, Richard A., and Reynolds, David K. Phenomenological reality and post-death contact. *Journal for the Scientific Study of Religion,* 1973, *12,* 209-221.

Kardiner, Abraham, and Lionel Ovesey. *The Mark of Oppression — Explorations in the Personality of the American Negro.* Cleveland, Ohio: The World Publishing Company, 1951.

Kastenbaum, Robert, and Aisenberg, Ruth B. *The Psychology of Death.* New York: Springer, 1972.

Kennard, E.A. Hopi reactions to death. *American Anthropologist,* 1937, *29,* 491-494.

Kiefer, Christie W. *Changing Cultures, Changing Lives.* San Francisco: Jossey-Bass, 1974.

Kitano, Harry H.L. *Japanese Americans.* Englewood Cliffs, New Jersey: Prentice Hall, 1969.

Kluckhohn, Florence Rockwood, and Fred L. Strodbeck. *Variations in Value Orientations.* Evanston, Illinois: Row, Peterson and Company, 1961.

Koenig, R.R. Anticipating death from cancer—physician and patient attitudes. *Michigan Medicine,* 1969, *68,* 899-905.

Koenig, R., Goldner, N.S., Kresojevich, R., and Lockwood, G. Ideas about illness of elderly black and white in an urban hospital. *Aging and Human Development,* 1971, *2,* 217-225.

Koestenbaum, Peter. The vitality of death. *Omega,* 1971, *2,* 253-271.

Kogan, Nathan, and Shelton, Florence. Images of "old people" and "people in general" in an older sample. *Journal of Genetic Psychology,* 1962, *100,* 3-21.

Lester, David. Attitudes toward death today and thirty-five years ago. *Omega,* 1971, *2,* 168-173.

Lewis, Hylan. Blackways of Kent: Religion and salvation. In Nelson, Hart M., et al., eds. *The Black Church in America.* New York: Basic Books, 1971.

Lewis, Oscar. *Life in a Mexican Village: Tepoztlan Restudied.* Urbana: University of Illinois, 1951.

Lewis, Oscar. *A Death in the Sanchez Family.* New York: Random House, 1969.

Lomax, Alan. The Homogeneity of African-Afro-American Musical Style. In: Norman E. Whitten and John F. Szwed, (eds.) *Afro-American Anthropology,* New York: The Free Press, 1970.

Lyman, Stanford. Generation and Character: the Case of the Japanese Americans. In Amy, Tachiki, et al. (eds.) *Roots: An Asian American Reader.* Los Angeles: University of California, 1971.

Madsen, William. *The Mexican-Americans of South Texas.* New York: Holt, Rinehart and Winston, 1964.

Martin, David S., and Wrightsman, Lawrence. The relationship between religious behavior and concern about death. *Journal of Social Psychology,* 1965, *65,* 317-323.

Middleton, W.C. Some reactions toward death among college students. *Journal of Abnormal and Social Psychology,* 1936, *31,* 165-173.

Mitford, Jessica. *The American Way of Death.* New York: Simon and Schuster, 1963.

Moberg, D.O. Religiosity in old age. *Gerontologist,* 1965, *2,* 78-87.

Moberg, D.O. Spiritual Well-Being. White House Conference on Aging Background and Issues. Washington, D.C.: Government Printing Office, 1971a.

Moberg, D.O. Religious practices. In M.P. Strommen, (ed.). *Research on Religious Development*. New York: Hawthorn, 1971b, p. 551-598.
Moore, Joan. The death culture of Mexico and Mexican-Americans. *Omega*, 1970a, *1*, 271-291.
Moore, Joan with Alfredo Cuellar. *Mexican Americans*. Englewood Cliffs, New Jersey: Prentice Hall, 1970b.
Nagano, Paul. Japanese Population Trends and Religious Analysis of Metropolitan Los Angeles, 1969, mimeo.
National Council on the Aging. *The Myth and Reality of Aging in America*. Washington, D.C.: National Council on the Aging, 1975.
Nehrke, M.F. Actual and perceived attitudes toward death and self concept in three-generational families. Paper presented at the 27th Annual Conference, Gerontological Society, Portland, Oregon, 1974.
Nelson, Hart M., et al., eds. *The Black Church in America*. New York: Basic Books, 1971.
Norbeck, Edward. *Changing Japan*. New York: Holt, Rinehart, Winston, 1965.
Osuna, Patricia. El funeral de mi tia Elena. *Omega*, 1970, *1*, 249-258.
Osuna, Patricia, and David K. Reynolds. A funeral in Mexico: Description and analysis. *Omega*, 1970, *1*, 249-269.
Pandey, R.E., and Templer, Donald I. Use of the death anxiety scale in an inter-racial setting. *Omega*, 1972, *3*, 127-130.
Parsons, Talcott, and Lidz, Victor, Death in American society. In E.S. Schneidman, (ed.), *Essays in Self-Destruction*. New York: Science House, 1967, 133-170.
Payne, Thelma L. Behavioral responses of Japanese patients to illness, birth, accidents, surgery and death. M.A. Thesis, California State University Los Angeles, 1970.
Paz, Octavio. *The Labyrinth of Solitude — Life and Thought in Mexico*. New York: Grove Press, 1961.
Phillips, D.P., and Feldman, K.A. A dip in deaths before ceremonial occasions: Some new relationships between social integration and mortality. *American Sociological Review*, 1973, *38*, 678-696.
Pinkney, Alphonso. *Black Americans*. Englewood Cliffs, New Jersey: Prentice Hall, 1969.
Raether, Howard C. The place of the funeral: The role of the funeral director in contemporary America. *Omega*, 1971, *2*, 150-153.
Redfield, Robert, and Alfonso Villa Rojas. *Chan Kom — a Maya Village*. Washington, D.C. Carnegie Institute, 1934, Publication #448.
Reynolds, D.K., Japanese American aging. Presentation to the Society for Applied Anthropology, 1971.
Reynolds, David K. Directed Behavior Change: *Japanese Psycho-*

therapy in a Private Mental Hospital. Unpublished doctoral dissertation. University of California, Los Angeles, 1969.

Reynolds, David K. A funeral in Mexico. *Omega,* 1970, *1,* 259-269.

Reynolds, David K. *Morita Psychotherapy.* Berkeley and Los Angeles: University of California Press, 1976.

Reynolds, David K., and Kalish, Richard A. Anticipation of futurity as a function of ethnicity and age. *Journal of Gerontology,* 1974, *29,* 224-231.

Reynolds, David K., and Kalish, Richard A. Content analysis of death portrayal in the ethnic press. *Ethnicity,* accepted for publication.

Rhudick, Paul J., and Dibner, A.S. Age, personality, and health correlates of death concerns in normal aged individuals. *Journal of Gerontology.* 1961, *16,* 44-49.

Riley, J.W., Jr. What people think about death. In O.G. Brim, Jr., H.E. Freeman, S. Levine, and N.A. Scotch (eds.), *The Dying Patient.* New York: Russell Sage Foundation, 1970, pp. 30-41.

Riley, Matilda, and Foner, Anne. *Aging and society: In An Inventory of Research Findings.* New York: Russell Sage Foundation, 1968.

Ross, Elisabeth K. *On Death and Dying.* New York: Macmillan, 1969.

Schoenberg, J., and Stichman, J. *How to Survive your Husband's Heart Attack.* New York: David McKay, 1974.

Scott, C.A. Old age and death. *American Journal of Psychology,* 1896, *8,* 54-122.

Seiden, R.H. We're driving young Blacks to suicide. *Psychology Today,* 1970, *4*(3), 24-28.

Shaffer, Thomas L. *Death, Property, and Lawyers: A Behavioral Approach.* New York: Dunellen, 1970.

Shanas, E. *The Health of Older People: A Social Survey.* Cambridge, Mass.: Harvard University Press, 1962.

Shneidman, Edwin S. The enemy. *Psychology Today,* 1970, *4*(8), 37-41.

Shneidman, Edwin S. You and death. *Psychology Today,* 1971, *5*(6), 43.

Simmons, Leo W. *The Role of the Aged in Primitive Society.* New Haven: Yale University Press, 1945.

Soustelle, Jacques. *Daily Life of the Aztecs.* New York: Macmillan, 1962.

Spicer, Edward H., Hansen, Asael T., Luomala, Katherine, and Opler, Marvin K., *Japanese-Americans in the Relocation Centers — Impounded People.* Tucson, Arizona: The University of Arizona Press, 1969.

Stack, Carol B. The Kindred of Viola Jackson: Residence and Family Organization of an Urban American Family. In Norman E. Whitten, and John F. Szweds, (eds.), *Afro-American Anthropology,* New York: The Free Press, 1970.

Steiner, Stan. *La Raza.* New York: Harper and Row, 1969.

Swanson, W.C., and Harter, C.L. How do elderly Blacks cope in New Orleans? *Aging and Human Development,* 1971, *2,* 210-216.

Swenson, Wendell M. Attitudes toward death among the aged. *Minnesota Medicine,* 1959, *42,* 399-402.

Swenson, Wendell M. Attitudes toward death in an aged population. *Journal of Gerontology,* 1961, *16,* 49-52.

Swenson, Wendell M. Approaches to the study of religion and aging. *In Religion and Aging,* Los Angeles: Andrus Gerontology Center, University of Southern California, 1967.

Tachiki, Amy et al., (eds.) *Roots: An Asian American Reader.* Berkeley and Los Angeles: University of California Press, 1971.

Templer, Donald Irvin. The construction and validation of a death anxiety scale. *Journal of General Psychology,* 1970, *82,* 165-177.

Templer, Donald Irvin, Death anxiety in religiously very involved persons. *Psychological Reports,* 1972, *31,* 361-362.

Templer, Donald Irvin, Ruff, Carol, and Frank, Cyril. Death anxiety: Age, sex, and parental resemblance in diverse populations. *Developmental Psychology,* 1971, *4* 198.

Vaillant, George C. *Aztecs of Mexico. Origin, Rise and Fall of the Aztec Nation.* Garden City, New York: Doubleday and Company, 1941.

Valentine, Charles A., and Valentine, Betty Lou. Making the scene, digging the action, and telling it like it is: Anthropologists at work in a dark ghetto. In Norman E. Whitten, and John F. Szwed, (eds.), *Afro-American Anthropology,* New York: The Free Press, 1970.

Vernon, Glenn M. *Sociology of Death: An Analysis of Death-related Behavior.* New York: Ronald Press, 1970.

Vogt, Evon Z., and Albert, Ethel M., (eds.), *People of Rimrock.* Cambridge, Mass.: Harvard University Press, 1966.

Wade, Richard C. Beyond the master's eye. In: Hart M. Nelson, al., (eds.), *The Black Church in America.* New York: Basic Books, 1970.

Weisman, Avery D., and Hackett, Thomas P. Predilection to death: Death and dying as a psychiatric problem. *Psychomatic Medicine,* 1961, *23,* 232-256.

World Almanac and Book of Facts. New York, New York: Newspaper Enterprise Association, 1971.

Yamamoto, Joe, and Imahara, John. America and Japan — two ways of mourning. Paper presented at 126th Annual Meeting of the American Psychiatric Association, May 13, 1970, San Francisco.

Yamamoto, Joe, Okonogi Keigo, Iwasaki Tetsuya, and Yoshimura Saburo. Mourning in Japan. *American Journal of Psychiatry,* 1969, *125,* 74-79.

Appendix

SUMMARY OF INTERVIEW RESULTS BY ETHNICITY, AGE, AND SEX*

Item No.	Question/Response	Ethnicity				Age			Sex	
		B.A.	J.A.	M.A.	A.A.	20-39	40-59	60+	Male	Female
001	How many years of school did you finish? (Mean years)									
		10.6	12.4	6.5	11.1	(.001)				
003	What is your current occupation?									
	Unskilled	38	14	25	15	18	22	29	27	19
	Skilled	34	46	34	41	34	38	46	58	20
	Professional/ Managerial	6	6	1	12	7	5	4	8	3
	Housewife	16	28	40	29	30	33	20	0	56
	Other	7	8	0	4	11	1	1	7	2
		(.001)				(.001)			(.001)	
004	What is your current age? (Mean chronological age)									
		45.7	49.0	47.0	47.6	(n.s.)				

*Unless otherwise indicated numbers in tables are percentages. Numbers in parentheses are chi square significance levels for the entire item table. B.A.=Black Americans, J.A.=Japanese Americans, M.A.=Mexican Americans, A.A.=Anglo Americans.

Item No.	Question/Response	Ethnicity				Age			Sex	
		B.A.	J.A.	M.A.	A.A.	20-39	40-59	60+	Male	Female
005	What is your current age? (Age groups)									
	20-39 years	36	32	39	40	(n.s.)				
	40-59 years	37	38	34	33					
	60+ years	27	31	28	28					
006	What is your religious affiliation?									
	Buddhist	0	51	0	2	11	15	15	12	14
	Catholic	6	1	90	18	33	28	27	30	29
	Protestant	86	32	8	65	40	51	50	45	49
	Other/None	7	16	3	16	16	6	8	14	7
		(.001)				(n.s.)			(n.s.)	
0Q7	Compared to most (INSERT RESPONDENT'S RELIGIOUS AFFILIATION HERE, E.G., CATHOLICS) do you feel you are									
	More devout	20	12	18	18	9	17	27	16	18
	About the same	64	52	50	46	49	53	59	52	54
	Less devout	16	36	33	36	43	30	15	32	28
		(.05)				(.001)			(n.s.)	
008	Which of these fits your marital status now?									
	Married	50	71	73	66	63	79	50	70	60
	Never Married	13	16	10	10	27	3	4	19	6
	Widowed	21	13	8	12	0	5	41	6	21
	Divorced/Separated	17	0	9	12	10	13	5	6	13
		(.001)				(.001)			(.001)	
009/010	Where were you born?									
	Los Angeles	5	11	12	5	10	12	2	9	7
	Elsewhere in California	5	25	12	13	18	18	2	15	12
	Elsewhere in U.S./ Canada (N=3)	91	20	14	70	45	53	46	48	49
	Outside U.S./ Canada	0	45	62	15	28	18	50	28	33
		(.001)				(.001)			(n.s.)	
013	How old is the oldest person living in this household? (Mean age)									
		51.3	53.8	50.2	49.0	(n.s.)				

Item No.	Question/Response	Ethnicity				Age			Sex	
		B.A.	J.A.	M.A.	A.A.	20-39	40-59	60+	Male	Female
014	How many persons that you knew personally died in the past two years?									
	None	10	17	19	26	25	17	10	17	19
	1-3	42	45	43	52	52	47	35	46	45
	4-7	23	24	29	14	15	21	33	22	23
	8+	25	15	9	8	8	14	22	15	13
		(.01)				(.001)			(n.s.)	
015	How many died by accident? (Based on those knowing at least one person who died, N=358)									
	None	60	77	66	71	60	70	74	64	72
	Any	40	23	34	29	40	30	26	36	28
		(.10)				(.10)			(n.s.)	
017	How many died in war? (Based on those knowing at least one person who died, N=358)									
	None	86	93	90	89	86	91	92	·87	93
	Any	2	7	10	11	14	9	8	13	7
		(n.s.)				(n.s.)			(n.s.)	
018	How many died by suicide? (Based on those knowing at least one person who died, N=358)									
	None	89	97	95	98	95	97	98	97	96
	Any	2	3	5	2	5	3	2	3	4
		(n.s.)				(n.s.)			(n.s.)	
019	How many died by homicide? (Based on those knowing at least one person who died, N=358)									
	None	89	100	96	100	91	99	97	96	96
	Any	11	0	4	0	9	1	3	4	4
		(.01)				(.01)			(n.s.)	
020	How many funerals have you attended in the past two years?									
	None	33	16	40	45	42	29	27	27	39
	1-3	44	52	43	45	51	49	36	51	41
	4-7	14	15	15	7	5	13	23	14	12
	8+	9	17	2	4	2	9	15	8	8
		(.001)				(.001)			(n.s.)	

Item No.	Question/Response	Ethnicity				Age			Sex	
		B.A.	J.A.	M.A.	A.A.	20-39	40-59	60+	Male	Female
022	How often have you visited someone's grave, other than during a burial service, during the past two years?									
	Never	71	35	56	59	70	50	43	56	54
	1-3	26	25	27	26	21	30	28	26	26
	4-10	2	22	8	10	3	12	17	11	10
	11+	2	17	9	5	6	8	12	7	10
		(.001)				(.001)			(n.s.)	
023	How many persons who were dying did you visit or talk with during the past two years?									
	None	62	58	61	68	72	59	55	59	65
	1	22	24	25	14	18	24	22	20	22
	2+	16	17	15	18	11	17	24	21	14
		(n.s.)				(n.s.)			(n.s.)	
024	About how often do you think about your own death?									
	Daily	25	4	27	13	15	11	29	14	21
	Weekly	10	6	11	12	9	10	9	10	10
	Monthly	15	12	14	18	16	16	11	13	17
	Yearly/Hardly Ever	36	45	39	35	39	46	29	39	38
	Never	14	33	10	22	20	16	22	24	15
		(.001)				(n.s.)				

Now I am going to ask you some questions about a few situations we have invented. First, imagine that a friend of yours is dying of cancer. He/she (MAKE THE FRIEND THE SAME SEX AS THE INFORMANT) is about your age. His/her family has been told by the physician that he/she will die soon.

Item No.	Question/Response	Ethnicity				Age			Sex	
027	Should your friend be told that he/she is going to die?									
	Yes	60	49	37	71	59	56	42	55	52
	No	29	39	58	24	34	31	53	36	39
	Depends	11	12	5	5	7	13	5	8	10
		(.001)				(.01)			(n.s.)	
028	(If yes or if it depends) Who should tell him/her?									
	Physician	65	55	67	65	56	70	60	65	61
	Family	25	29	20	16	30	17	19	19	26
	Clergy	4	3	11	9	6	5	9	6	6
	Other	7	14	2	11	8	8	11	10	8
		(n.s.)				(n.s.)			(n.s.)	

Item No.	Question/Response	Ethnicity				Age			Sex	
		B.A.	J.A.	M.A.	A.A.	20-39	40-59	60+	Male	Female
030	Do you think a person dying of cancer probably senses he's dying anyway without being told?									
	Yes	81	80	78	89	79	86	80	74	90
	No	11	15	19	7	14	12	14	20	7
	Depends	8	5	3	4	7	3	6	6	3
		(n.s.)				(n.s.)			(.01)	
*031	If you were dying, would you want to be told?									
	Yes	72	81	60	77	71	74	71	72	70
		(.01)				(n.s.)			(n.s.)	
032	Do you actually know of someone who was dying in circumstances like these, so that a decision was made to tell him or not to tell him that he would shortly die?									
	Yes	40	29	45	42	31	50	36	32	46
		(.10)				(.01)			(.01)	
033	(If yes) Was he/she actually told he/she was going to die? (IF MORE THAN ONE PERSON WAS KNOWN TO RESPONDENT USE THE MOST RECENT CASE FOR THESE QUESTIONS)									
	Yes	63	60	44	69	68	51	58	61	55
		(.10)								
	(Based on "Yes" responses to #032, N=159)					(n.s.)			(n.s.)	
034	(If yes) Who told him/her?									
	Physician	74	67	64	89	77	71	76	68	80
	Family	17	22	23	7	19	24	4	18	16
	Other	9	11	14	4	3	6	20	15	4
		(n.s.)				(.10)			(n.s.)	
	(Based on "Yes" responses to #033, N=90)									
035	Did you ever tell someone he was about to die?									
	No	93	94	97	96	99	93	92	93	96
		(n.s.)				(.05)			(n.s.)	

*For this and all other items providing only one alternative, non-responders have been eliminated, so that unaccounted-for respondents gave opposite answer, in this instance "No."

Item No.	Question/Response	Ethnicity				Age			Sex	
		B.A.	J.A.	M.A.	A.A.	20-39	40-59	60+	Male	Female
036	(If no) Could you tell someone he was about to die?									
	Yes	51	47	19	52	45	37	43	52	32
	No	39	46	77	41	46	56	54	42	61
	Depends	10	7	4	7	9	7	4	6	8
		(.001)				(n.s.)			(.001)	

(Based on "No" responses to #035, N=407)

Item No.	Question/Response	B.A.	J.A.	M.A.	A.A.	20-39	40-59	60+	Male	Female
037	If you were told that you had a terminal disease and six months to live, how would you want to spend your time until you died?									
	Marked change	16	24	11	17	24	15	9	23	11
	Withdraw/inner-life	26	20	24	12	14	14	37	17	24
	Concern with others	14	15	38	23	29	25	12	16	29
	Complete project	6	8	13	6	11	10	3	9	8
	No change	31	25	12	36	17	29	31	28	24
	Other	8	8	3	7	5	6	8	7	6
		(.01)				(.001)			(.01)	
039	Would you tend to accept death peacefully or fight death actively?									
	Accept	59	66	65	63	53	65	74	59	68
	Fight	39	34	36	33	46	32	25	41	30
	Depends	2	1	0	4	1	3	1	1	2
		(n.s.)				(.01)			(.01)	
040	Would you tend to endure pain in silence or tell someone of your pain?									
	Endure	38	37	56	51	47	43	47	47	44
	Tell	61	61	44	41	52	53	51	52	52
	Depends	1	3	0	8	1	5	2	1	4
		(.001)				(n.s.)			(n.s.)	
041	Would you encourage your family to spend time with you even if it was a little inconvenient for them?									
	Yes	32	36	56	44	42	38	46	42	42
	No	67	62	44	53	56	60	53	56	58
	Depends	1	2	0	3	2	1	1	2	1
		(.01)				(n.s.)			(n.s.)	
042	Would you call for a priest/minister?									
	Yes	64	51	88	53	63	66	64	57	72
	No	34	47	10	45	35	31	34	40	27
	Depends	3	2	2	2	2	3	2	3	1
		(.001)				(n.s.)			(.01)	

Item No.	Question/Response	Ethnicity				Age			Sex	
		B.A.	J.A.	M.A.	A.A.	20-39	40-59	60+	Male	Female
043	Would you allow children under 10 years of age to visit you?									
	Yes/yes with qualification	64	78	66	75	74	67	69	44	42
		(.05)				(n.s.)			(n.s.)	
044	Would you worry if you couldn't cry?									
	Yes	42	42	59	42	48	41	51	44	49
	No	59	55	39	58	52	57	47	55	50
	Depends	0	3	2	0	1	1	2	2	1
		(.05)				(n.s.)			(n.s.)	
045	Would you try very hard to control the way you showed your emotions in public?									
	Yes	79	82	64	74	74	76	75	80	70
		(.05)				(n.s.)			(.05)	
046	Would you let yourself go and cry yourself out (in private or in public or both)?									
	Yes	64	71	88	70	82	75	60	63	83
	No	34	26	12	30	17	22	40	34	17
	Depends	2	3	0	0	1	3	0	2	1
		(.01)				(.001)			(.001)	
047	Would you be likely to touch the body at any of the funeral services?									
	Yes	51	31	76	51	57	45	55	50	55
		(.001)				(n.s.)			(n.s.)	
048	Would you be likely to kiss the body at any of the funeral services?									
	Yes	13	12	59	33	36	25	26	29	29
		(.001)				(n.s.)			(n.s.)	
049	Would you carry out your husband's/wife's last wishes even if they seemed to be senseless to you and caused some inconvenience?									
	Yes	65	85	78	80	81	73	76	78	77
	No	31	13	16	17	15	22	20	20	18
	Depends	4	2	6	3	3	4	3	2	6
		(.05)				(n.s.)			(n.s.)	
050	Who would you be likely to turn to for comfort?									
	Family member	53	51	54	50	58	58	37	48	56
	Clergy/God	32	22	33	28	19	24	48	28	29
	Friend	6	14	8	13	11	12	7	13	7

Item No.	Question/Response	Ethnicity				Age			Sex	
		B.A.	J.A.	M.A.	A.A.	20-39	40-59	60+	Male	Female
050	Continued									
	Physician/ funeral director	4	0	0	2	2	1	1	1	1
	No one	5	14	4	8	10	6	7	9	6
		(.10)				(.001)			(n.s.)	

052　Who would be likely to help you with such problems as preparing meals, babysitting, shopping, cleaning house, and things like that?

		B.A.	J.A.	M.A.	A.A.	20-39	40-59	60+	Male	Female
	Family member	50	74	65	45	63	63	48	54	63
	Friend	42	9	14	45	22	28	33	26	28
	No one	9	17	21	10	16	9	19	19	9
		(.001)				(.05)			(.05)	

068　Sudden death or slow death, which seems more tragic?

		B.A.	J.A.	M.A.	A.A.	20-39	40-59	60+	Male	Female
	Sudden	39	43	41	20	31	36	45	34	39
	Slow	58	50	50	68	62	59	45	58	54
	Equal	3	7	9	12	7	6	9	8	7
		(.01)				(.10)			(n.s.)	

069　An infant's death (up to 1 year), a child's death (around 7 years old), a young person's death (around 25 years old), a middle-aged person's death (around 40 years old), and an elderly person's death (around 75 years old). Which seems most tragic?

		B.A.	J.A.	M.A.	A.A.	20-39	40-59	60+	Male	Female
	Infant	14	8	13	17	18	8	13	13	13
	Child	26	24	25	44	38	27	21	28	31
	Young person	45	43	48	32	32	48	49	42	42
	Middle-aged person	8	22	6	5	7	11	13	12	9
	Elderly person	6	1	6	0	2	5	3	3	3
	Depends	1	3	3	1	4	1	1	2	2
		(.001)				(.01)			(n.s.)	

073　Which seems least tragic?

		B.A.	J.A.	M.A.	A.A.	20-39	40-59	60+	Male	Female
	Infant	24	18	25	14	12	26	23	24	17
	Child	5	2	1	0	3	0	3	3	1
	Young person	2	1	0	2	1	2	1	2	1
	Middle-aged person	2	2	5	1	3	2	2	2	3
	Elderly person	67	74	69	82	80	68	70	70	76
	Depends	1	3	1	1	1	2	1	1	2
		(n.s.)				(.10)			(.10)	

Item No.	Question/Response	Ethnicity				Age			Sex	
		B.A.	J.A.	M.A.	A.A.	20-39	40-59	60+	Male	Female
074	Which seems more tragic, the death of a man or the death of a woman?									
	Man	10	34	9	16	15	24	13	14	20
	Woman	38	29	36	25	39	26	32	34	31
	Equal	50	36	55	52	44	49	52	40	46
	Other	2	2	0	7	3	2	3	2	3
		(.001)				(n.s.)			(n.s.)	
075	Which seems most tragic: natural death, accidental death, suicidal death, homicidal death, or death in war?									
	Natural	0	1	5	1	0	1	5	2	1
	Accidental	34	32	19	16	16	28	33	29	21
	Suicidal	9	10	8	12	12	9	8	9	11
	Homicidal	21	32	33	48	35	34	29	37	30
	War	36	25	35	22	37	28	24	23	37
		(.001)				(.01)			(.01)	
079	Which seems least tragic: natural death, accidental death, suicidal death, homicidal death, or death in war?									
	Natural	76	64	83	87	76	74	83	77	77
	Accidental	1	2	2	0	1	1	2	1	2
	Suicidal	14	26	14	7	16	19	10	15	16
	Homicidal	3	2	0	1	2	1	2	1	1
	War	6	7	2	5	5	6	3	7	3
		(.05)				(.01)			(.01)	

Here are some reasons why people don't want to die. Tell me whether they are important to you, very important to you, or not important to you personally.

Item No.	Question/Response	B.A.	J.A.	M.A.	A.A.	20-39	40-59	60+	Male	Female
080	I am afraid of what might happen to my body after death.									
	Very Important	3	5	8	5	3	4	10	4	6
	Important	6	11	9	11	10	6	13	11	8
	Not Important	91	84	83	84	88	90	78	85	86
		(n.s.)				(.05)			(n.s.)	
081	I could no longer care for my dependents.									
	Very Important	26	42	47	44	49	48	19	42	39
	Important	26	33	29	29	33	25	30	30	28
	Not Important	48	25	24	26	19	27	52	28	33
		(.01)				(.001)			(n.s.)	

Item No.	Question/Response	Ethnicity				Age			Sex	
		B.A.	J.A.	M.A.	A.A.	20-39	40-59	60+	Male	Female
082	I am uncertain as to what might happen to me.									
	Very Important	9	14	11	9	10	13	10	11	11
	Important	16	19	21	19	23	13	21	19	19
	Not Important	75	66	68	72	67	75	69	71	70
		(n.s.)				(n.s.)			(n.s.)	
083	I could no longer have any experiences.									
	Very Important	3	11	7	6	11	6	3	8	6
	Important	9	26	27	23	25	24	14	20	23
	Not Important	88	63	66	70	65	70	83	72	71
		(.01)				(.05)			(n.s.)	
084	My death would cause grief to my relatives and friends.									
	Very Important	3	11	7	6	24	30	20	26	24
	Important	9	26	27	23	57	43	43	48	48
	Not Important	88	63	66	70	19	28	38	26	28
		(.001)				(.05)			(n.s.)	
085	All my plans and projects would come to an end.									
	Very Important	10	14	15	14	13	17	9	15	12
	Important	24	43	34	22	34	30	29	34	28
	Not Important	66	44	51	64	53	53	63	51	60
		(.05)				(n.s.)			(n.s.)	
086	The process of dying might be painful.									
	Very Important	13	18	30	18	20	21	18	17	22
	Important	41	38	27	36	33	36	38	37	34
	Not Important	46	44	43	46	47	43	45	46	44
		(.05)				(n.s.)			(n.s.)	
088	Some people say they are afraid to die and others say they are not. How do you feel?									
	Afraid/terrified	19	31	33	22	40	26	10	27	26
	Neither afraid nor unafraid	28	13	13	24	21	20	17	22	16
	Unafraid/eager	50	50	54	53	36	52	71	47	55
	Depends	3	6	1	2	3	3	2	3	2
		(.05)				(.001)			(n.s.)	

Item No.	Question/Response	Ethnicity				Age			Sex	
		B.A.	J.A.	M.A.	A.A.	20-39	40-59	60+	Male	Female
089	Of the following, which one has influenced your attitudes toward death the most?									
	Being or thinking you were close to death	10	22	18	14	19	14	16	18	14
	Death of someone else	26	41	39	35	33	42	30	34	37
	Reading	7	2	5	6	7	6	1	5	5
	Conversations	3	4	7	5	7	5	2	4	6
	Religion/including mystical experiences	40	15	23	25	15	25	39	23	28
	Funerals and other rituals	3	6	0	8	6	3	5	5	4
	Media	2	3	4	2	5	1	2	3	2
	Other	10	8	4	6	10	4	7	9	4
		(.01)				(.001)			(n.s.)	
091	Have you ever felt that you were close to dying?									
	Yes	48	31	49	37	42	42	39	43	39
		(.05)				(n.s.)			(n.s.)	
092	Did that experience affect your way of living or philosophy of life? (Based on "Yes" responses to #091, N=181)									
	Yes	50	50	45	43	49	44	48	49	45
		(n.s.)				(n.s.)			(n.s.)	
	Here are some ideas we have heard in our preliminary interviews. Do you agree or disagree with them?									
095	People can hasten or slow their own death through a will to live or a will to die.									
	Agree	88	85	62	83	80	82	74	75	83
		(.001)				(n.s.)			(.10)	
096	Death may someday be eliminated									
	Agree	12	22	16	13	17	7	25	17	15
		(n.s.)				(.001)			(n.s.)	
097	Accidental deaths show the hand of God working among men.									
	Agree	63	63	71	56	64	60	68	60	67
		(n.s.)				(n.s.)			(n.s.)	
098	Most people who live to be 90 years old or older must have been morally good people.									
	Agree	40	43	40	20	24	35	55	35	37
		(.01)				(.001)			(n.s.)	

Item No.	Question/Response	Ethnicity				Age			Sex	
		B.A.	J.A.	M.A.	A.A.	20-39	40-59	60+	Male	Female

The next set of questions concerns plans and preparations you might have made for your death.

100 Have you taken out life insurance?

	B.A.	J.A.	M.A.	A.A.	20-39	40-59	60+	Male	Female
Yes	84	70	52	65	61	76	66	73	63
	(.001)				(.05)			(.05)	

101 Have you made out a will?

	B.A.	J.A.	M.A.	A.A.	20-39	40-59	60+	Male	Female
Yes	22	21	12	36	10	22	39	26	19
	(.001)				(.001)			(.10)	

102 Have you made arrangements to donate your body or parts of it to medicine?

	B.A.	J.A.	M.A.	A.A.	20-39	40-59	60+	Male	Female
Yes	2	3	1	8	3	4	3	5	2
	(.05)				(n.s.)			(n.s.)	

103 Have you made funeral arrangements?

	B.A.	J.A.	M.A.	A.A.	20-39	40-59	60+	Male	Female
Yes	13	11	8	14	3	11	24	13	10
	(.05)				(.001)			(n.s.)	

105 Have you paid for or are you now paying for a cemetary plot?

	B.A.	J.A.	M.A.	A.A.	20-39	40-59	60+	Male	Female
Yes	22	26	12	25	7	17	44	20	22
	(.10)				(.001)			(n.s.)	

106 Have you seriously talked with anyone about your experiencing death someday?

	B.A.	J.A.	M.A.	A.A.	20-39	40-59	60+	Male	Female
Yes	27	16	33	37	28	28	29	28	28
	(.01)				(n.s.)			(n.s.)	

107 If yes, who? (Based on "Yes" response to #106, N=119)

	B.A.	J.A.	M.A.	A.A.	20-39	40-59	60+	Male	Female
Family member	52	35	80	42	40	76	50	41	69
Friend	37	53	18	36	54	12	32	40	26
Clergy	7	6	3	19	2	10	18	14	5
Other	4	6	0	3	5	2	0	5	0
	(.05)				(.001)			(.01)	

109 Have you arranged for someone to handle your affairs?

	B.A.	J.A.	M.A.	A.A.	20-39	40-59	60+	Male	Female
Yes	24	17	25	42	13	27	44	26	28
	(.001)				(.001)			(n.s.)	

Item No.	Question/Response	Ethnicity				Age			Sex	
		B.A.	J.A.	M.A.	A.A.	20-39	40-59	60+	Male	Female

People may have certain expectations of a (widow-widower). The next few questions are about someone who has just lost (his/her) spouse.

In general, after what period of time would you personally consider it all right for a (young/middle aged/elderly) (Black American/Japanese American/Mexican American/Catholic/Protestant) (man/woman) . . .

Item No.	Question/Response	B.A.	J.A.	M.A.	A.A.	20-39	40-59	60+	Male	Female
110	To remarry?									
	Unimportant to wait	34	14	22	26	23	27	20	26	22
	1 week-6 mos.	15	3	1	23	11	9	10	9	11
	1 year	25	30	38	34	32	36	26	30	33
	2 years +	11	26	20	11	22	17	11	17	17
	Other (including never/depends)	16	28	19	7	12	10	34	17	18
		(.001)				(.001)			(n.s.)	
111	To stop wearing black?									
	Unimportant to wait	62	42	52	53	49	57	50	57	48
	1 day-4 mos.	24	26	11	31	27	23	15	24	21
	6 months +	11	21	35	6	17	18	22	14	23
	Other/depends	4	11	3	11	7	3	12	6	8
		(.001)				(.05)			(.10)	
112	To return to his/her place of employment?									
	Unimportant to wait	39	22	27	47	28	38	33	32	34
	1 day-1 week	39	28	37	35	37	37	28	40	29
	1 month +	17	35	27	9	24	19	24	17	28
	Other/depends	6	16	9	10	11	7	14	11	9
		(.001)				(n.s.)			(.05)	
113	To start going out with other men/women?									
	Unimportant to wait	30	17	17	25	19	25	23	24	20
	1 week-1 mo.	14	8	4	9	10	8	7	10	7
	6 months	24	22	22	29	25	24	22	25	23
	1 year +	11	34	40	21	30	29	20	23	30
	Other/depends	21	19	18	17	15	14	28	17	20
		(.001)				(.10)			(n.s.)	

Item No.	Question/Response	Ethnicity				Age			Sex	
		B.A.	J.A.	M.A.	A.A.	20-39	40-59	60+	Male	Female

114 What do you feel is the fewest number of times he/she should visit his/her spouse's grave during the *first* year — not counting the burial service?

	B.A.	J.A.	M.A.	A.A.	20-39	40-59	60+	Male	Female
Unimportant	39	7	11	35	21	22	23	24	20
1-2 times	32	18	19	11	23	20	16	20	20
3-5 times	16	18	12	18	15	18	13	16	15
6+ times	13	58	59	35	41	39	48	40	45
(Don't know, etc.)	(11)	(6)	(3)	(19)	(9)	(10)	(9)	(12)	(7)
	(.001)				(n.s.)			(n.s.)	

115 What do you feel is the fewest number of times he/she should visit his/her spouse's grave during the fifth year after the death?

	B.A.	J.A.	M.A.	A.A.	20-39	40-59	60+	Male	Female
Unimportant	52	8	20	43	29	26	34	30	28
1-2 times	30	47	39	35	40	43	30	40	36
3-5 times	9	16	22	15	17	16	14	15	16
6+ times	10	30	18	6	14	15	23	14	19
(Don't know, etc.)	(14)	(6)	(4)	(22)	(11)	(12)	(11)	(15)	(8)
	(.001)				(n.s.)			(n.s.)	

116 In general, do you think that others in *your family* would be more strict, about the same, less strict, or other (don't know, etc.) in their expectations of this widow/widower?

	B.A.	J.A.	M.A.	A.A.	20-39	40-59	60+	Male	Female
More	15	26	38	26	37	25	16	31	23
About the same	57	45	43	63	44	50	63	46	56
Less	22	29	18	11	18	22	20	21	19
Other	6	0	1	0	1	2	2	2	2
(Don't know, etc.)	(21)	(3)	(4)	(0)	(6)	(7)	(11)	(9)	(6)
	(.001)				(.01)			(n.s.)	

117 In general, do you think others in *your neighborhood* would be more strict, about the same, less strict, or other (don't know, etc.) in their expectations of this widow/widower?

	B.A.	J.A.	M.A.	A.A.	20-39	40-59	60+	Male	Female
More	20	21	38	23	27	27	23	30	23
About the same	30	36	41	51	42	32	48	37	42
Less	32	43	20	51	26	36	27	30	30
Other	19	0	2	3	5	5	2	4	5
(Don't know, etc.)	(51)	(12)	(16)	(22)	(18)	(25)	(33)	(27)	(22)
	(.001)				(n.s.)			(n.s.)	

Item No.	Question/Response	Ethnicity				Age			Sex	
		B.A.	J.A.	M.A.	A.A.	20-39	40-59	60+	Male	Female

People differ in the *ways* they show grief and the *length of time* they mourn.

118 How do you know when someone is *not* grieving normally and needs help?

	B.A.	J.A.	M.A.	A.A.	20-39	40-59	60+	Male	Female
Withdrawal/apathy	33	15	16	25	20	24	24		
Death preoccupation	8	7	5	4	5	5	3		
Exaggerated expression of grief	3	7	14	15	13	6	8		
Abnormal behavior	51	29	27	27	30	35	38		
No reaction	5	4	34	15	30	35	38		
Other	7	40	5	14	12	18	17		
(Don't know, etc.)	(24)	(34)	(28)	(28)	(23)	(28)	(28)		
	(.001)				(n.s.)				

119 When would you begin worrying that someone had been crying, grieving, and sorrowful for *too* long?

	B.A.	J.A.	M.A.	A.A.	20-39	40-59	60+	Male	Female
2 weeks or less	38	29	24	27	34	32	19	34	25
1-3 months	40	40	42	38	42	37	42	44	37
6 months +	22	31	34	34	24	31	39	22	38
(Don't know, etc.)	(22)	(27)	(12)	(28)	(17)	(20)	(32)	(25)	(19)
	(n.s.)				(.10)			(.01)	

Next we have some questions about life after death.

120 Do you believe you will live on in some form after death?

	B.A.	J.A.	M.A.	A.A.	20-39	40-59	60+	Male	Female
Yes	59	47	40	66	48	48	64	52	53
	(.001)				(.01)			(n.s.)	

121 If yes, what form?

	B.A.	J.A.	M.A.	A.A.	20-39	40-59	60+	Male	Female
Thru children/works/ memory	20	33	27	30	33	22	27	25	30
Return to earth in spirit form	9	43	7	7	16	15	16	15	16
In heaven, paradise	70	24	67	63	51	63	57	60	54
	(.001)				(n.s.)			(n.s.)	

(Based on those responding "Yes" to #120, N=227)

122 (If Heaven) Do you believe those in heaven watch over earth or have no concern for earth?

	B.A.	J.A.	M.A.	A.A.	20-39	40-59	60+	Male	Female
Watch over	39	100	82	83	81	65	66	72	68
	(.001)				(n.s.)			(n.s.)	

(Based on those responding "Yes" to #120, N=227)

Item No.	Question/Response	Ethnicity				Age			Sex	
		B.A.	J.A.	M.A.	A.A.	20-39	40-59	60+	Male	Female
124	(If "No" to #120) What is death to you?									
	Nothingness	60	33	68	59	53	56	57	60	50
	Other	40	67	32	41	47	44	43	40	50
		(.01)				(n.s.)			(n.s.)	
	(Based on those responding "No" to #120, N=205)									
125	Regardless of your *belief* about life after death, what is your *wish* about it?									
	Wish there were	80	51	69	83	71	67	73	71	69
	Indifferent	14	30	18	9	19	17	17	17	19
	Wish there were not	6	19	14	8	9	16	10	11	13
		(.001)				(n.s.)			(n.s.)	
126	Have you ever experienced or felt the presence of anyone after he had died?									
	Yes	55	29	54	38	41	45	46	37	51
		(.001)				(n.s.)			(.01)	
127	(If "Yes") What type of experience?									
	Dream	65	63	74	45	55	64	34	68	60
	Visit	29	6	21	42	29	25	22	17	32
	Seance	0	0	3	3	2	3	0	1	2
	Other	6	31	2	11	15	9	5	14	7
		(.001)				(n.s.)			(.10)	
	(Based on those responding "Yes" to #126, N=193)									
128	What was the quality of the experience?									
	Appeared/spoke	68	69	75	82	71	67	83	80	68
	Psychologically felt	26	25	16	16	23	26	12	15	25
	Sensed by touch	6	6	8	3	6	7	5	5	7
		(n.s.)				(n.s.)			(.05)	
	(Based on those responding "Yes" to #126, N=193)									
129	How did you feel at the time?									
	Pleasant	55	41	57	63	41	59	66	62	50
	Fearful	31	19	36	13	41	22	17	19	33
	Mystical	7	16	3	13	8	9	9	8	9
	Other	8	25	3	11	11	10	9	11	9
		(.01)				(.10)			(n.s.)	
	(Based on those responding "Yes" to #126, N=193)									

Item No.	Question/Response	Ethnicity				Age			Sex	
		B.A.	J.A.	M.A.	A.A.	20-39	40-59	60+	Male	Female
132	Other than during dreams, have you ever had the unexplainable feeling that you were about to die?									
	Yes	15	12	34	15	26	15	15	15	23
		(.01)				(.05)			(.10)	
133	Have you ever had this feeling about someone else?									
	Yes	37	17	38	30	32	28	31	25	36
		(.01)				(n.s.)			(.05)	
134	(If "Yes") Did they actually die subsequently?									
	Always	60	47	51	60	43	63	63	52	58
	Sometimes	13	21	23	13	16	14	24	19	17
	No	28	32	26	27	41	23	13	30	26
		(n.s.)				(.05)			(n.s.)	
	(Based on those responding "Yes" to #133, N=132)									
135	How often do you dream about your own death or dying?									
	Never	78	80	64	62	62	75	81	73	70
		(n.s.)				(.01)			(n.s.)	
136	Would you want a big, elaborate funeral?									
	Yes	10	6	6	8	10	4	7	9	6
	No	79	92	89	89	84	90	83	85	87
	Indifferent	12	3	5	3	6	6	10	7	7
						(n.s.)			(n.s.)	
137	Do you expect that many of your friends and/or relatives will help share in the expense of your funeral?									
	Yes	27	43	30	27	40	31	23	30	34
	No	71	56	69	69	58	68	74	66	66
	Indifferent	2	1	1	5	2	1	3	3	1
		(.05)				(.05)			(n.s.)	
138	Would you rather have a large funeral with lots of friends and acquaintances or one in which only relatives and close acquaintances attended?									
	Lots of friends	21	9	33	9	22	17	15	18	19
	Only close friends	58	81	58	67	61	68	69	61	69
	Indifferent, neither	22	10	10	24	16	16	16	22	13
		(.05)				(.05)			(n.s.)	

Item No.	Question/Response	Ethnicity				Age			Sex	
		B.A.	J.A.	M.A.	A.A.	20-39	40-59	60+	Male	Female
139	Do you want the selection of a priest/minister for the funeral to be made by your family after you've gone?									
	Yes	62	79	74	68	70	72	70	73	69
	No	14	15	11	19	16	12	16	10	19
	Indifferent	25	6	15	13	14	16	14	17	12
		(.01)				(n.s.)			(.05)	
140	Do you want the priest/minister to be of your own ethnic group?									
	Yes	40	73	56	52	53	49	66	57	54
	No	7	2	4	4	5	4	5	5	4
	Indifferent	52	26	40	44	43	47	29	38	43
		(.001)				(.05)			(n.s.)	
141	Do you feel that a large percentage of your life insurance should go toward paying your funeral expenses?									
	Yes	35	39	47	25	30	36	47	32	41
	No	62	56	37	65	61	57	42	57	51
	Indifferent	4	6	17	11	9	7	12	10	8
		(.001)				(.05)			(n.s.)	
142	Would you prefer to have your casket open provided there were no disfigurement?									
	Yes	51	59	51	39	49	51	50	50	51
	No	9	26	33	31	27	23	24	18	31
	Indifferent	40	15	17	31	25	26	26	32	18
		(.001)				(n.s.)			(.001)	
143	Would you prefer that your funeral director be of your own ethnic group?									
	Yes	39	65	47	40	47	40	60	51	44
	No	7	4	4	6	6	6	4	5	6
	Indifferent	54	32	48	54	48	54	36	44	50
		(.01)				(.05)			(n.s.)	
144	About how much do you feel an adequate funeral would cost?									
	Mean cost	1075	1948	1209	1179					
145	Funeral cost categories									
	0-$700	30	9	29	31	28	20	28	20	30
	$701-$1400	53	30	44	40	36	47	44	43	41
	$1401+	17	61	28	29	36	32	29	37	29
	(Don't know)	(7)	(21)	(16)	(11)	(14)	(7)	(18)	(12)	(13)
		(.001)				(n.s.)			(.001)	

Item No.	Question/Response	Ethnicity				Age			Sex	
		B.A.	J.A.	M.A.	A.A.	20-39	40-59	60+	Male	Female
146	Would you want children under 10 years old to attend your funeral?									
	Yes	55	55	41	56	53	51	50	56	47
	No	15	31	47	27	30	30	31	22	39
	Indifferent	30	15	11	17	17	18	20	22	14
		(.001)				(n.s.)			(.001)	
147	Do you want a wake to be held before the funeral service?									
	Yes	25	41	68	22	43	40	37	39	41
	No	15	31	47	27	44	46	46	42	49
	Indifferent	22	14	17	5	14	15	17	19	11
		(.001)				(n.s.)			(.10)	
148	(If yes) Where do you want your wake to be held: at a funeral home, at a church, at your home, or someplace else?									
	Funeral home	49	24	68	53	49	56	47	49	53
	Church	27	50	21	16	20	30	41	27	32
	Own home	24	26	11	32	30	14	12	23	16
		(.001)				(.10)			(n.s.)	
	(Based on those responding "Yes" to #147, N=178)									
149	Do you expect that there will be some drinking of liquor during your wake or funeral service?									
	Yes	36	15	39	23	35	33	15	38	19
		(.001)				(.001)			(.001)	
151	Do you expect that others will take tranquilizers to keep calm during your wake or funeral?									
	Yes	38	16	50	41	42	34	29	40	31
		(.001)				(.10)			(.10)	
153	Where do you want your funeral service to be held: at a funeral home, at a church, at your home, or someplace else?									
	Funeral home	18	18	47	50	29	38	31	29	37
	Church	64	73	47	36	56	53	59	54	57
	Own home	5	3	4	5	8	2	3	6	2
	Indifferent/no funeral	13	6	3	10	8	7	8	11	4
		(.001)				(n.s.)			(.01)	

Item No.	Question/Response	Ethnicity				Age			Sex	
		B.A.	J.A.	M.A.	A.A.	20-39	40-59	60+	Male	Female
154	Would you object to having an autopsy performed on your body?									
	Yes	25	33	32	23	25	28	33	28	28
	No	64	59	55	67	68	63	50	60	63
	Indifferent/Undecided	11	8	13	10	7	9	17	13	9
		(n.s.)				(.05)			(n.s.)	
155	Would you object to being embalmed?									
	Yes	8	29	22	18	22	16	20	21	18
	No	84	58	59	69	68	71	62	68	67
	Indifferent	7	13	19	13	10	12	18	12	15
		(.001)				(n.s.)			(n.s.)	
156	How would you like your body to be disposed of?									
	Buried	84	33	89	66	65	71	68	68	69
	Cremated	4	53	5	18	20	16	24	18	22
	Donated	6	4	3	9	9	3	2	4	6
	Indifferent/undecided	6	11	4	7	6	10	5	10	4
		(.001)				(n.s.)			(.10)	
157	Where would you like your body/ashes to be disposed of?									
	Los Angeles	54	60	67	51	43	66	69	59	58
	Elsewhere/U.S.	26	12	6	24	21	15	14	16	18
	Outside/U.S.	1	11	20	3	17	3	6	8	10
	Ocean	1	8	2	8	8	3	2	6	3
	Other/Indifferent	18	8	5	4	12	12	9	12	11
		(.001)				(.001)			(n.s.)	
160	At what age do you expect to die?									
	Mean Age	79.0	74.3	71.9	73.9					
162	Now, if you could choose, to what age would you like to live?									
	Mean Age	88.6	80.1	75.8	79.7					
165	Where would you like to die?									
	At home	44	72	54	61	63	49	63	55	60
	In hospital	21	16	34	14	15	32	18	17	26
	Other	35	12	11	25	23	19	20	27	14
		(.001)				(.01)			(.001)	

Item No.	Question/Response	Ethnicity				Age			Sex	
		B.A.	J.A.	M.A.	A.A.	20-39	40-59	60+	Male	Female
167	Do you feel people should be allowed to die if they want to?									
	Yes	53	49	31	61	53	50	40	46	50
		(.001)				(.10)			(n.s.)	
168	(If yes) Under what circumstances should they be allowed to die?									
	In pain	36	23	31	14	27	26	21	26	24
	Dying anyway	33	49	57	59	50	50	46	43	54
	Unproductive/unhappy	9	2	3	0	2	4	4	5	2
	No feelings or sensations	4	4	3	10	5	4	8	6	5
	Because they want to	18	8	6	16	16	8	15	12	13
	Other	0	15	0	2	0	8	6	7	2
		(.001)				(n.s.)			(n.s.)	

(Based on those responding "Yes" to #167, N=206)

Item No.	Question/Response	B.A.	J.A.	M.A.	A.A.	20-39	40-59	60+	Male	Female
169	(If no) Why do you feel this way?									
	Only God has the right to take life	54	23	63	49	51	44	51	48	50
	Sake of others	2	4	6	5	4	4	6	5	4
	Always hope	31	39	30	28	29	36	31	29	35
	Other	13	35	1	18	17	15	13	18	11
		(.001)				(n.s.)			(n.s.)	

(Based on those responding "No" to #167, N=217)

Item No.	Question/Response	B.A.	J.A.	M.A.	A.A.	20-39	40-59	60+	Male	Female
170	Have you ever considered that all human life might be eliminated from earth?									
	Yes	62	42	56	58	63	50	48	55	53
		(.05)				(.05)			(n.s.)	
171	(If yes) How?									
	Nuclear explosion	37	51	34	48	45	49	27	47	37
	War (not nuclear)	3	4	3	2	4	3	2	3	3
	Ecologically	8	19	6	17	12	12	12	13	11
	Cosmic natural event	36	11	41	25	27	29	48	26	33
	Other	10	4	8	3	7	9	3	6	8
						(n.s.)			(n.s.)	

(Based on those responding "Yes" to #170, N=237)

Item No.	Question/Response	Ethnicity B.A.	J.A.	M.A.	A.A.	Age 20-39	40-59	60+	Sex Male	Female
172	What effect has this interview had on you?									
	Positive	33	34	73	35	46	45	42	44	44
	Neutral	58	48	24	54	45	43	49	48	43
	Negative	9	18	4	11	9	13	10	8	13
		(.001)				(n.s.)			(n.s.)	
176	About what percentage of the people on this block would you say are of your own ethnic group?									
	75-100	87	11	64	61	56	54	59	52	60
	25-74	11	30	27	16	20	20	23	22	20
	0-24	2	60	9	23	25	25	18	26	20
		(.001)				(n.s.)			(n.s.)	
178	This interview was conducted in									
	English (mostly)	100	61	35	100	79	84	51	74	73
	Japanese	—	39	—	—	6	3	24	10	10
	Spanish	—	—	65	—	15	13	24	17	17
		(.001)				(.001)			(n.s.)	

ELDERLY SERVICES LIBRARY,
THE COUNSELING CENTER

INDEX

Page